211 BLUE

The Story of the Chameleon Cop

William Engle with Taylor Engle

211 Blue: The Story of the Chameleon Cop
Copyright @ 2022 by William Engle and Taylor Engle

Published by

Bitterroot Mountain Publishing House LLC
P.O. Box 3508, Hayden, ID 83835
Visit our website at www.BMPHmedia.com

1st edition 2022
Interior and cover design by Jera Publishing
Photographs: All images in author's collection
Editing by Suzanne Holland, M.S.

For questions or information regarding permission for excerpts please contact Bitterroot Mountain Publishing House at Editor@BMPHmedia.com.

This is a work of creative non-fiction. Although the author and publisher have made every effort to endure the accuracy and completeness of information contained in this book, we assume no responsibility for errors, inaccuracies, omissions, or any inconsistency herein. Any slights of people places, organizations are unintentional. Many names have been changed, but the situations were real.

Library of Congress Control Number: 2023901048

ISBNs:
978-1-960059-03-1 (ebook)
978-1-960059-04-8 (softcover)
978-1-96005905-5 (hardcover)

1. True Crime 2. Crime Memoir 3. Police Crime

Printed in the United States of America

ACKNOWLEDGEMENTS

Thank you to the entire team at Bitterroot Mountain Publishing House—most notably, Anna and Suzanne—for helping me bring this to life on my father's behalf, and the unconditional support of my loved ones throughout the process (you know who you are).

Finally, and most importantly, I want to thank my daddy for the honor of writing his life story alongside him. Writing with him taught me about who I am, who he was, and most importantly, who we were together. I thank him for this incredible privilege, and I am forever grateful for the gifts he has given me.

INTRODUCTION

A chameleon is known for its incredible ability to change colors – blending into its surroundings and constantly adapting in order to survive. Such is the legacy of my Daddy, Bill Engle: a man who lived countless lives in one, pivoting the very instant you thought you had him pinned him down.

Seven years ago, my father came to me with a few pages of a manuscript – one he claimed was going to tell the incredible, unbelievable story of his life. Until then, his past was something I'd only heard about in tiny bits and pieces, constantly teased and alluded to, but never expanded on. I was always "too young," and when prodded for details, the answer was always, "I'll tell you when you're older."

I was a very curious child, and this was maddening to grow up with. The mystery of my dad's secret dark past loomed over my head for years, and I was constantly on the hunt for clues. Constantly waiting and watching for someone to slip up and mention something, anything. But it remained a mystery.

As I grew older and he continued to tease, I became annoyed and resentful, like his refusal to expand on his past life – which he always claimed was "wilder than you could ever imagine" – was a direct reflection of the trust he had in me. So, when he came to me with the manuscript and asked for my help, I saw it as an opportunity to finally unpack the skeletons in his closet and size them up for what they were. I agreed without hesitation.

My father and I have always shared a deep love for storytelling, and writing this story together was cathartic for both of us.

For him, he saw this as a chance to share the invaluable lesson he learned decades ago and carried with him for the rest of his life: that no matter how royally you screw things up, salvation can never be ruled out. Life is beautiful, terrifying, crazy, and full of possibility, and for every wild and unprecedented direction his went in, he never gave up hope. He never stopped chasing the end goal of true contentment, and for that very reason, he earned it.

For me, this project began solely as a chance to finally know my Daddy – the good, and the bad. But through that pursuit of family knowledge, I was able to absorb that same lesson in a different way. That in order to produce something beautiful, you have to stick through the ugliness–a.k.a., the parts of your writing you absolutely despise. I learned to be patient with the process, and have enough foresight to trust myself and where I'm headed with my words.

In this book's complete form, I now see the universalness of the lesson my dad spent years of his life learning, and then passing along to me. This story of salvation holds value for everyone: that no matter where you are in life, you can keep going, changing color, and adapting to the environment you want to create for yourself. That no matter how dark and hopeless things may appear at first glance, you're not really at the end of your rope. No, on the contrary; you're at the beginning of a brand new one.

Taylor and Bill Engle

1

1970 - ROBBERY IN PROGRESS...

This story didn't really start here, but by now I've realized nothing ever really starts where you think it does. It was closing time at the Buena Park Kmart store. Presumably, a core store where they shot commercials or trained new employees in a dingy little conference room behind the swinging black "Employee Only" doors.

The year was 1970, although it could easily have been 1950 in Buena Park, by the way the community resisted the cultural revolution underway. Town center was Knott's Berry Farm...hardly cutting edge. Sideburns were trimmed to mid-ear in this part of the country. The Sunday evening September air had just begun to crisp up Orange County, back when California still had a hint of the change of season.

The Vons next door to Kmart would be closing at 7:30 p.m. But, people didn't have to look at their watches to know it was almost that time. Shoppers started to move faster as they mentally prepared for the closing of the store, yearning for one last *Blue Light Special*.

Customers from both stores slowly filtered out the front doors, making their way to the comfort of their vehicles. With bags, parcels and purses in hand (wallets much lighter), a band of parents finished school shopping for the evening.

Two hundred fifty feet from the Kmart entrance, a man and woman in their late twenties sat in the front seats of a 1969 white Volkswagen bug. Purposely nondescript, both remained frozen still, intensely watching the storefront doors…both slightly inclining forward, each in their own way. A blatant contrast existed between their physical stillness and the focused movement of weary customers in a hurry to get home and settle in for the night. No one seemed to notice these two statues.

Through the front store windows, it was fairly easy to see the staff going about their closing duties. Most wouldn't glance twice, a scene truly unworthy of two glances; but the boredom was quite misleading.

In the meantime, an unknown, terrifying storm gathered within the store.

Twenty minutes later, a majority of the staff hurried through the front door with a mutual elation of shift-end. They couldn't be happier at leaving the jungle of retail for the night. One staff member silently raised her fist in the air as though victorious in escaping the drudgery of another shift. As she left, her hair bounced off her shoulders.

An unarmed security guard hastily locked the entrance doors from the outside, sliding the key into his pocket as he made way to his Honda. He had a slight limp and seemed to be hypersensitive to other people staring at it, although probably no one was. Sometimes it made him an asshole to be around. But that, he didn't seem to notice. He loudly cleared his throat.

At this time, six people were still in the store. This was more than usual for a typical Sunday evening closing.

INSIDE KMART ...

Joe Burns' ebony face glistened with sticky sweat as inner fear threatened to overwhelm him. His left hand twitched as he tried to stop blinking hard. He stretched slightly, thinking this could ebb the tremors. It didn't. Instead, the movement released a cloud of pungent body odors. His brow furrowed. He curled up, smelling his upper lip in a slightly obsessive-compulsive sort of way.

Hunched down unnaturally, as if attempting to hide from someone, Joe awkwardly nestled his body in the gardening section, behind hoses and pesticides and a storage shed façade. *The stress these events offer could possibly cause one to deviate from a perfect plan . . . and fuck everything up. Stay aware.* These earlier words from his *boss* reverberated through his mind with perfect clarity.

Not far away, Scott Miller also contorted in hiding. Being even taller and thirteen years older than Joe, made his feat particularly difficult. Scott leaned forward, tightly holding a .38 caliber revolver to his chest. The tips of his fingers met the grooves of his wedding ring, sending a wave of shock through his taut body. He'd never done anything like this before. He leaned forward even further, pressing his lips together, trying to detect any movement.

Scott was strategically placed in the aisle between the bathroom supplies and cleaning products. He gave himself plenty of room to move around without detection. He could roam if hunching became too hard on his tall body or if his legs got too restless. More importantly, Scott had a perfect view of the large store interior as he moved around.

Accessed only from the store warehouse, the employee locker room sat in the northeast corner of the store. It was there for the employees' convenience to relax and change in and out of their work clothes. The locker room contained a dressing area and a separate large bathroom. The north wall of the bathroom held the door to a broom closet, where the janitors kept their cleaning supplies.

Alone, Fernando Garcia reluctantly slid his thick legs into his pants, pulled them up, and tightened his belt. He yawned and vaguely glanced at the shiny beige metal lockers, while putting on his *Kmart Custodian* shirt. No reflection was available, but he didn't expect any.

"I hate this fucking job," he muttered.

Chipped lime-green walls backed the wooden bench he sat on. Bolted to the floor at every opportunity, it ran the length of the lockers. This locker room avoided giving one hope for career advancement from any angle, but it helped with employee retention.

On the bright side, there was always that broom closet—a room with no corporate eye, a necessity for Fernando's mood lightening, pre-shift toke ritual.

Six remaining employees peppered the northeast corner of the store. They waited by Store Manager Bob Mosher's office for him and security to finish the register closing duties. Bob felt very proud of handling deposits, going over receipts, and taking cash and checks for the armored truck's arrival. This level of responsibility was a big accomplishment for Bob.

The two final employees arrived simultaneously from different areas of the store. The unsuspecting eight engaged in small talk as they waited, completely unaware of what was happening beyond.

They spoke in end-of-day talk, store talk, the kind of talk they only had to be half-conscious for—offering smiles that faded weakly. Heads nodded to affirm speakers were heard. The bored employees were of both sexes and a range of ages. Bob had been delayed, but they weren't too concerned; he was often late.

Joe still lingered in the gardening section, squirming around in his cramped space. He tried to dim the pounding of his heart in his head. Careful not to make a sound, he attempted to uncurl his body for any semblance of relief. The air grew heavier, making it hard for him to breathe. A .32 caliber revolver hung from his right hand.

2

SUMMER 1964

Even by Southern Californian standards, it was a crazy summer. The Beatles exploded onto the scene with The Rolling Stones close behind. Cassius Clay knocked out Sonny Liston with a punch few saw, and Richard Burton married Elizabeth Taylor. The nation's head spun around. A huge cultural shift began.

Wearing my best suit, I waited on a hard visitor's bench in the lobby of the Stanton City Police Department, a mild challenge for my bony butt. I never graced a police lobby before in my life.

Two other guys in their mid-twenties sat with me. We waited quiet and still. Through my peripheral vision, I caught each of them wiping their sweaty palms on their pants. *Little nervous, are you?* I smiled inwardly. It kind of reminded me of kids waiting outside the principal's office.

We waited for the oral interview portion of the testing process to become a city police officer. From an original field of over a hundred, only three would be selected out of a remaining ten. That showed in our lack of conversation and our body language, each one of us feigning disinterest to the other two, but inwardly aching for success.

I felt *passionate* about my need for this particular job. All the remaining applicants had their own needs for the job, I'm sure. But, mine was desperation, an urgency. The stakes were high for my family and me.

I fidgeted a bit on that hard surface, even though I considered my chances here pretty good. I had a background in theater and felt very comfortable in front of groups. The exam board consisted of three members. *That's a group,* I reassured myself.

My written exam scores were the highest. I'd studied to get there. On paper, it appeared I had the right stuff.

This was one of the very few jobs where I could work, perform, and support a rapidly growing family, *and* complete my graduate education full-time in a reasonable amount of time. At twenty-five years old, with almost three kids, I had serious catching up to do. It made me anxious, gave me an empty feeling in my stomach when I thought about it. Fight or flight remained my new normal. My goals were clear, but my path wasn't.

Working full-time regular hours, I believed there was no way I would graduate fast enough to avoid being irrelevant in my career… or almost *any* career.

Other than those enticing hours, the life of a police officer wasn't very attractive to me. *The worst-case scenario could be death,* I thought. That wasn't very comforting. At that age, I was still quietly conservative about the unknown. I hadn't allowed myself to be tested in response to blood, violence, or tragedy. I still danced my way around those tunes.

Hadn't been there, didn't miss it. Sure, I came from the blue-collar South Bay area, but when the other guys were at their requisite gang fights, I was home watching Fred Astaire or Bob Hope.

The way I saw it now, I didn't have much of a choice. I needed this job. The other guys there probably daydreamed about catching bad guys back on the playground. For me, that was just part of the job description. I fantasized about the *financial support.*

For as long as I could remember, my goal remained to teach college-level speech and drama and then expand into professional acting and directing. That was my playground fantasy.

My shattered dreams could only be put together again with hard work. Everything I aimed for required both time and money. Time spent studying for college exams and memorizing lines. Money for courses and books, costs of starting my acting career, and financing a family. My battle definitely ran uphill.

I was a walking *Sisyphus*.

The mysterious door to the interview room suddenly opened, and a young man, sweating a bit on his forehead, exited into the lobby. Not looking at any of us, he walked out directly, chewing his lower lip in apparent ponderous confusion.

That action slightly widened our eyes, as we glanced around the room nervously, making only fleeting eye contact. We wondered what happened to him in there, and who'd be next?

Minutes later, police Captain Hawks appeared with the answer, "William Ellis, please." Hawks, a large man with thick white hair and two catcher's mitts for hands, extended his right one in welcome. He wore a brown plaid sport coat with wrinkled tan pants and black shoes large enough to make you stare. I lost my hand somewhere in his while he shook. Together we entered the room.

Inside, two other men looked like cops cut from the same cookie cutter: short hair, clean shaven with an "in charge" attitude. They stood behind a long, bare table, watching my entrance with wary interest. (I later found cops look at most *everyone* with a wary interest). In front of the table sat only a metal folding chair, which I'm sure was symbolic of how they wanted the interviewee to feel.

I'd never been in front of three police officers of any rank in a room before. *This whole interview process was designed to be intimidating.* I noticed a spotlight glaring down from the ceiling. The single chair glowed. For one ludicrous second, I thought my ass would be scorched the second I lowered myself into it.

I nervously glanced around the room, less like an interviewee, more like the victim of an interrogation. This sure wasn't my usual audience. If *this* audience didn't like your show, they could put your butt in jail, or send you home without a job.

Stifle those thoughts and focus on the captains. I pulled my shoulders back, scooted to the back of the chair, and tried to look relaxed, but attentive.

They asked about my past and present work, school history, accomplishments and goals, family and wife relationships, leisure time activities, and so on. They showed interest in what I was telling them, nodding along, and even asking follow-up questions. They encouraged me to share my position on various social issues, with them probing deeper on a few.

The interest they showed in my answers made me feel comfortable. It even started to puff me up a bit. I felt relaxed in this sea of uniformed police captains.

It took about fifty minutes and seemed to be a pleasant interview. Relieved, I barely caught Hawks and Captain Brewer exchanging glances. Hawks raised his eyebrows. I took that to mean they had what they needed, either that or he needed a potty break.

But, he leaned forward and lowered those eyebrows, "You told us earlier you were against police brutality, is that right?"

A simple question I saw as the obligatory wrap-up to a successful interview.

"Yes, sir," I answered, settling back into the chair.

Hawks only slightly smiled as the others now watched. I was too comfortable with myself to realize the smile never reached his eyes, and that he talked right through it.

"Let me ask a few questions to see how you might react in certain scenarios . . . ."

"Sure," I nodded.

"Okay. You're a police detective. You got a few snitches working with you. You know, informants?"

A virgin to police work, I tried to visualize such a possibility as Brewer described, "If any cop needs crucial information out of *any* snitch, and the snitch won't give it, you okay to beat him to get that info?"

I did my best to mask the fact this type of scenario was freaking unimaginable to me. I'd only ever seen anything like that in the movies. The closest I'd personally been to a beating was when Jimmy Kendall cold-cocked that bully in the ninth grade.

"No, sir." *I thought we covered this.*

Captain Hawks, "Right . . . it's against the law. You'd enforce the law if hired, correct?"

I nodded again. Inside I felt apprehension, and my nerves lightly hummed.

"A man and his wife come to the police station to report their four-year-old daughter has been kidnapped. Kidnappers demand twenty-five grand to return the girl, unharmed. They give all the drop details and swear to deliver one of the child's cut-off fingers each day the money isn't paid."

My nerve-hum heightened as Brewer continued his scenario, "As they tell their story, you realize one of your snitches probably knows who the kidnappers are. Probably." He leaned back in his chair and stared at me a moment.

"He won't just give this to you. No, they don't do that. But, you've been working him a while, so you know his weak spot." He leaned forward again as if conspiring. "It's that he can't take a physical beating. Not a bad one. He'll give up everything he's got."

"So, do you beat him?"

There was a brief silence, and I could feel the weight of each captain looking my way. The interview became less pleasant.

I gulped. "I'm against police brutality. I'd try other ways." *Is this a memory test?*

Brewer commented, "Right. That's what you told us."

Something seemed off. It seemed as though they were speaking those words, but their faces were telling me something completely different. I felt like a kid spun around rapidly before being pushed to the ground. Vertigo.

"You and other detectives can't dig up a lead. You try everything. Snitch isn't giving you shit, but you know for sure he knows." A slight pause before, "Still, you don't beat him?" Eyes were boring into my skull from three different directions. My head felt hot.

"No, sir." I quietly cleared my throat and shifted my weight in the chair.

"Okay, then. A day passes . . . " He eye-balled me as though he expected me to finish the line.

"Parents receive a small box, special delivery. It's their daughter's right index finger…"

Holy shit.

Hawks continued, the rest leaned forward in an effort to will me into an answer. "Do you beat him now?"

"Well. I'd… " I paused and felt my face beginning to fluster. *What the hell do they want?*

"Does your silence mean you wouldn't beat him?"

My jaw tightened involuntarily, upper teeth clutching lower teeth. It was an effort to continue looking at him and still concentrate. But how could I not?

"Okay then, another day goes by." *Oh, okay asshole, another day goes by. Now what?* "Parents get a *second* finger. What do you do?"

You bastard!

"We already got that you're against police brutality, your snitch is still giving you nothing. What do you do?" Hawks pressed. Enough for me to know he'd had a lot of garlic in last night's dinner.

Remaining still, seated beneath the spotlight which only seemed to brighten, I'd been backed into a corner, and it became obvious to me that *any* response I came up with would be the wrong one. It was designed that way, I was sure.

What they wanted in the very beginning was, "I'll beat the living hell out of that snitch. I'll beat him until he can't stand up. A career is nothing compared to keeping a child safe." And *Mighty Mouse* music would play in the background, "Here I come to save the day!" Truth has no place here.

I resented the ambush, but eventually I got what it was about. I think it was beyond a police career, beyond the family. This wasn't about wearing the cool badge, about providing for your daughters and your passion. This was about quickly acting on the right decision for the greater good. Every time.

As I sat in the hot seat and mulled this *Don Quixote* epiphany, my present-self was unaware this realization would stay with me strongly and help guide my entire life. For better *and* for worse.

With the interview completed, I drove home crumpled and still in a daze. The more I thought about it, the worse I felt about myself. My entire life's trajectory-correction was riding on a winning interview I was so damn confident I had. Instead, I blew it.

I firmly set my gaze on the horizon, ignored the traffic noises, gripped the steering wheel and promised myself out loud this hesitation was the first and last.

After a few days, I wasn't surprised to learn by mail that I failed the exam. I'd have questioned their standards had I passed. But, it still stung. Failure was foreign to me.

I learned from that and quickly gave it a second try. This time, I was hired by the City of Buena Park as Police Officer William F. Ellis on March 26, 1965.

Thrilled, I punched my right fist into the air when I read the letter, "Yes! Yes!" My goals and dreams were alive again, and the jolting interview was forgotten for the moment.

Although joyful, the news did bring thoughts of a considerable unknown directly in front of me. Was I prepared?

I wouldn't have to wait long to realize the truth.

3

JUNE 11, 1965

My eyes involuntarily widened as it hit me again. Everywhere I looked, it was all I could see: the banners, the audience, the murmuring. I was graduating from the Orange County Peace Officers Academy. *I'm going to be a cop. Can I really handle this?*

I could hear my breathing shorten as I looked around the room and felt the pomp and circumstance of it all. I slowly nodded my head allowing a silent self-congratulation for completing *step number one.*

Maintaining a full college schedule in addition to the full-time Academy requirements, I felt worn the hell out. I could barely see straight thinking about it—probably from my long-term lack of sleep. It felt as though sand was stuck beneath my eyelids. I pinched my thigh with my thumb and forefinger in an attempt to get out of my head and snap back into the moment. *Hello, reality?*

Everyone was in uniform and looking tip-top, including visiting police management from various cities; all with cropped hair, ironed pant legs, and bright white smiles. That is, if you discount the random nicotine stains on teeth.

We wore our excitement on our ironed sleeves.

So many cops in one room. The seniors gazed at us with a soft nostalgia in their eyes. We returned their looks with our excitement for the near future. The energy was bouncing off the walls. It made sleepy Orange County feel like New York City.

My goals finally began to feel reachable again. I'd been living and breathing law enforcement for the past few months (in addition to the academy, I went on "ride-a-longs"), and it had become a large part of me. It filled all of my waking and even some of my sleeping hours.

Learning of the responsibility and power that came with wearing the badge was huge, but then again, how much can a rookie really know at his academy graduation ceremony? I hadn't been much beyond the book part, yet. I hadn't even written a traffic ticket.

I could see Mom with my wife, Sarah, and our two daughters, all beaming with pride. I also saw my father- and mother-in-law. His name was Dick, and he had the tendency to act like one. Clearly, he was surprised I'd actually made it this far—he didn't do a great job of hiding that sentiment. To be honest, I don't think he really tried.

He once saw me dance ballet in tights, and from that point forward never ascribed anything alpha to me. In his eyes, I'd always be *Og the leprechaun*...from *Finian's Rainbow*, not a dedicated college student, the father of his grandchildren, and now a police officer. Just some boy in tights.

My mother-in-law, Lucille, seemed completely disinterested in the ceremony, and why not? Several years ago, she'd put a 10-gauge shotgun on the family dining room table to shoot and kill herself. She placed the barrel against her stomach, and reaching with her toe to pull the trigger, she unintentionally twisted, partially missed, and failed. I had to clean her stomach parts off the dining room wall right after my twentieth birthday, to the accompaniment of weeping and pointing.

The graduation must have been pretty dull in comparison.

I vaguely heard the MC introduce Buena Park Police Chief Ralph Sedley. The salt-and-pepper-mustached man rose from his seat and walked to the podium with perfect posture, as he was welcomed with nice applause.

The chief stood at the podium, spreading a few papers out and clearing his throat. He smiled paternally at the audience, as they finished clapping. He had this way of smiling at a room, and everyone present believed he was speaking directly to them.

I felt my face drifting into a smile in return, eager to hear what he had to say.

"Thank you very much, Don. You know, it's an honor to be asked to speak here today," Sedley began, giving an appreciative nod. "Orange County Peace Officers Academy does a wonderful job in training our young police officers of tomorrow. I often sat in on classes, and I've got to tell you, folks, these men graduating this afternoon know their law enforcement. Our communities are well-served. And, Buena Park PD is very happy to be associated with the program. Our city has four officers graduating today, including Officer Ellis with honors. We expect every one of you graduates will have long and honorable careers."

He turned his head to the graduating group and nodded, affirming, and scanning the eyes of all. He gave two "thumbs-up," and with enthusiasm, turned back to the now applauding audience.

Sedley spoke with a soft yet firm sort of grace, making the four of us feel properly acknowledged and respected. All eyes were on him, nodding along with his words as he continued, addressing law enforcement and 1965 cultural conflicts, and monumental changes in almost all aspects of this country. Woodstock and young men burning their draft cards, the Birmingham marches, Vietnam escalating, and Bob Dylan going electric were among his topics.

Sedley's address eventually ended and everybody received their certificates to more audience applause and cheering. Moments later, I stood tall and talked with my family just like every other officer in the room. To my surprise, Chief Sedley approached our group. I introduced him to everyone; the intense effort had become fulfilling, replacing exhaustion.

The Chief smiled at Sarah as he shook her hand, "You must be very proud of your husband."

"I am. He worked hard," Sarah answered with a proud smile. "Full load at school... "

"And honors, here," Sedley added. "I'm impressed." He turned his attention to me, "Ellis, you're the type we need in law enforcement. You'll do fine. Hang in there." He patted my shoulder and gave me a friendly wink. "Nice to meet you all. Enjoy the rest of the evening."

Dick was beaming now and not trying to hide it, as if he thought I'd suddenly entered manhood. His chest thrust out; he grinned as though he knew a secret. Like maybe all that tights-wearing was okay if you also have a big-ass police badge!

That evening, Sarah and I sat close together on the couch in our Anaheim apartment. It was two-bedroom, sparsely furnished and a little worn in, but it was ours. Our two girls were also in the living room/dining area. Four-year-old Mary was curled up pawing through a picture book while Annie, two-years-old, quietly gazed at the television.

"We still have a week at the PD with Sergeant Keaton before they throw us out there on the streets," I said with a vacancy.

Sarah tilted her head, giving me a quick peck on the chin, "I'm proud of you."

I squeezed my arms around her in silent thanks and held her as I rested my chin on her head and continued staring at the wall.

"Lots of things are going through my mind, babe. Being a police officer is a whole new world that is going to help get me through college faster…and get things to where they should be. But I need to have a whole different worldview now. Parts of which, I didn't even know existed before the Academy and those ride-a-longs."

She slowly moved her hand up my leg, patting me gently with comfort. "You're going to be fine. You'll adapt. I've got faith in you."

I buried my hand in her blonde hair and reached the nape of her neck, pulling her face to mine. "I've got faith in you, too."

4

Two weeks later, I'd been on my own for a week. My police car hauled ass down La Palma Avenue, with flashing emergency lights and siren (Code three). I'd been assigned an "unknown trouble," medical-aid type emergency, and was making my way to 1247 San Marino Avenue.

Drivers did their best to pull out of the way of my siren, but mostly, they seemed confused. Sirens did that. My eyes were steady on the 2 p.m. traffic, and my heart slammed against my chest. I thought of the trusty first aid kit and silently hoped I wouldn't have to use it.

I felt like I could see at a 360-degree angle—I was superhuman, a huge rush. Nervous, but very alive, colors were brighter, building edges were sharper—like everything was on steroids.

The deep, calm voice of Sid the dispatcher continued from the auto speaker, the soundtrack to my unknown mission. "Now confirmed headshot. Victim reported as a four-year-old white female. Possible accidental shooting by a six-year-old boy, unknown further details at this time. Proceed with caution. Ambulance en route. Your ten-twenty?"

"Westbound on La Palma at Western. ETA one and a half."

I recognized Sergeant Cooley's voice as it crackled in the air hovering around my car radio, "Twenty-three ten, following up at Beach and Orangethorpe. ETA about three." I felt slightly relieved that he traveled close behind me.

I'd been doing this just long enough to know a world can change in a second. We patrolled in one-man units, and the concept of back-up was somewhat comforting on an "unknown trouble" code three call. Especially the first one.

I arrived near the scene to find a woman frantically pacing back and forth on the curb. As soon as she noticed my black and white, she began waving her arms, motioning for me to come forward. I accelerated to her and parked, exiting the car and grabbing my first aid kit from the trunk.

The woman moved toward me, looking ready to melt at my feet, her body trembling. She had to clamp a hand over her mouth to quell her hiccupping sobs for just long enough to blurt, "A-a little boy sh-shot her. It was a-an accident. You-you-g-got to h-help her. It's really b-bad." She sat hard directly on the ground beneath her, her hands finding their way to her head.

"Where's the gun?" I asked firmly, moving toward the front door of the home.

"I-I don't know. It's in there. The girl is in th-the last b-bedroom."

"Okay, please stay put and tell the next officer that gets here where I am," I said, locking eyes with her before turning to disappear inside.

I walked down the hallway, filled with a newfound caution, going over all the information and possibilities in my head. The first aid kit in my left hand, my right on my holstered weapon. I still didn't know where the gun was or who was now in possession of it—important to know while in a police uniform and actively on duty.

I pushed inexperience aside and acted as though I knew exactly what I was doing. *Oh, a little girl was shot? No problem, I've had three or four of these calls this week alone,* I rambled to myself. *Yeah, right. You've got no clue what you're doing yet.*

I forced myself out of my head and into the present, focused to make a positive impact on the situation. If not to prove something necessary to myself, then for the sake of this hysterical woman and the poor, unlucky little girl. Thoughts of my two young daughters flashed before me as I picked up my pace, whipping my head from left to right to rapidly check the state of each open door.

Everything was strangely quiet until the last bedroom. Before I had the chance to peer through the doorway, a hysterical woman with dark blood staining the arms of her blouse and her hands hurried through, almost running into me in the process. I felt the heat of panic and sweat and blood on her…and the chaos flowing from within the room.

"You have to help my baby girl. Please, sir. She's dying!" the woman gasped through sobs.

I stared at her incredulously as she spoke, hit with further learning that this *was* life. This was an early part of my unknown. One minute you could be sitting down watching television, wondering what to cook for dinner, and the next minute you're covered in your child's blood, wondering whether or not she was going to live to eat dinner.

I just want to be in plays.

I gently and quickly moved past the woman and entered the room to find a tiny girl lying on the floor bleeding. There was no confusion. She'd been shot in the head. The blood pooling beneath her head married to the mustard-colored shag carpet.

There were two other women in the room who looked in a daze, and a teenage boy with long hair, his entire body shaking, tears streaking his face.

Police training made it almost autonomic for a glinting .38 revolver to catch my eye. It was lying about a foot from the girl's head wound. In one fluid motion, I retrieved the gun, then kneeled and opened my first aid kit, getting supplies to treat the wound.

As soon as I'd finished dressing her wound the best I could, I gently touched the girl's small, smooth chin and looked into her childlike eyes, growing glassier with each passing moment, each drop of blood leaving her head.

"You're going to be okay, darling," Quietly, as though we were the only two people in the room. "Can you do me a favor?"

The girl managed to flicker her eyelids, imitating a nod.

"Just breathe very slowly for me. It'll all be okay soon." I turned my head to the women, still standing in the same spot and staring at us. "Where's the boy?"

One seemed as though she was opening her mouth to speak when Sgt. Cooley burst into the room. He knelt on the other side of the child, quickly checking the head wound.

"Shit, we don't have time to wait for the ambulance. You hold her, I'll drive. Let's move." The last two words were said over his shoulder as he grabbed the gun I'd retrieved and disappeared back into the hallway.

I scooped up the girl, and we hurried to his squad car through a parting crowd of both horrified and fascinated people. He dove in behind the wheel. I awkwardly took the passenger's seat, holding the child on my lap, while her sticky warm blood slowly seeped through my shirt.

A squeal of tires and a familiar shriek with the emergency lights sounded as we peeled out of the neighborhood, bound for the emergency room. I continued applying gentle pressure to the girl's head. She focused on me with concern and questions in her eyes.

For the first time, I noticed the name "Jenny" carefully embroidered onto her shirt.

"You're going to be okay, Jenny. We're going to the hospital, sweetheart. You're going to be just fine," convincing myself as much as I meant to convince her.

A tiny hand reached up to touch my face but didn't quite make it, so I met it halfway and grabbed onto it with my own, which was heartbreakingly larger. I couldn't cry for her benefit.

That took effort.

Cooley grabbed his radio mic, "Twenty-three ten, we're transporting the victim to Lincoln Hospital. Can't wait for the ambulance.

Have two units preserve the scene." He put his radio back in the cradle and sighed, looking out the window as we sped past traffic.

"So, Ellis, what happened to the little boy at the scene?"

Silence.

"I'm talking to you. Hello?"

He looked over at me, annoyed I was ignoring his question, but I hadn't heard a word he'd said because I was busy staring at the girl's eyes. Something didn't feel right. I squeezed her little hand, which was still in mine. It felt limp, lifeless and so small.

I closed my eyes and suddenly knew it didn't matter how quickly we got to the hospital.

It didn't make a difference that we didn't wait for the ambulance because Jenny couldn't wait for us either.

The ultimate effects of violent tragedy had found me early.

5

SUMMER 1959

My little brother slept in his small twin bed, with me lying down to his right in mine. Eventually, I drifted off to sleep, until I woke up to a strange presence hovering over me.

I instinctively squinted to adjust to the darkness, confused at what was going on. Holding my breath, I wondered, *Is there someone in this room?* What were the odds that someone was in our bedroom in the middle of the night? Yet, I sensed movement.

Enter beautiful Sarah Stark, sitting on the edge of my bed smiling and watching me sleep—or rather, now watching me stare at her.

Sarah and I met when I was seventeen and she was fourteen. We quickly fell into young love. She was gorgeous with beyond shoulder-length, honey-blonde hair, a face like Grace Kelley and a body full of sensuality.

Having lunch together at school, holding hands in the hallways, walking home together, and losing interest in any surroundings when near each other. It became as consuming as a high school love could get. I'd had girlfriends before, but none of them ever really stood out. When I met Sarah, her presence demanded I notice her and love her almost immediately. She carried herself with a strong sense of confidence and assertiveness that either attracted or intimidated almost everyone, yet fascinated me. Instantly, love hooked me.

"Did I wake you?" she purred, stroking the fabric of my blanket next to her thigh. I felt the heat of her body run through the mattress and up into mine.

"What're you doing here?" I whispered, my face frozen in fear. I glanced over at my sleeping brother, Tim. He hadn't budged. Still fast asleep, snoring lightly.

Maybe I'm imagining her.

"Since Daddy won't let you come see me, thought I'd come see you," she responded with ease. I wasn't imagining anything.

"What time is it right now?" I didn't even know why I was asking this. My voice was higher than intended, and I don't think I could have processed the answer. I'd never had a girl break into my home and bedroom before.

"About two, I guess. Does it matter? We both know there's not an hour in the day Daddy would let me come over here."

Images of her father flashed into my mind. He with his thick hands around my throat, his face redder than mine, even though I'm the one suffocating...or he's swinging at me with a baseball bat, maybe loading his automatic and aiming it between my eyes with a menacing visage, all with Hitchcock-approved music, of course.

When I gave Sarah a "going steady" ring, he forbade me from seeing her for six months. Telephone calls only. A huge load. It had been two weeks of school-only sightings.

"What if my mom hears you? How'd you even get in?" I hushed even lower, beginning to perspire a bit.

Tim turned over in bed and his light snoring stopped. *Is he awake?*

Sarah slid along the bed as quiet as a mouse, sliding her hand up my chest and moving her lips to my ear. "Bathroom window.

You should lock it," she moved her head back to give me a little wink. "I'm going to get in bed with you." She used her toe to kick back my covers, never breaking eye contact.

"What? No! And lower your voice. You're going to wake Tim," I hissed, feeling my heartbeat in my hands. "Let's go outside."

Momentarily pushing away that fear of getting caught, I led an amused Sarah by the hand through the house and into the backyard. She carried her tennis shoes in one hand, tiptoeing so as not to make a single sound. I shut the back door silently, and we made our way into the life-size playhouse from childhood, located deep in the rear yard.

As I shut the playhouse door, Sarah was on me, kissing passionately and running her hands all over me. I returned the kiss, losing myself in her lusciousness.

"How did you get all the way over here in the middle of the night, anyway?" I gasped about an hour later, once we'd come up for air. Trying to grasp anything that made sense. None of my blood was currently in my brain.

"I rode Katie's bike," she murmured, eyes still closed and lips seeking mine.

My mouth melted into hers as I considered how ridiculous it was for a fifteen-year-old girl to ride a young child's bike six miles through the black-blue night wearing nothing but a nightgown and a jacket.

"You can never do this again," I managed to get out, mouth pressed against hers.

Her still-hot lips cracked into a smile. "Scout's honor. Now, I guess you'd better drive me home? But, not yet."

Sometime later, I piled her and the bike into my car, cruising through the night back toward her house. It was a rather silent ride, me dwelling on the fear that had swelled inside me and hadn't quite acquiesced.

I didn't know it at the time, but this definitely would not be her last late-night visit. Her boldness, the taking of what she wanted, was almost as inspiring as it was crazy.

About a year into dating, Sarah and I finally made love (a *very* huge deal in that time). We'd gone into the relationship earnestly promising each other that we'd wait until marriage to have sex, but the tension between us was much too strong and tempting.

The social-sexual-revolution notoriously associated with the 60's was still on the horizon; we loved when the world was still about suppressing your desires and emotions. Failing to maintain at least a perception of virginity was frowned upon by everyone around us. I'd even written to *Dear Abby* for advice to help us contain our passions.

Eventually, we couldn't wait any longer.

Like most first times, it was very passionate, but also a bit scary and awkward. It was overwhelming to finally have that freedom. So much, that by the time I got used to doing things, it was over. But the taste and the smell of our love permeated everything. Several minutes later, we laid next to each other, still breathing hard and looking at the ceiling in mutual disbelief. I had no idea I could sweat so much in such a short time.

I put an arm around her delicate shoulders and pulled her closer to me. It felt amazing, better than a second curtain call. I could feel the love and devotion dripping off of us both. We were walled off from the rest of the world.

Deep down though, I still felt scared and guilty. What would Mom think? My precious mother, who raised five children on her own and only wanted the best for me….What did God think? But, I foolishly pushed these thoughts out of my mind, holding closer and closer to my golden love that had just given herself to me.

"We're married now," Sarah said softly, picking up one of my hands to play with my fingers. "We're married under the eyes of God. Pastor says, 'Whenever a man and a woman come together...' and we have. I pronounce us *man and wife*."

She glanced up at me. Her eyes sparkling and shining.

I was speechless. She'd obviously been paying closer attention in church than me. I was there every week, but the words hardly touched me. I was more interested in her.

"Okay, but we're still waiting to do it officially," I proclaimed. "I've got to finish college, and you have to finish high school before we can even think of marriage. My acting career has to be going, too. That's the most important thing."

Sarah pulled my face to hers, kissing me long and hard. She slowly climbed on top of me, moving her body sensually until once again, we moved together. That time, a lot less awkward. That time, much more pleasure.

In retrospect, Sarah never did respond to my important proclamation.

Over the next year, we enjoyed each other as often as possible. If we were attached before, now we were inseparable. We'd have lunch together every day and meet in the dollhouse almost every night like clockwork. Throughout the year, I continued to reassure both of us that we still had to wait for marriage, *until after I've graduated from college and have my acting career started.* I repeated this point many times over the next several months.

She still never quite responded.

I began working full time, while cutting back to one class at community college, telling myself I was building a good foundation for my acting career. But, it was hard for me to believe it...no matter how sincerely or how often I said it.

I was starting to feel pretty stressed. At the rate I was going, I'd be in school for at least the next decade. Sarah was supportive, telling me she'd drop out of school and get a job to help support us while I finished college full-time. "We could marry officially," she said. She was sixteen years old.

After months and months of discussions, we finally decided together not to wait any longer. We were already married in our own eyes (or so we thought), so we might as well make it public. Everything else would just work out. All we could see was each other.

We believed the only way to do this with the necessary parental approval was to get Sarah pregnant. Neither side would give us permission now, but both sides would insist on marriage if she became pregnant. That was our logic, and it became our goal. Statutory rape charges were at best a vague concern. It didn't take long.

THREE MONTHS LATER...

"Mr. Ellis?"

I ran a hand over my face, the ringing phone woke me from a mid-afternoon flu-nap. My body ached all over and I smelled like sleep. "Yes?"

"Your wife gave us this number for contact. This is Doctor Matthews, and I'm calling with good news, Mr. Ellis. The test results are in, and your wife is pregnant."

I glanced up at the ceiling, momentarily bewildered and not thinking of the aches, fighting for clarity. *Wife? Pregnant?* Flashback to a few days ago: "I'm late. This could be it. I'll go into the clinic, have a test," she whispered excitedly over the phone.

"Congratulations to the both of you."

I was nineteen. Sarah was sixteen.

"Mom. Something I have to tell you." My voice was hesitant, tentative. We were in the kitchen, in the midst of a relaxing day, two weeks later. She prepared dinner, while I sat at the table with my hands folded, palms sweating and hot. The edges of both hands stuck to the linoleum table top.

She stood with her back to me before the sink, letting potato skins fall as she peeled them with her special mom-skill.

"What's that?" she asked, continuing to peel. Mom got things done. She worked six days a week and still cooked for her five children, did the laundry, and made it to every event.

My body felt like a pile of bricks. I couldn't have moved my arms if I tried. I took a deep breath and with great difficulty, "Sarah's pregnant, Mom...I am so sorry."

The air in the room died. It felt as though I'd just kicked her in the stomach.

Her back remained to me, but she let the potato and knife slip out of her hands and bump into the sink. Her body melted onto the counter. She propped herself up. "Oh, God, Bill. What have you done? What about your future?" she choked out. My heart was breaking.

"It'll all still happen," my words came out in a hurry. "I promise. Those plans haven't changed, Mom. Sarah and I promised each other." I continued to stare at her back, waiting for her to turn around. She did, slowly.

"It won't happen," looking me in the eyes, and shaking her head. "I knew that girl was going to do this to you, Bill. I knew it all along."

"No, Mom. Please. We did it to each other. We did it on purpose," I said softly. "She's telling her parents right now. I'm sure her dad will be knocking on our door any minute."

She watched me, continuing to shake her head as she processed the "on purpose" part. She looked so pained, tears starting to run. "He's crazy anyway. Damn redneck. This'll probably send him over the edge."

Just then the phone rang. It was Sarah, calling to tell me about her confessional experience, telling me her dad was indeed angry and on his way over. I looked at Mom, gripped with the reality: nothing good can happen right now. He might go nuts and try to kill me. The phrase "shotgun weddings" had an origin, and I was about to directly learn why.

But, what could I do? This was the plan. Our wise idea. I knew this part had to happen and could only wish for the best.

Uncle Bill, almost the size of Sarah's father, was visiting for the week. Mom was in the middle of explaining my dilemma to him when Pissed Dad pulled into the driveway and got out of the car. He slowly approached the house, pausing a moment before knocking on the door. *Taking deep breaths*, I hoped.

I answered his knock quickly. He stood there, looking at me for a few seconds, "Come on out here. We need to talk." He hardly moved his lips.

He smoldered from behind, turning and walking to his car without another word. I glanced at Uncle Bill, and he was nodding. I had to do this. He muttered, "I'll be watching from the window. Don't let him drive away with you."

That wasn't warm and fuzzy.

I walked to the car, opened the door and got in, settling awkwardly into the passenger seat. My stomach was churning. My mind was racing but going nowhere.

Both his hands were gripping the steering wheel so tightly that all the blood seemed to have left his knuckles. I thought he was concerned that if he let go, he might strangle me.

But we went on to discuss it like adults. I respected him for respecting me enough to have a conversation.

We somehow worked it out, and we found ourselves in the same corner. My inner-shaking calmed somewhat. He was not going to kill me.

After we told our parents about the pregnancy, we were married in *less than a week* in a Methodist church in Hawthorne. A church where no one knew us. Certainly not the Baptist church we frequented with her parents. They didn't want anyone talking.

At this point, we had no idea what damage we'd created in our lives.

The wedding was small of course. My grandfather, Pappy, stood in as my best man, and one of Sarah's school friends was her maid of honor. You could count the total attendance on one-and-a-half-hands. Exactly three black and white Polaroids were taken to commemorate the day. One was a shot of the newlyweds with the groom's mother and the bride's parents, a dark look of dismay crackling beneath everyone's plastic façade.

A few other guests were there, more for support and sympathy than anything else. It wasn't exactly a big happy celebration.

It should have dawned on me that we *might* be marrying too early when registering at the front desk for our honeymoon at the *Disneyland Hotel*. The only thing that would have made it more hilarious would've been if we were wearing Mickey Mouse ears. I was sweating and hemming and hawing like crazy; meanwhile Sarah couldn't and wouldn't make eye-contact with the deskman. *No, we didn't just sneak out of the Sadie Hawkins dance.*

He insisted we provide our birth and marriage certificates, as if we were middle-schoolers trying to pull one over on him. Even after proudly showing him our papers, he continued eyeing us warily. Couldn't blame him.

We were, after all, children.

After our one-night honeymoon (which felt guilty and anti-climactic when you consider we'd been having sex for over a year), we settled into a very tiny one-bedroom house in someone's backyard in Inglewood. I started a second night job, and picked up some Saturday work at my main job, a shipping clerk at an electronics firm in Los Angeles.

I soon had to drop out of all of my theater training classes, too: dance, vocal, acting. I still auditioned for acting roles here and there, but not nearly enough as I wanted. No time in a forty-eight-hour work week, and I was unwilling to spend any of that hard-earned money on anything but the bare necessities. Life was getting blurry to me.

We continued to lose ground in money owed. It seemed like when one thing was fixed, another got broken. I didn't have any skills when it came to mechanical, electrical, or plumbing repairs…I knew nothing. And to top it off, neither of us knew anything about handling finances. We were two kids without a clue. I had no father to guide me, and she was a Southern belle and all that goes with it, like okra and a limited sense of humor.

Our first daughter, Mary was born in June of 1961. She was beautiful to us, a strawberry-blonde doll. We smothered her with love, happy to feel like successful adults for a fleeting moment.

It didn't last very long. We went further into debt.

Sarah started encouraging me to consider suspending my dream of acting and teaching and just concentrate on the current job. I'd become a very young supervisor at work, but it wasn't my idea of a goal. *A career in aerospace?* I knew what my goals were.

I also couldn't stop thinking about my mother and how far a cry this was from the things she knew I'd be able to accomplish. She had worked overtime to pay for my dance and vocal training. It was all the help and support a single mother of five could afford.

Several months passed and our marriage became less blissful. Sarah's original pledge to support my quest was now seldom found.

It seemed as if I never spoke of becoming an actor/director or teacher in the first place. Without trying to, I'd started to feel betrayed.

"This wasn't our deal, Sarah. Remember? It wasn't subject to change. That was a huge part of our marriage decision," I said to her one day, frustrated I'd let things get this out of control and desperately needing us to re-clarify our positions.

She heard me out and let me know she remembered and understood, making me feel as though the ship was righted. But over the next several weeks, I didn't see much change in her attitude. In fact, she'd barely noticed my theater work, except for her unreasonable jealousy of any female actresses I worked with. That was consistent.

But, the bottom line was that she was partially right in her attitude toward my attention to theater. I had the responsibility of raising a child. I couldn't come first anymore. That sure as hell was not a part of the plan, and we didn't have a new one, yet.

6

1970 - ROBBERY IN PROGRESS...

Scott suddenly appeared in the aisle, startling Joe as he stage-whispered, "Stick to the plan, dammit. You got to get *the clean-up guy.* Hurry-it-up." His eyes flashed menacingly, masking his inner feelings of fear and dread.

Joe's palms up and eyebrows raised, "That's where I was going, okay?"

Joe glided through aisle after aisle, head pivoting in every direction. Carefully, he made his way toward the locker room, where the clean-up guy (Fernando) was supposed to be.

Like a choreographed dance, Fernando simultaneously stepped into his "private place" as Joe arrived at the outer doorway.

Fernando took a deep breath and smiled. He was almost in his heaven: the deep, wide, well-ventilated broom closet. He was more than ready to indulge in his nightly pattern of sneaking a pre-shift toke, and this was the only place he felt safe doing it.

It made his job so much nicer. Asshole customers amused him rather than angered him, the relentless demands of his manager were much more bearable, and the crappy burrito he always ate at lunch break, tasted like it was made in a real Mexican restaurant.

With the movement of a few boxes, the dingy closet transformed into his well-appointed spot for these types of breaks. He smiled at his little space as if thanking it for having him yet again. Fernando was no stranger to this room, and neither was his box of weed.

He switched on a purposely dim light, a bulb he tinkered with a while ago for moments of peace like this. Smiling, he silently closed the door and locked the deadbolt from inside; it was all muscle memory.

He sat and opened the lid of a small box with a half-ounce baggie of pot and a small pipe, which he nicknamed *Conchita*. Taking one in each hand, with obvious and pleasurable anticipation in his eyes, he took a moment to admire the rich green of the marijuana, that wonderful pungent smell, and silently thanked his cousin for hooking him up with that "top-shelf shit."

With his weapon drawn, Joe made it into the locker room. He didn't see anyone, even though the plan read that he would. Surprised, he quickly scanned the room for any evidence that might point to what was going on in here.

One of the locker doors stood open and empty. He cautiously approached, unprofessionally slamming it shut...which alerted Fernando that he was not alone.

Joe scratched his head in frustrated confusion. Nothing to indicate that anyone had been in here in the last hour.

He tiptoed his way to the restroom door, listening for movement. With the hopeful element of shock up his sleeve, he suddenly opened it...but saw no one.

Joe creeped his way to the single toilet stall, quickly kicking the door open with his foot while brandishing the firearm with both hands. No one.

He squinted his eyes in thought, anxious to find his man. *I'll show you I don't need your help,* he thought to himself, recalling a conversation from earlier.

Just as he began to consider a next step, Joe noticed the broom closet door. He walked over and tried the knob. It didn't give. *What the hell?* He jiggled the knob.

On the other side of the door, Fernando's eyes darted from the weed to the deadbolt. He sat, frozen in place, clutching his baggie and Conchita, hoping the light was dim enough not to leak under the door. His huge eyes continued to widen and threaten to burst.

Joe tried the door twice more, thinking maybe if he twisted hard enough, it might miraculously open.

"Anybody in there? This is corporate security. Open the door right now. Anybody?" Nothing. He again looked at the un-changed sign, "Broom Closet."

He evaluated it with pursed lips; it was a small locked closet. *No one's probably touched it all day,* he decided with his ear pressed against the door.

After all, his visit was sudden. A potential someone wouldn't have time to rush into the closet and deadbolt it shut. No, he'd definitely have heard something.

He straightened. Satisfied with his thought process, Joe left the restroom, took the locker room in five silent strides, and whispered his feet across the floor to Scott's side.

Meanwhile, Fernando remained paralyzed in the broom closet, terrified security might discover his guilty secret. His heart seemed to be bouncing out of his chest and his throat at the same time. *Shit, Maya will kill me. I need this job. What am I gonna do?* He snapped out of his paralysis and forced himself into action, carefully hiding the evidence in miscellaneous boxes. All the while, he sweated profusely with the fear of someone busting down that impenetrable door.

"He isn't there. Maybe he didn't come to work today or something, but he's not there."

Scott's eyes widened in alarm, "Shit, we have to have him. Did you look in the storage area?"

Joe clenched his jaw, unused to being challenged. "He's *not* here, man." His jaw un-clenched almost immediately as he realized that being right in this particular situation isn't exactly what they want.

The two men stood face to face, staring in shock and confusion… trying to remember if they had a backup plan.

7

"What, Hon?" I asked, slowly coming back from my increasingly common reminiscence of the past. The struggle to regain what was willfully lost never seemed to leave me.

She moved toward me, concern in her eyes, "You thinking about that call, again?"

"Huh? Oh, no, I'm going over these 'late payment demands' and 'last warning' letters. It keeps getting worse." I looked up at her, "And we keep having kids."

We both then smiled that electric smile we shared. It seemed adversity turned us on to each other even more. It felt like we were soldering ourselves together and combining strengths, moving through life as a singular force against the chaos. It overwhelmed all logic.

The sound of a young girl giggling twinkled in the background like wind chimes. That healthy, wholesome, childlike laughter always brought a smile to my face. Everything was dark. I felt robbed of my senses, except for the ability to hear that melodious laughter. The joy echoed throughout my being.

The laughter grew louder, eventually morphing into a desperate and terrifying scream, a scream so horrific my butt puckered. Nothing was dark anymore. I was floating. No, I was drowning.

I forced my eyes open and frantically looked around until it registered that I was drowning in a pool of bloody children, each screaming for help, each only moments away from death. I locked eyes with a little girl. She was beautiful, yet drenched in her own blood. A startling contrast to her pasty complexion. She stared at me as she silently howled for help. Her eyes were screaming what she couldn't amidst the bloodied water. *Please help me*, her eyes begged. *I'm dying. Please help.*

I opened my mouth to tell her that everything's going to be okay. To tell her she was beautiful and young and she was going to live a long and happy life. I opened my mouth to tell her that, of course, I'd help her, *Yes, little girl, I'll do anything to help you*, but the words refused to come out. No matter how hard I tried, I couldn't make a sound.

I directed my arm to shoot out and grab her, but by the time I expected my hand to be firmly wrapped around her elbow, it still lingered by my side. I tried to twist my body to hurl myself closer to the dying child, but only moving about a tenth as fast as I needed to be. The harder I tried to move, the slower I became, and the farther away the girl drifted. Her eyes branded themselves into my soul, screaming, begging me, without saying a word. I wanted to scream for help, but was now immobile and useless.

Suddenly, my body shot upright. Forcing my eyes open, I looked around my bedroom in the dark. I was drenched in sweat and panting. I couldn't get enough air, as if I'd just emerged after being underwater for several minutes.

A sleepy Sarah sat up. With concern in her voice she asked, "Are you all right?" She searched my face with her palm to my forehead.

"I'm fine," I answered, avoiding eye contact. "Just another damn bad dream. I'll be fine."

Sarah rested her hand on my shoulder, "Maybe you should get up for a bit. Clear your head? I'll get up with you, if you'd like."

"Thanks, but I don't have time. I need to get some sleep. Three hours before I have to be up for finals. It's okay. Really. I'm fine now." I still wasn't looking at her, illogically haunted at my inability to save the children that kept appearing at night. *When does this stop?*

Sarah put her hands on each side of my jaw and gently turned my head to look at her. "Honey, please. You can slow down a bit. No one's racing you, you know."

"Can't imagine who'd want to." I turned over and made sounds of sleep, so she'd stop worrying about me and relax. All the while, I was staring into oblivion, trying to force those dreams out of my head. I had to figure out a way to deal with disturbing calls like that better.

8

It was almost time for swing shift's briefing, when Lt. Crown took one last look at his notes. He sat behind a large desk facing eight police officers that had notebooks in their hands with pens ready. This was serious stuff. It was like a hungry salesperson getting leads. *Who's wanted? What's happened? Hot sheet info?*

It's about protecting the public. It also gave me a sense of excitement about what might lay ahead that shift.

The lieutenant took less than twenty minutes to inspect our uniforms and advise us of unusual crimes and incidents that'd gone down in Buena Park since the close of shift the day before. The beats (area of responsibility), were assigned for the night. We were like a football team, following the plays separately, but together. Hopefully, to leave the town a tiny bit better than it was before we began.

"Get that paper I handed out," he ordered, exuding impatience until each of us located it. While waiting with him, I noticed his face was rodent-like, his little eyes beady and red. His face remained in a workplace grimace.

His nose began to redden, "You guys still have a problem with writing complete, thorough, reports. The simple 'who, what, why, where, when and how' parts. Some of you in this room have even lost cases in court simply because of your own damn reports." He paused to hitch his thumbs into his belt and walk the length of the front. He faced the guys and shook his head. Somehow his nose seemed to add a shade of purple.

"The D.A.'s don't like you, men. You make their jobs harder. Defense has a ball with you, of course. A suspect you know is *guilty* gets to hit the streets 'cause of your poorly written crime report. A technicality you created by yourself, and bam...*they're* back outside. We all know this. How does that feel? Anyone want to tell us how your fucked-up report let a criminal walk free and how that made you feel deep down? Anyone?"

He looked around the room, taking his time and letting the shame soak in. "You're getting better, but according to the chief and the numbers, you're not there yet. And, you've got to get there. So, take a look at this incident report, written by 'still wet-behind-the-ears Ellis,' here."

I was seated alongside everyone else, and blind-sided. No one told me I was going to be called out in front of all my shift-mates. As a rookie, that's something you want to know ahead of time. I was elated with the attention, but curious about which report it would be. My face was frozen, blocking out everyone else the best I could.

Lieutenant spun around on his brown cowboy boots and made his way back to front and center. "Guys, have you no shame?" He pointed in my direction. "He's been on the streets one month—ONE, and Chief says to use his reports to help *you* write yours. Something wrong with that? Isn't that out of the natural order?" He stared at each of us, I guess daring someone to challenge him.

"Hey, Lieutenant, I call Ellis Webster. You know, the dictionary," heavy Baxter Barnes laughed good-naturedly. He looked around to see who was joining in with him.

"No one fucking cares, Barnes. I'm talking. You shut the hell up."

Barnes wilted in his seat, corn-fed thighs hanging over the sides.

"Everyone, listen up and follow along. It's getting late, and you men embarrass me. But, we're going to read through this together before you hit the streets. Chief's orders."

He sounded reluctant and put out.

But, with that introduction, he began to read. I recognized my report on a simple disturbing the peace complaint from a few days earlier. It sounded weird coming from Crown's mouth. Of course, your own words always sound weird when someone else is speaking them. Crown stopped on occasion to point out what he was told was important in the report. *At least that's what the Chief says*, he thought to himself. He was just the messenger. Like so many other times in his career.

By the time he finished reading the report, Crown understood why the Chief ordered it for training. It was better than he expected from a mint-fresh rookie.

He looked around the room now, almost pumped up. As if he'd had anything to do with the report. His mouth formed a semi-smile. "Any questions?"

In the back of the room, Sergeants Keaton and McKinley stood, leaning against the back wall. Their arms were folded, as they'd been during the entire briefing.

McKinley leaned over while still looking straight ahead at Crown, whispered, "What's this Ellis about?"

Keaton thought for a moment. "I liked having him on my shift. He's smart, good attitude. Writes excellent reports so far. Look at his report and match it with most of yours."

He looked over to see the expression on McKinley's face and quietly snickered, "Kidding, John. You write great reports."

Keaton moved a couple of steps away.

McKinley didn't seem to hear Keaton's words. He was rapt listening to the Lieutenant and watching me with irritation, while chewing the inside of his cheek.

It's too early to give him attention, he's a fucking rookie, he thought to himself as he watched me incredulously. *A month, for shit's sake.*

9

Catcalls echoed in my ears and reverberated through the hallways as I walked up the stairs from the briefing room. The kind you'd expect from other cops. "Ooh-hoo, Ellis. 'The Chief's new butt-boy.' 'Shakespeare.' 'Suck-ass,'" they crooned with delight.

I'd already caught on and knew I couldn't let this go on for much longer. I turned around, raising my eyebrows and using my higher position on the stairs, "By the way, let me know if you need any help spelling big words, guys…like, oh, 'humiliating?' I mean if you were to describe tonight's briefing to anyone, you probably want to use that word."

I gave them a feigned laugh to show I wasn't taking seriously the fact their incompetent reports apparently resulted in criminals running free, and we prepared to leave for patrol. You sure couldn't let it seem like you were taking yourself too seriously. But, I figured that would apply only to the first year, until they got to know me.

Walking toward our vehicles, Officer Jack Paxton said, "Hey, Ellis. Good report, man. No kidding. I'm going to have you start writing my grocery list, you little fucker." He waved his helmet toward his unit. "Let's go get some coffee and talk about it." He grinned and stopped in front of me, waiting for a response. Eyeballing him back, I noticed his very short, almost severe, black hair sat atop his cherubic face and stocky body.

"We can't stop for coffee the first hour."

"Aw, bullshit," Paxton shot back, keeping that grin on his face.

"Maybe for you. I'm new. I have to follow rules. See you in an hour and a half, if you want."

I put my briefcase in the car and started inspecting the vehicle prior to duty, as was procedure. I searched the inside for hidden weapons or overlooked contraband, perused the outside for any marks or dents. A cop must always be aware of his surroundings, and that included close knowledge of his vehicle and weapons at all times.

Believe me, we were tested on these procedures. Management would occasionally hide *faux* weapons in our units to test us. I saw the benefit of it. Our alertness to situational danger proved to be rather important, if we wanted to make it home to our families after each shift.

"Hey everybody. Look at Ellis. Checking the car! Like a pro. You're doing great work, little hustler. Maybe sometime you can show me how to check my car just like that." He looked at my work with pseudo-admiration as he sidled up to me with a sly grin on his face.

Something in me told me to be wary. It crawled up and down my skin.

During our first week on the street, we were under the watch and supervision of fellow officers for further training and observation. Those with sufficient experience and at least a perceived ability to mentor were chosen for the task. I'd had Paxton the first day.

At the end of watch, I'd stopped at the intersection of Orangethorpe and Stanton, waiting for the light to change and continued on my way to the city yard. At end of shift, it was each officer's responsibility to "gas-up" the vehicle for the oncoming shift.

Paxton began talking more oddly in a way that ramped up my feeling something else was afoot.

"Hey, Ellis. You're incredible, man. You are doing so great. You're fantastic. Everybody in this busy intersection knows it, too," he gestured toward others. "Look around. Look at these people, how interested in you they are." He had the half-grin of mischief on his face.

Looking around the intersection, I saw that most every person whether in a car or on foot was staring at me expectantly, like they were waiting to be entertained.

"Look at 'em, Ellis. Look how fucking admired you are. No one's even moving."

Sure enough, neither direction of traffic was moving. They'd all stopped at the intersection, joining this newly formed gaggle of gawkers. I felt I was supposed to be doing something, to be finding something. My eyes searched the car wildly, checking for a sign. My discomfort was increasing by the second.

Finally, the clue was staring at me in the reflection of a store window. My overhead emergency red lights were on, and flashing all over the place.

Oh, great. Now everyone's going to know just how new I am.

Before I could react, Paxton leaned over and activated my siren with his left hand. The sudden, loud screech startled me.

Now, everyone looked confused, and few of them looked terrified. I was sweating the embarrassment out all over my uniform. Everyone was looking for a leader.

"You'd better get going. You got to move. Lights and siren!" He shouted. "Hurry up. Get out of here, Ellis. You look like a fool." He laughed derisively, obviously delighted with himself.

I accelerated and moved through the intersection, continuing east on Orangethorpe Ave. I soared for three blocks as quickly as I could. He, continuing his laughter—me, humiliated and clammy.

Suddenly, I made a right hand turn into a residential area, and disappeared from the Orangethorpe traffic with a great sense of relief. Now, I could slow down and turn off the emergency equipment, quiet my inner-siren, and maybe dry my shirt. I took a deep breath and pulled over entirely.

I wanted to be pissed off, but couldn't help but laugh with Paxton. The son of a bitch really got me. I took off my helmet, the sweat running down my face was significant.

"It's part of the training, Ellis. Got to see how you handle pressure." I was still pretty embarrassed, but wasn't going to let him know it. He was already enjoying it too much.

I willed my Wonder Bread skin not to turn a telltale pink shade as I dried my face with my sleeve. *What a rookie moment that was.*

An hour later, I pulled up to Winchell's doughnut shop at Beach and Manchester to meet Paxton, as promised. He was already there and looked like he'd been for a while. As I walked up to him he said, "I usually don't do this, but I'm dead tired tonight. Got to get some coffee in me. Don't snitch, bitch."

"I'm not your mother," I shot back, walking up to the counter. It was a shiny aluminum surface with little jars holding packets of sweeteners and sugar packs, creamers and wooden stir sticks.

"You kind of look like her." He moved next to me at the counter window.

A dumpy, but sort of attractive-in-the-right-light kind of lady, about twenty-three, approached the window and mechanically asked, "Hi, what can I get you?"

"Small coffee, please." I pushed a dollar bill toward her on the counter. She pushed it back without expression, except maybe boredom.

"Sorry, we don't take money for coffee from police officers. Corporate policy. You can buy doughnuts, but not coffee. That's only available for free." What she said was exciting and confusing to me, but she was sneering at me through her tousled, stringy bangs. A single wrinkle in her forehead indicated it was my turn.

It was my first experience with this type of perk, and I felt like a celebrity. I stood there self-consciously, hoping no one could see the tremble I felt in my plastered-on smile.

Paxton was enjoying my reaction. Even the waitress looked like she was starting to wake up a bit. She cracked a smile, bearing witness to my fresh-faced inner conflict.

"Hey, it works out. Don't feel bad. Ever hear of a Winchell's Doughnut House getting robbed? Think about it," she gave me a sly wink.

"Yeah. Think about that, Ellis. Nobody robs Winchell's," Paxton reiterated slowly, allowing it to sink in.

Perhaps faulty reasoning, but we were talking about a damn cup of coffee.

"Okay, then. Thank you. Please give me a glazed doughnut and take it out of this." I handed back the dollar bill.

I turned to face the 2 a.m. traffic as Paxton muttered, "Don't let any of the guys at the PD bother you. They're just messing with you. Besides, only I'm allowed to really screw with you," he added with a half-grin.

"I got that figured out. Thought you knew I had a sense of humor. You didn't know that?" I prodded.

"Yeah, you're a damn card, Ellis."

The waitress arrived at the counter window with coffee and a glazed doughnut.

Seeming to just remember she was at work, she handed them to me, adding, "Can I get anything more for you?"

Paxton leaned on the counter before I could answer, "Yeah. Sure. How about a piece of jaw?" He chuckled at himself and had that grin.

She looked directly at him, snorted and turned around to begin wiping the counter top. Dismissing our presence.

I walked away to distance myself from that aura, but he followed, still chuckling quietly. "See Ellis? That's how you handle business."

He enjoyed my look of disgust. "Oh, calm down. I'm just messing with you. Don't be such a puss. She's a friend of mine. She knew ahead of time I was going to do that, okay? Oh, man. Are you easy, or what?" He laughed good-naturedly.

I slowly shook my head, "Your idea of comedy is…really different."

"I know, so I'm told." He paused for a moment as we ate. "Hey, I saw your shooting scores. What the hell happened with you? Started out shooting like an eight-year-old girl and then, boom. You race up the damn chart." He stepped back as though in amazement. Then he smiled again.

"FBI taught us at the academy. And, I'm going to get even better, so don't piss me off," I said, closing one eye to aim my thumb and index finger between his eyes.

"You better watch out. Keep this up, the brass might ask you to join the competition shooting team. Don't do it, though," his cadence slowed as he stepped forward, "because you'll blow it. No, I'm being serious with you, you'll tense up and blow it. And, everybody will be intensely watching *you*. Everyone. I'm telling you, man. Very competitive. All the best shooters in the county. Way too much pressure for a rookie. You won't be able to handle it. You'll fuck it up in front of everyone and you'll *disgrace* the department. I know you will," he laughed tauntingly, hoping he'd gotten to me. And he did. I guess that was his idea of hazing.

"But you ought to drop by the house. I live close to you. Show you how I reload ammunition. Make a man out of you."

"You have your own reloading equipment?" I asked, brushing right over his attempt to sap my self-worth. I was surprised. I never knew anyone who made ammunition in their garage before. My life was really opening up.

"Yep. Come by one day and I'll show you. Hey, I'm gonna hit the streets. Let's get together around four, if it's slow enough. We can go over to Knott's and mace chickens."

Just when I thought I was done being shocked by Paxton, he said something to knock me on my ass. I couldn't help my expression as I looked up at him.

He raised his eyebrows at my startled response.

I couldn't tell if he was joking or not. "How do you do that?" I leaned back in mild disbelief.

"It's easy. Just roll up and park the unit and they eventually walk up to you. Or, sometimes I throw a little bread. They come up pecking their damn beaks to get that bread and zap. I mace their ass. It's fun, man. They run around like crazy."

"You're kidding me," unaware my jaw had dropped to my chest.

"I don't think it hurts them much. They just run around in a circle for a while. It's funnier than hell, Ellis. You just have to get into it." He laughed slyly, and I still wasn't sure if he meant it or not. Maybe it showed on my face.

"What's so bad about it? People hunt. I'm just having fun. I'm not *killing* them. Just helping them lose weight." He paused briefly in consideration, "But how do we know the little bastards don't deserve to die? They never say shit. Never warm up to you. They're shifty. That's guilt, dude."

Paxton seemed a little off-center, but funny and bright as hell— except about chickens.

10

Two men were present in the chief's luxurious wood-paneled office. Credentials, awards and photos overwhelmed the huge wall behind him. Three separate flags were on full display within the office: The United States, State of California, and City of Buena Park flags. It was all brazenly, almost ostentatiously patriotic. God Bless America. God Bless Buena Park. God Bless Us All.

It was so overwhelming, I half-expected to see a breeze making the flags ripple to the beat of America: "My Country, 'Tis of Thee."

The chief's massive slab desk of heavy maple wood rested on dark blue carpet. Two visitor chairs faced the chief's desk, and in them sat Lt. Burns and Sgt. Houser. A staff meeting just concluded, but the chief had asked Burns and Hauser to hang back. The door shut behind a group that seemed curious about the closed-door meeting, and didn't want to leave—their feet dragging most of the way.

"What do we have?" Chief leaned back in his executive chair, arms crossed over his belly, his face gaunt and braced, like he was preparing himself for bad news.

Houser hesitantly turned to Burns, "You want to start?"

"No. You go ahead." He seemed just as wary, clearing his throat.

Houser nodded. "For what it's worth, Ellis will make a good cop. I'm pretty sure of that. He's had some hairy calls and does well. Guys like him, and most supervisors like him." He paused for a second to allow any questions, and seeing none, proceeded.

"Here's my memo about Ellis and the Rules and Regulations thing." He stood and handed the memo to Sedley.

"I can't remember for sure, so I can't say he did ask me for a copy." He shook his head. "I can't believe he wasn't issued one. But, apparently none of the new hires were."

Sedley leaned forward, "Why the hell would a new officer not have a copy of rules and regulations? That's nuts. Where's Lenny?"

"The captain is speaking to the Ladies' Club. He should be back in a couple of hours," said Burns.

"What do you have?"

Burns slid a printed memo across the desk to Chief Sedley. "Here's Ellis' response. Looks like we all fell down a bit on this. PD sure did. And this kid's in a pile of financial shit. Took a big pay cut to come here.

"Financially, it didn't work out. It'll take him a while to dig his way out of this. But, just maybe he can. He has a second job. If he declares bankruptcy, the problem goes away."

Chief looked over the documents for a moment and then leaned forward in his chair. "Thank you, gentlemen. I'm going to give him a second chance on this. He can document everything as it happens for us. Everything. Any further credit issues come up, we let him go. And, I'll talk to him." He looked up, "Any thoughts?"

everal months later, I was sitting in my personal car, hoping the pounding rain would subside. It was going like hell out there, and I didn't want to put myself through that just yet. We Southern Californians don't do well in the rain. *I'll give it a minute. Briefing doesn't start for a half-hour. Hell, I can give it ten minutes.*

My seat was reclined for ultimate relaxation, allowing me to procrastinate my obligations for the moment. *I could just relax for ten minutes and…*suddenly I jolted upright as the thought ran through my mind, *Wait, this is the only time I have to study.*

Although the thoughts were causing me some anxiety, I decided to shut that down for the moment. I leaned back into my seat again, desperate to let go of the stress of the moment. I knew I had a lot of years ahead of me with this same kind of maniacal schedule before I reached my goals.

I constantly raced from shift duty to school and from a second job to court. Also, my gigantic family always asked for its fair share of attention—my wife and loving daughters. But, everything was so tight. Sleep had become a stranger to me.

I'd adjusted to police work, though. I sailed through my rookie year. I was confident and assertive in extreme situations. I'd become one of the best shooters on the PD, and there was little I hadn't seen. If a call came in that involved a death, and it wasn't given to me, I would get permission to visit the crime scene for my own edification. Certainly not because I enjoyed it, but because exposing myself to the horror helped me grow increasingly numb to it. Adrenaline still raced through my body before most hairy calls, but who doesn't love a good code three chase?

I glanced at my watch. *I've got a couple more minutes.*

It would be a long run into the department with heavy rain banging on my shoulders. My thoughts went straight to my olive-green raincoat currently hanging in my locker with a mocking smile. *Why would anyone ever expect rain?*

Staring out the window, I saw a movie about my life playing on the sheets of rain. The sky was dark midnight, and the parking lot lamps cast a glow across the tops of cars and the wet pavement, causing a reflection of wavering light against the night.

I began to think of my daughter Annie and how small and delicate she was, and how much I loved holding her in my arms and making her feel protected. Dancing through my head were visions of Mary, my eldest, showing me a new story she'd written

My thoughts settled on Sarah. She'd grown from girl to an even more beautiful woman these past years. Men literally stopped in their tracks and turned around just to get another look at her…of her long blonde hair and her entitled attitude. Even at church, their gazes lingered beyond reason. I just grinned and shook my head. Five years ago, I would have been intensely angry catching a man staring at her.

It was so much more relaxing to know that now I could simply shoot him in the face. I could also just shoot his foot. There were always options.

The rain started to ease a bit, and it seemed to be my chance to duck in, so I ventured out to reach the PD back entrance, where I'd work swing shift that night. Lt. Dilbert Gorsh was watch commander. I had no idea the impact we would eventually have on each other's life.

I'd become friendly with him, which was kind of different in its own right, because he was disliked by most officers. He was famous for sending what most called, "Gorsh-a-Grams." It was his way of correcting questionable report writing, and he enthusiastically did so with a bright red pen. He loved it. He lived for it.

When ready, the marked-up report was placed where everyone could read it. Cops could be thin-skinned when it came to giving a shit about what their peers thought. They hated Gorsh-a-Grams and the shame that came with it. Peer pressure ran amok.

He'd yet to send me one, thus far. This surprised him, and he liked to joke with me about it. He was a big man, six-foot-eight, and seemingly an intellectual, in the police arena, at least. I guess that's not saying much. He enjoyed my sense of humor, as I did his. Gorsh became an early mentor of mine…of sorts.

One night, several months into police life, I guess I was feeling a bit down. The constant exposure to people, and what they did to each other and to themselves became an endless loop of the full-range horrors of humanity. The darkness. The evil. They tried to prepare you for this in training, but they couldn't. I began to realize it wasn't going to get any better. Man's inhumanity to man was not going away.

I'd just finished working a family fight that turned violent, but don't they all? This one included the severed finger of a woman that was the casualty of her man slamming his car door on it. This was during an earlier argument as he fled to the bar. She didn't want him to…and so it goes.

Days later, the man walked into the house, dropped the severed finger in his wife's lap and laughed, "Oops. Lose something?" Not surprisingly, quite the confrontation ensued.

As usual, she decided to not charge him, so I didn't have to bag the day-old severed finger. They seemed to be making up as I left their home. Probably made them hot. Next time, it'll be an arm or a leg.

While I finished up the report, Gorsh summoned me into his office and asked a few questions about the call. I answered a little absentmindedly.

"I swear, sometimes it looks like the world is about to end. There're crazy-ass people out there. A whole lot different than I thought they were—way worse than I thought. I didn't know there were so many that insanely different." I chuckled, but inside I was deadly serious.

Gorsh shook his head. "You got the Rookie Blues, Ellis, my man." He leaned back in his chair to postulate. "See what you got to do is, you always got to think like this: You're dealing with the lower two percent of the population, the shit of society, ninety-eight percent of the time. And, when you deal with normal people, there's some type of emergency, or you're giving them bad news, or a ticket, so they want nothing to do with you. Once you get that down, you can come off suicide watch."

He laughed in his boisterous way. But it did help. It brought me a bit of perspective. He tossed me a life raft while I figured things out.

About that time, Keaton stuck his head into the office, "Hey Ellis…I saw in the newspaper you won the State College Speaking Championships." He brought the rest of his body along, "Good for you."

He smiled at Gorsh. "If anyone has good instincts, it's me," as he put his hand out to shake mine. Just what I needed.

12

"**U**nit twenty-three twelve." Sid's voice always sounded like velvet over the police car radio.

I was assigned to Beat Three tonight. My call identification was 2313, and I was assigned to patrol the middle-east portion of the city. I loved Beat Three, which included the Knott's Berry Farm area. It was always an adventure: a mass of people, all demographics, action happening all around. I felt more alive than ever in this area of the city, more aware.

At 1 a.m., I traveled southbound on Dale Ave., approaching Crescent. I intuitively changed to the right lane, preparing to be a potential backup to 2312.

The air felt crisp, wiped clean from the rain earlier. The streets smelled like freshly applied asphalt, almost free of crime. *Yeah, right.* By now, I was well aware that kind of clean didn't exist. In fact, if it did exist, I'd be out of a job. I needed people to do bad things, just until I finished my degree.

Sid continued, "Twenty-three twelve, you have a four-fifteen bar fight in progress. At the *Aw Come In*, 6200 block of Beach Blvd. Multiple people involved. Twenty-three eleven and twenty-three thirteen, follow up."

"En route from Beach, north of Manchester," announced Bob Casey. "ETA two."

I picked up my own microphone, confirming to everyone listening that I was also on the way. I whipped my wheel to the right, turning on Crescent and increased the speed.

I wasn't assigned Code 3 status, but this type of call demanded a rapid response. Andy (twenty-three eleven) was going to get there alone before any backup did. You've got to help your brother. But, also, everyone knew it could be them in that situation next time, and they'd want the same speed of response.

There wasn't much traffic, but anyone still out for the night might not be as aware as usual. I activated the overhead emergency lights, taking care not to turn on the siren, but increased my speed further.

I turned right on Beach Blvd, barely pausing for red traffic lights. Whether a brother, officer asked for help not, you got there as soon as possible. At least, most of us did.

"Twenty-three twelve, ten ninety-seven front." Andy announced his arrival at the front of the bar.

I sped toward the *Aw Come In*, remembering it was notorious for bar fights. It was a country western bar with rednecks and bikers (as if there was a difference) and casual binge-drinking. The weekend crowd was usually large and boisterous, spilling out onto an asphalt backlot, which turned into an alley. Everyone wore black. Not a friendly group at first sight.

Too much open space for that many dark angry drunks. This gang was even angry through laughter, if you can imagine that. Trouble always brewed there.

Slowing through the intersection of Orangethorpe Ave., I noticed a police car parked in the street, extreme right lane. Parking lights were on with the engine running. I could see a silhouette of a head, but no movement. *What the hell?*

I deactivated the emergency lights and slowed the speed even more, a bit concerned. The bar fight was only half a mile away, where one of our officers was surely in the middle of it right now. *Why would this black and white be parked and running?* Was something wrong? As I got closer, I could see someone in the driver's seat, but I was unsure who it was.

The silhouette still sat unmoving, like he was just relaxing on the side of the road after a long drive somewhere. I pulled up to the driver's window to get a better look.

Crawling closer, I suddenly realized it was Sgt. McKinley. I squinted my eyes, instinctively searching for some sort of explanation. He was sitting idly in the car with the motor running, blatantly making no progress toward the *Aw Come In*.

"2312, 10-97, rear. Fighting in the parking lot, too," cracked the radio.

I looked down in a daze, remembering what I was in the middle of. It dawned on me McKinley had no intention of answering that call in a timely manner. It looked as though he was making sure all other units got there long before he did. This was concerning to me. He probably could have reached the bar at the same time as Andy. *What the fuck is the matter with you?* I wanted to scream out the window.

Instead, I shouted, "You okay?" desperate for him to prove me wrong.

McKinley waved me forward with his left arm, while he continued to stare straight ahead. Not once did his eyes meet mine. They just fixated lifelessly into the abyss.

I accelerated, glancing in the rearview mirror. McKinley remained parked. No movement. I couldn't believe my eyes. My blood went cold.

"Twenty-three-seventeen respond," Sid smoothly commanded. 2317 was Mike Gunner, so I was positive he was already en route. Any time there was a physical altercation or any other danger, Mike wanted to be the first on the scene. Me, too. Oftentimes I would feel as though we were in a race. We never spoke of it, but we both knew. Somehow, I couldn't see McKinley in the same race, any race.

Fifteen seconds later I arrived, dismissing McKinley from my mind, "2313, 10-97, rear."

"10-4."

I moved out of the vehicle and rushed into the alcohol-fueled chaos, amid flashes of staggering legs and slurred words. Typical commotion for a drunken bar in full swing, but the air was tinged with something extra.

Bob had inserted himself between two fighters, both bruised and slightly bloodied. They appeared very relieved to be able to stop fighting. Out of shape and worn out, they were both panting hard in a daze. Bob had no trouble keeping the two apart.

"You guys, knock it off or you're going to jail. We've got a special room for you." Bob declared, butting out his chin in an alpha manner that always seemed to come naturally to him.

A loud screech was heard outside as Mike Gunner's black and white came to a dramatic stop at the curb. He leapt from the squad car, placing his nightstick into its holder and darted toward the parking lot. He was high on adrenaline. Moving quickly, his head freshly shaved and his mood ever aggressive.

"Dispatch says someone has a knife," he spat, eyes flying all over the scene. Ready for anything. *Semper Fi.*

"Help Casey, I'll go inside."

The sentence wasn't even finished before Gunner began making his way. "Shout if you need me," he said as he moved into the middle of the group. He was the captain in this element. Without missing a beat, he commanded, "Let's see some ID, people. Right now!"

Entering the *Aw Come In* was always an experience. The typical bar smell of beer, cigarettes, cheap perfume and sweat, rose to another level when mixed with blood and vomit. In full bloom tonight, it was distinct, to say the least. This odor never, ever seemed to falter. I knew I'd never forget it.

In the bar dimly lit, I took notice of some sort of floor struggle on the far side of the bar. I couldn't see over the bar clutter of open beer bottles, shot glasses, and lipstick stained cocktail napkins, but I could hear.

"Over here," Andy called.

Multiple pairs of feet thrashing together indicated at least a few people on the floor were fighting. I powered over in that direction, keeping my eyes glued on the ten to twelve possibly armed people watching me.

Some of them loved this action. You could smell it on them. You could hear it in their breathing rhythm. Much like Gunner, they were in their element, just in a slightly different way. He was in it for justice, sometimes as declared by Gunner himself. They were in it for...well, I didn't really want to find out what they got out it.

Others were shifting around uncomfortably, thinking of where else they'd rather be. Their escape impulse had kicked in, and they were anxious.

My progress toward the fight was slightly halted by the sight and loud sound of a large switch-blade knife hitting the barroom floor. Apparently, someone didn't want it anymore. I scooped it up without pausing. "Don't anyone leave here," I ordered with volume, causing everyone in the place to sincerely plan on leaving.

As I came around the bar, the raucous brawlers were rising to their feet.

Andy had control of one man. The other two still be fought each other as well as the man Andy was controlling. Exposed butt cracks, hairy backs, rolls of fat, and bad breath created a repulsive mess.

I grabbed both fighters as they grappled. "Stop it. Police. Knock it off." I shoved them apart while avoiding thrown fists, until they were too far apart to make contact with one another.

The fighter on my left was determined to continue, unfazed that a police officer had just ordered him to stop. The clueless and buzzed antagonist in this fight slowly cocked his drunken right fist to sucker-punch the other man.

I decided to end it, and hit him hard with my right fist, square in the lower chest. *Karma, shit ball.* With the wind knocked out of him, he bent over trying to get it back.

"What the fuck did I do?" *Belccch.* "What's going on? This hurts." He struggled between retching and coughing when his knees gave way, and he slumped to the ground. He put one hand to his chest, the another to his throat, and gasped for air.

"What the fuck? What did you hit him for, cop? He didn't do shit to you," a man from the shadows slurred.

"You stay out of this." I pointed in his direction, adrenaline practically shooting out through my fingertips. *We're not all McKinley.*

"Oh, yeah? Tough guy. Take your fucking badge off, and let's see how tough you are." The volume of his voice told me he was moving toward me, judgment clouded.

Suddenly, out of the corner of my eye, the flash of a quickly moving Mike Gunner appeared. I didn't bother responding to the man. At this point it would have been futile.

Meanwhile, Mike was in a slow and calculated trot. The kind field-goal kickers made as they approached the ball. Mike's ball was this man's menacing head.

He hit the man full stride, fist to the side of his temple. It looked as though he tried to punch through the man's head, which he probably was. There was a loud, melon thumping sound. The brawler's head jerked back, threatening to spin completely around. He fell hard on the floor. Loud enough to stop all action in the bar.

"Ow! That hurt. You son of a bitch," Mike muttered, looking at his right fist and shaking it out. The man on the floor wasn't moving much. Gunner glared at him with contempt for daring to injure his hand with his head. He was a kick.

I returned my attention to my subject, still moaning and holding his chest.

"Roll over on your stomach and spread your arms and legs," I barked. "Right now."

He slowly complied. His knuckles were red and his pants looked and smelled like they were covered in urine. I wondered if it had been my punch that caused him to piss his pants. He was still breathing hard, but beginning to calm down as he stretched out.

Andy had someone in custody, cuffed behind.

Gunner had acquired quite an audience, and he stared menacingly at them. Holding onto his right hand, his glare daring anyone to say *anything* about what had just happened.

Silence overtook the crowd. Not so much in fear as in enjoyment of the show. They wanted to see everything. What the hell, this was Friday night!

"Everybody get your ID out, right now," Mike newly demanded. No one seemed to know for sure if he was doing this to punish them for the way they looked (rednecks and bikers), but they'd been through the drill before, and knew they had to do it regardless. The crowd began getting out driver's licenses while grumbling about police interference, throwing passive-aggressive insults as loudly as they could get away with without actually being noticed.

Two other officers showed up for further backup. One of them was Sgt. McKinley. Their arrival was basically useless now, except the numbers looked way better. Now, the police were in control. But "control" was still in question as McKinley sat in his parked squad car staring straight ahead, listening to radio traffic and refusing to move.

I quickly put that thought behind me, where it belonged.

Gunner had organized his small crowd of party animals, and I began helping him check IDs. Casey and two other officers had the back secured. Everything else appeared to be tentatively organized.

I could feel and see McKinley furtively glancing at me from time to time.

But, this wasn't the time or place, and I simmered alone.

13

A t 4 a.m., I wearily pulled into the PD parking lot and parked my black and white. "Twenty-three thirteen, ten-nineteen." I'd arrived at the station. With slow hands, I shut off the engine and grabbed my notebook to take into the report room and complete my paperwork.

For a fleeting few seconds, I felt distracted by the amount of metal and cage and weapons loaded in this car, the amount of raw power. I'd come to enjoy this feeling. I returned to the task at hand, tucking my notes for the report into the crook of my arm and closing the car door. I turned to enter the PD.

McKinley was standing in the station's rear bay area, often used to take in prisoners. Arrestees could be physically taken from a vehicle directly through a steel cell door, which was an actual necessity every few assholes or so. He stood with his hands on his hips, seemingly waiting for me.

I paused briefly upon seeing him, still disgusted with his behavior from the last call. My mind raced with possibilities. Had he done something like this before? He's a twelve-year veteran, for fuck's sake.

What if next time, I was the one in a sticky call forced to rely on him for backup? After letting these thoughts go through my mind, I decided there was no better option than to walk straight into the fire.

So, I changed direction ever so slightly and headed toward McKinley. He was forty-six years old with close cropped salt and pepper hair, the type of 'do you'd see on a retired Marine, or maybe on a sketchy dogfight trainer. He had several nervous ticks. *Surely, well-earned.*

Mac's mouth rested in a slightly wary grin. He lowered his hands as I approached. His fingers nervously tapped his pant legs as he watched me with anticipation in his eyes.

"Get everything you need for the report?" he asked, brow furrowed and voice gruff as ever. Probably trying to mask the tick. But, his mouth was very dry.

"I was just following up. I'm doing an incident report, separate from the arrest reports. Have it pretty quickly," I said, hesitant to look him in the eye; didn't want him to read the disgust on my face. I didn't want the cotton from his mouth to touch me.

"Yeah right," he muttered, barely aware of what we were speaking about. "Hey. I got to talk to you about earlier." He folded his arms and leaned forward. "You know Ellis, sometimes we think we see things we don't really see." His eyes were watching mine carefully.

"O-kay." I almost felt embarrassed for him.

"We don't always know what's going on in situations. Even someone as smart as you."

I couldn't help but detect a hint of mockery in his tone. "Not sure what you're talking about," I said, squaring my jaw, keeping my eyes cold.

Mac put his hands in his front pants pockets and looked around to make sure no one was a witness. He leaned in. "Earlier. Passing by the car and not sure what was going on?" he rambled with his arms now half-raised, his palms facing me. He looked guilty.

I shrugged. "I don't care what was going on. That's your business, Sergeant. I do care about how we could've lost control of that situation because you weren't there, and you could have been there. That's what I care about, sir."

He sucked in his pock-marked cheeks and sighed, "There were reasons."

I shook my head. "I just don't know of any reason that'd stop you from responding to an *officer needs help* situation."

McKinley had both hands out again as if he was trying to hold back my thoughts. "Just keep this quiet, Ellis. You don't know. Okay? You don't know." It seemed as though he was trying to convince me he was on a secret mission and couldn't divulge his presence, and that I should keep it quiet.

"Know what, Sergeant? I think I *do* know. If someone asks me, I'm going to tell them. It won't be in my report, but we need know what's going on with back-up out there. I'm not going to lie for you. That's critical, and I just know what I saw." I was as pissed now as when I first saw him hiding out in his black and white. "You can tell them your side. Like you said, I don't know about that."

"Well, just be very careful. I suggest you think this over," he said, his tone venturing into the realm of threatening.

"I just hope I'm never in trouble in need of backup, and they send you," I bristled, now passionate enough to verbalize what I'd really been thinking earlier.

"What do you mean?" he asked quietly, squinting his eyes and moving his face a little closer to mine.

I was sure he knew what I meant. I shook my head again. I wanted to punch him in the face and tried to show that to him in my eyes. Both my hands were vibrating with the urge to strike.

"Nothing, sir. I got to get in and file my report. Lt. Gorsh wants it." I turned to walk away before I did or said something I would later regret.

McKinley mumbled in a condescending tone, but he was already too far behind for me to hear him clearly.

14

1970 – ROBBERY IN PROGRESS...

"I can't believe this," Scott exclaimed, his jaw slackened. "You wait here. I want to take another look."

Shaking his head in frustrated dismissal, the anger at anyone questioning him flushed Joe's face, quite a feat for a man with skin as dark as his. "No way I missed him. Come on, we're running out of time."

Scott arched his eyebrows, then shook his head, "We have two minutes. I need to double check this. Then we go." He spun on his heels and began to race to the employee locker room.

"Wait." Joe held up his right hand, "What if you don't find him?"

Scott whirled around, exasperation oozed from every inch of him. "We're locked in the store, asshole. Remember? No choice. I'll be right back."

Maybe she got it wrong. Maybe we can't pull this off, flashed through his mind as he continued to move toward the locker room, more nervous now than he could ever remember being in his life. *It was so much easier with the boss here.*

Fernando closed and re-locked the broom closet door from the restroom side as silently as he was capable of. He planned on working his shift like any other night, as though nothing happened. *No pot smell—technically nothing did happen*, he thought.

Yeah, he felt confident in his plan. His life had been filled with the necessity of covering for himself. He had a pattern going, a rhythm. He hurried through the restroom with a large dusting mop, desperate to get away from the crime scene before security returned. Poking his head into the locker room to make sure no one was around, he inched in, which turned into an all-out sprint once he realized he was in the clear.

Scott, two-thirds of the way to the locker room, heard a staff member shouting, "Please hurry up, Bob. I gotta get home. I have a sick kid."

Manager Bob shouted an answer, "We'll be right there. Sorry."

The exchange stopped Scott in his tracks. "Shit!" He twirled around and hurried back to his original hiding position.

"It's time now, okay?" Joe anxiously pleaded, "Let's go." His clenched fists and raised shoulders were telltale signs of his anxiety.

Scott held up his right hand without a word, miming for Joe to *shut up and take pause*. He again listened for movement as he glowered at Joe.

Soon, there were sounds of the manager arriving at his office and the happy voices of staff relieved to see him. They could finally leave for the night.

Scott's brows knitted into a scowl for Joe, "See? That's why we have a plan."

Fernando left the locker room and entered the store-proper, holding his mop like a sword of triumph. He kept walking, hearing the voices of his chatty fellow employees. The paranoia dripped out of him in syrupy perspiration.

The group of murmuring staff were now six aisles away from Fernando. He purposely mopped out of sight, behind the men's shoe racks.

West of Fernando stood Joe and Scott, also listening to the staff chatter and trying to time their pounce.

Three dramatically different energies electrified the air: the soft paranoia of Fernando, the restrained desperation of the staff to leave, and the fear and anticipation of Joe and Scott. Not connecting, yet connected. A visual three ring circus. A collision seen in advance.

Bob fumbled for his keys. He stopped suddenly and looked up, feigning surprise. "Oh no, I lost my keys!" He hunched his shoulders. "Now what'll we do?"

Christy, the store cashier manager, was eager to go. She rolled her eyes vehemently. "Come on, Bob. Please. You always do this. I want to go home."

"Okay, Okay." He looked at the floor a bit offended by her directness as he took the keys from his pocket. "Just having a little fun at the end of the day is all."

Christy rolled her eyes yet again, "Doesn't work the fourth time around, Bob."

Other store staff began to offer their deep thoughts on end-of-day joking, and how it might have impacted their lives.

Joe and Scott progressed to within thirty feet of the manager's office. Both, with bandanas covering their faces, had weapons drawn and raised. Their heads swiveled to see everywhere with pained stares as they approached further.

As the last employee began to enter the office, Scott suddenly appeared from hiding and pushed her into the office. She stumbled forward, heaving a grunt, but not falling. He and Joe entered the room filled to the brim with surprised staff, most of them shuffling back a step or two.

The first employee muffled a small yelp. Guns still drawn, the two weapons held eye-contact with everyone in the room except for Joe and Scott, who wildly stared at the breathless strangers.

"Everybody shut up and freeze! This is a robbery! Look at the floor right now. No one needs to get hurt. Right now! Look at the damn floor!" He moved closer with a menacing stare, and settled into his role.

15

David Moore and I hit it off the day we met in our theater history class. Clean-cut cops typically clashed with the long-haired stoner types, especially back then. But, he was the only person in college who made any sense to me. I always looked forward to seeing him.

He saw me as Bill, the actor/student/person. The guy who'd go to great lengths for a self-perceived good laugh. I saw him as an entertainer, songwriter, and aspiring actor. He swiftly became my best friend.

At his home not far from the college, David often sat at an upright piano in his living room and played original songs like, "Good Time Jill" and "Blue Lightning." I was blown away with his music and lyrics. I'd always enjoyed live music, but his songs and performances had me mesmerized. I was instantly convinced this guy would be a star.

He thought the same of me. He'd tell me he had no idea why I was wasting my time being a cop when a great performing career was "waiting in the wings." This had all the makings of a fine friendship as far as I was concerned. We hung out together almost daily in school and out, relishing in our shared love of the performing arts—something my uniformed brothers could never understand.

My police cruiser turned into the parking lot of Ralph's Market. I crept up next to an older Dodge van parked a distance from the store and the street; it sat in the dark because the parking lot light wasn't functioning.

As I parked and started to get out of the cruiser, two young men became visible while standing behind the van. They awkwardly abandoned their sodas, shifted their feet and looked at me through unruly locks of hair. One looked at me with a sense of recognition, which he quickly and mischievously masked. I moved toward them.

"Oh no. We're fucked now," David quietly exclaimed. "This is a cop. But, he's not the cop-friend I was expecting."

The other head of hair stood wide-eyed and rigid. His life seemed to be flashing before his eyes. His hand pressed against his chest with splayed fingers. Right when it seemed he was about ready to bolt into the distance, David burst out laughing.

"We're messing with you, Parse." He collected himself. "Tom, meet my dear friend, Officer Ellis," David sang, moving toward me and patting me lightly on the shoulder.

"Wow," said Parse without moving. "Oh, my God. This is pretty amazing. You weren't shitting, dude."

David's friendship was beginning to provide me with a unique escape. It allowed me to completely express myself through comedy, something I'd always been able to do, until I joined the humorless police department. And David, well, our friendship allowed him to freak out his friends, which amused both of us.

"Come on. It'll be hilarious." He raised his eyebrows at me, enticing as I looked around the lot. He always encouraged my characters and impressions, and now he wanted me to perform a few of them right here in the parking lot for him and Parse.

He was right. I thought about the possibility of a random person driving by and catching two long-haired stoners with their van and surfboards watching a police-uniformed leprechaun dancing around on parking lot asphalt. Almost as if David and Parse were hallucinating, but everyone else could see it too.

It was hilarious. I loved the visual.

16

Seated in the living room with her mother and father, Sarah read aloud with white knuckles from a newspaper article. "And I quote the Chief, when asked for reaction to Bill's success, 'I'm naturally very pleased. Many of our officers attend school to enrich their education, and when one succeeds in such a dramatic way, it's something we're all proud of.'"

She rose and handed the article to Dick, pointing to the photo. "Here, look at them shaking hands. It was nice of the chief to say that, but Bill says reactions at the PD have been mixed, to say the least." She began rubbing her hands together to remove the dryness of the paper.

Dick looked up from the article, his eyebrows furrowed, "What do you mean?"

She chose her words carefully, thrilled her father was finally asking questions about me and felt eager to impress him. "I don't know exactly. The Chief loves what's been happening. You know, winning the State Speaking Championships? He thinks it's good for the community to see a police officer in a human-interest light. He says when Bill wins the nationals in Texas next month, he's going to meet him at the airport with a band.

"The other guys get a kick out of it and razz Bill." She paused slightly as she took a seat. "That's if they know. A lot of them don't even know about it."

Dick leaned forward, his head cocked to the left, "They don't?"

Sarah very much enjoyed being *the source*, which made Bill's position on the police department that much more fulfilling for her. Being well-informed agreed with her commanding personality. She paused a little, dangling the information in front of her father with a playful smirk.

"Some of them don't live in town, Daddy. They don't see our news. It's pretty much not acknowledged by any of his coworkers." She looked away, trying to quell the fire starting inside her. *I worry about this bastard's problems more than he does. That's how much I love him,* she thought to herself with a little smile.

Dick scoffed, his management background fueling his take on the matter. "Ignored? Well, that's kind of dumb. If it's supposed to be a police human interest story, you should have your officers armed with at least a little bit of this news. I mean, that's poor. If the chief of police thought it interesting enough to take time for a photo and statement, to me, you engage the public. That's only common sense."

Sarah affirmed with a vigorous head nod, "That's what Bill says. He says for some reason, there's a bit of negative reaction from management types. You know, sergeants, lieutenants." She couldn't hold back her smile—she was so relieved to finally hear Dick agreeing with her husband. At least, with her version of him. She crossed her legs, hyperaware that she had just peed herself the tiniest bit.

"What do you mean?"

"Seriously. He says it makes him feel a bit paranoid. You know he's a little out front anyway."

Dick snorted. "He's out front, all right. You can't be a smart aleck in that job."

"No, Daddy, that's wrong," Sarah shot back, anxious to maintain what she perceived as Dick's new and improved respect. She paused slightly. "A couple of them really want him to fall flat on his face."

"Well…that's not good," Lucille slurred. She reached into her purse and retrieved a pack of Marlboro cigarettes with only three left. She held the pack in her hand, smiling vacantly at Dick and Sarah. They both stared at her with blinking eyes, almost as if they had forgotten she was there. Apparently, she felt this, and protected her last three smokes.

"He says they don't understand him, and to hell with them," Sarah continued as though Lucille hadn't spoken. "The persona of a cop who happens to act and likes public speaking and goes to college full time? They only understand the cop part," she shrugged.

"He's out there doing the best he can and it's right to him, even if it *is* different. And, it benefits the city." She shook her head, "He isn't going to change anyway, not unless he wants to." A light wave of something washed over Sarah, but she quickly tucked it away in the back corner of her mind, unwittingly, almost subconsciously saving it for later.

"They'll get used to it…or they won't," Lucille chimed in, her eyes locked into that almost empty pack of Marlboros with her shotgun and booze-addled intellect.

"It'll be okay," proclaimed Dick, as if that made it so. "He's doing what they wanted. I heard at that graduation this was a 'new breed' of cop to reach out and bring the community together. Right? That's what he's doing. So, they'll get over it."

He tapped his index finger against the newspaper photo a few times, "Shaking hands with the chief and that big article…I can see where it could be a pain to some. That happens. But, not with the rank and file." He raised his wrist to eye level and gazed at his watch. "You said he's in class now? When'll he get home?"

Sarah confessed with a weak smile, "About eight-thirty tomorrow morning. He has rehearsals in Hollywood right after classes, and then works graveyard shift."

"Wow," muttered Lucille, finally lighting her Marlboro with a candle lighter.

Sarah continued, suddenly a lot quieter. She stared, not at anything in particular, just stared. "That's if he doesn't have court. If he has court, I don't know when he'll be home. And, final exams are close. Another day's sleep lost, I'm sure."

With his elbows on his knees and a concerned look on his face, Dick softly spoke, "You know, you can't burn the candle at both ends for very long. He's been going strong for quite a while now. Maybe he should enroll in less classes, take it easier."

Sarah shook her head. "I've talked to him. He's driven to get through school fast as possible, and see what he can do here at the PD. He's doing everything like he's chasing something."

Suddenly, all of the passionate fire perpetually burning in Sarah dimmed, and she was seen for the one thing she never really got to be. A teenage girl. Her arms crossed over her chest defensively, her gaze automatically went to her shoes.

Dick took his daughter's hands in his and waited until she looked him in the eye. When she did, he said, "If I know him honey, he'll catch it."

17

It was a June evening three months later at the Elks Club. Reserved specifically for officers and wives, they held a night to come together as "brothers in blue." It was an opportunity to meet the women we all went home to at the end of every shift (some more than others, of course).

I wore a charcoal gray suit and a red tie, two holdovers from my earlier business life. Sarah was a knockout in her powder blue dress. Her eyes sparkled with the joy of being on a date. She was content with anything, as long as we were together. She laughed at every joke, even my worst, and heads did not stop turning to gaze at her all night.

Well-decorated for a local hall, the club was not so well air-conditioned. But, it sort of lit up at night. The huge stucco white building had a large ballroom floor with a kitchen and bar. Other than that, there wasn't much to recommend it.

I'd been here before with many of my fellow officers, only that time the scene was a lot different. A riot had broken out from the antics of over a hundred twenty-year-olds, who had no interest in complying with the club's party rules. Things got ugly. I couldn't help but smile to myself. It was amazing to think both events, the riot and this subdued little blue-brother ball, took place in the same room.

Wives, equipped with toothpaste commercial smiles, casually fanned themselves as they mingled, careful not to sweat through their makeup.

Tables, large enough to seat eight, were peppered around the large room. Each table, covered by an emerald green tablecloth, had a facsimile of a Buena Park Police badge as a centerpiece.

Cops moved from table to table as they traded over-told, tough-guy jokes that had been worn out through generations of men, trying to impress colleagues and please management. Most furtively glanced about to spot any clues of acceptance.

I was a little surprised to see some of the guys sucking up in the "true blue" arena. I thought the police department would be different from an everyday nine-to-five company—less about politics and more about the bravado. But, I guess little work sagas existed in every job and sucking up was basically universal, reinforced wherever you looked (except in the mirror).

We'd just finished a reasonable dinner of chicken, mashed potatoes and gravy. As we picked up our drinks and began to mix with others, Sergeant Pense approached us with an elegantly dressed woman.

"Ellis, meet my wife, Alice." He smiled at Sarah. Sarah smiled back.

Sarah smiled at Alice. Alice smiled at Sarah. I smiled at everyone, not really sure what else to do. Thirty seconds in, and I had been through enough social exchanges to make my head spin.

After even more pleasantries, Pense cheerfully said to his wife, "Ellis here is already a member of the *Bator* squad. Aren't you?" He rocked back on his heels taking a sip of his beer with a wide grin, his eyes creasing, like he knew some big punch line.

"Bator squad?" asked Sarah. "He hasn't mentioned anything about it." She looked at me, "What's that, honey?" Her eyes were innocent and curious.

Pense choked on a mouthful of beer, his eyes lighting up with amusement. He was clearly ready to give Sarah his answer. Before he had a chance, I flashed him a look of man-to-man pleading. He winked at me, shaking his head and grinning. Sarah glanced at me, still puzzled. She was about to speak again when the blaring rustle of a microphone being adjusted cut her off.

Chief Sedley's voice boomed over the microphone in front of the room, saving us from Pense's unbearable punchline. "Will everyone please take your seats for a bit longer? I have a couple things I want to say about this past year."

Everyone began returning to their seats as I quietly answered Sarah, "It's a terrible joke he's told me about fifty times. You know when I got my Master Level shooting medal?"

She nodded her head, but her eyes were telling me she wasn't connecting yet.

I went on, feeling a little flushed in the cheeks at having to explain this stupid joke to my incredible wife. "Master? Bator? Isn't that a scream?"

She looked at me blankly.

"Actually, it was sort of funny the first time." I shook my head with a flat smile, awkwardly turning away, searching for a distraction.

As we took our seats, I glanced around the room at my comrades and their wives, drinking and gossiping like teenagers. Even the older cops had that mischievous sort of look on their faces, like we were in a high school lunchroom and a food fight was about to break out.

I wasn't too far into my career before I realized that cop life was kind of like high school—everyone trying to impress each other with their wives and their stories. The herd mentality was proven to be inescapable. I wanted to be in the herd, but I suspected it wouldn't be long before I realized it wasn't for me.

Chief Sedley began once more, "I hope everyone enjoyed their meal." He patted his belly. "I know I did. And, we're very grateful for all the hard work that was done in the kitchen tonight." He nodded toward staff, which was followed by mild-mannered applause.

He continued rambling as my mind began to focus on the fact that he was dressed like an older Jack Webb, smoking a cigar. The whole room began to look like an early 1950s movie.

The clichéd smoky haze rose as many exercised their after-dinner ritual. The smoking men had moved their chairs back from the table as though that would help anything, but it was at least a semblance of effort. They obviously felt grand in their grace.

I smiled at Sarah as the presentation continued. But, my mind soon wandered to rehearsals for a play I was cast in at school. I found myself going over lines in my head before I realized what was happening.

Sedley droned on and on.

I couldn't help feeling I was almost where I wanted to be at that point in my struggles. A great job, a loving wife, two beautiful daughters, graduation near. And of course, my career was finally beginning to pay off.

".... and Detective Roy Stern is selected as *Officer of the Year.* Come on up here, Roy."

A huge applause erupted. I jerked my head around, searching with everyone else for the man of honor. Stern was an excellent cop, well respected by everyone. Thirty-five with the muscular, agile body of a fighter. The man moved like a panther. He had a square, granite chin and was "as tough as nails," as Sedley described him. He was already an icon to me from what I'd seen and heard.

My mind wandered to one of the first interactions I ever had with Stern. I'd only been hired on for two months at that time, and a homicide occurred in the *Berry track.* Infamously known as one of the toughest areas of town, filled with gangs and the violence that typically followed. We found a messy murder scene of multiple stabbings and shootings. We were barely able to identify the mangled, bloody body. It turned out to be another husband unsatisfied with his wife. Perhaps she was late with dinner or engaged in some anti-macho statements.

I practically trembled with excitement as Stern came into the station. I wanted to talk to him and find out everything about the scene. It was how we learned.

I recalled approaching Stern as he sat himself before the long counter used for report writing. I was buzzing, adrenaline rushed through my body as if I had been there with him. He looked a bit worn down, shifting around his notes and documents to prepare for the writing task. Most cops do *not* like to write police reports, and he appeared no different.

"I heard about your call," I managed to get out. I barely knew Roy at this point. It was ballsy for a rookie to approach a revered veteran like that; we knew that from the beginning. But I was desperate for some insight from the more experienced cops. The caste system wasn't for me, didn't have time for it. I had to catch up.

He looked up at me with disinterested eyes, or maybe in his mind, he was still at the crime scene, "What call?" His dull eyes flew back to his papers.

Was he blowing me off because I was new, or was this the real him? I decided to probe further. "Oh, I'm sorry. I thought you had the 187 (murder) in the Berry track."

"Yeah, that was my call." He opened his briefcase on the desk and took out a copy of the penal code without looking at me.

"I heard it was really bad. Messy." I started to sound desperate for a response, but I didn't care. *Tell me something.*

Stern glanced at me with a bored expression, dry as a bone, as he opened the book to section 187. He opened his mouth to underplay, "Just a Mexican divorce." He sniffed as if that had said it all.

Then he just looked at me.

The expression on my face as I processed his words was enough to crack his granite face into the slightest semblance of a "gotcha" smile. In a flash it was gone, and he was right back to his seat and his report.

It both startled and impressed me how light he could be in a situation like that. That leap from tragedy to comedy in the blink of an eye, a coping mechanism, a secret to getting through it. It made sense to me: *An epiphany.*

Chief Sedley's voice continued after Ray's short acceptance, snapping me back to the present. "And…*the Rookie of The Year Award* goes to…Officer Bill Ellis."

My eyes widened, Stern's 187 still on my mind. I was used to being called "Rookie" by now, but never heard '*of the year*' go after it. I didn't even know it was a category. There were only five of us.

Sarah looked at me with surprise, which she quickly hid to make it seem as though she'd expected it. *Take that*, I thought as I squeezed her hand, smiling sweetly. She smiled back without her teeth, motioning for me to get up and accept.

Sedley waited as I somehow made my way up to the podium without tripping, shaking, or sweating through my gray suit. I heard words of congratulations during my journey, but I couldn't shake a foreboding feeling that there were a few who wouldn't mind watching me trip.

18

"Why do you have to go on your one day off?" Sarah pleaded from her place on the couch. I tugged on my light jacket for the rare Southern California chill, took her hands and looked into her blue eyes, "Babe, I told you. He asked me to. I think I can learn from him."

A gurgling noise announced itself from the bedroom, followed by high-pitched giggling.

"Let me get her," dropping Sarah's hands and moving to the noise. Relief washed over my body, whether I was aware of it or not.

I strode down our short hallway into the bedroom and gently scooped Katie (third and latest addition to our family), up in my arms. "Hey, little girl. How're you doing? I love you." I swayed back and forth as I held her to my chest, rocking her to a sense of ease. She was naturally happy and content. It was contagious, and I soaked it in.

I lived for that warm feeling of holding a child of my own—like everything became perfect. I couldn't help but put my face to hers and breathe in that soft clean baby smell. Nothing in the world smelled better than my baby's head.

I reluctantly returned to the living room, handing Katie to her mother,

"I'll be about two hours."

My insane schedule would give many the impression that about now all I cared about was school, working and acting…and reaching for more. But I loved being with my daughters. When all three of them were on my lap staring up at me with their eyes all full of life or we were playing around together on the floor, I could hardly take it. I was addicted to their alert faces, their resounding laughter, and their innocent touch when they hugged me as if I was the only man they'd ever need.

As for my wife, it was becoming difficult to be in the same room sometimes. The chasm between us grew wider than ever. Just as I started to feel everything was coming together, I noticed further strain between us. A strain I was in denial of, perhaps in effort to try and will my life closer to perfection. My constant pursuit, and the time it was taking, was bringing up a lot of half-buried resentment on both sides. Not to mention the increasing changes in my personality due to what I was exposed to every day. *Man's inhumanity to man.*

I felt quite distant from her then; like she couldn't possibly understand me anymore. I felt like very few people could. And, I was right. Looking back, it might be self-defense had run amok. But I couldn't see past it at the time.

"Click," I said to her one night in the midst of one of our arguments, touching my right-index finger to the side of my head. We were lying in bed next to each other, and she'd already blown through one of her monologues about how tough I'd been making life for her.

"What?!" She cut herself off mid-sentence and stared at me with her mouth open, clearly taken back.

"Click," I repeated. "I'm done. I've turned off my switch. I don't even know what you're talking about right now. I left." I looked at her with blank eyes, my face unmoving. "Truly gone."

Sarah just continued to stare at me, her mouth still open in bewilderment.

I turned over on my side and closed my eyes, determined to get some sleep.

I'd definitely changed. Disassociation skills learned for survival in police work, had now marched their way into my personal life.

And I liked it.

I parked the station wagon in front of Gorsh's house, stepped out and stretched my arms a bit. My eyes wandered around the neighborhood, mildly surprised. All the homes surrounding his were in immaculate shape: lush green lawns, fresh layers of paint and tidy driveways. But, I didn't even need to know Gorsh's address to spot his place—it stuck out like a sore thumb. A shredded window screen leaned against the exterior of his house, which was swarmed by homely patches of brown grass complemented by just the right amount of...more dirt.

I could see his house paint peeling from the sidewalk, and dust and cobwebs surrounded the entrance. The entire spectacle made me embarrassed for Gorsh. I approached the porch with a set jaw, trying to control my reaction. Police officers were supposed to be model citizens, and this surely didn't look good to his neighbors. At the time, I strongly believed in always representing, especially a lieutenant.

As if everything I'd seen thus far wasn't enough, the front door was ajar, taking in a light breeze. The only thing separating Police Lt. Dilbert Gorsh's private life from the street was a rusty old screen door, not quite closed, and sort of off-center. It was barely hanging on by the hinges (kind of like he would be one day).

Surely this wasn't what they meant by neighborhood watch.

I started in the direction of the front door, but before reaching the top porch step, the mystifying man himself threw open the screen door with a flourish.

"Why, it's Ellis. Come in, if you dare," he bellowed in his baritone, made-for-stage voice, stretching his inordinately tall body to its fullest extent. Gorsh glared at me from the height of his tip toes, looking like an angry clown. He really got a kick out of turning himself into a real-life version of Frankenstein, whether for awkward comic relief or intimidation behind the badge.

He chuckled and returned to his normal, but arguably still massive height. As I entered the house, Gorsh craned his neck to scan the neighborhood, possibly looking for anyone who might have followed me or knew either one of us from the PD. As our relationship had extended from mentor to friend, we'd kept it to ourselves to avoid others thinking there was any favoritism going on. There wasn't, but we both knew people always needed a reason to talk. We rarely worked the same shifts. "But one can't be too careful," he told me.

Seemingly satisfied I hadn't been tailed or noticed, he returned his gaze to me. "Go in and have a seat, young man. Sit at the feet of the master."

He'd offered to take his casual mentoring beyond just the PD now, and I was willing. Maybe he needed someone to practice on, and there was always a chance of me actually learning something.

A quirky and knowledgeable man, our conversations had gusto. We brushed over stocks and bonds trading (which I zoned out during), politics (the John Birch Society was far too liberal for him), and police department politics (to which he gave bellicose and sarcastic opinions almost always), and a little bit of everything else in life in between.

Something flickered in the corner of my eye: the quiet, feminine movement of his wife. She moved through the room quickly as I entered, like a six-foot whisper, a flash of flannel. She avoided eye contact. Then she was gone. The complete opposite of her booming, in-your-face husband.

The floors were bare, and somehow I didn't think they were going for the new "mod minimalism." Parts of the slab floor were showing through, except for the few areas covered by old throw rugs.

As for the furniture, it appeared to be from a 1930s flea market. If I hadn't seen Gorsh and his wife yet, you could have convinced me the house had been abandoned decades ago.

The dining room table was full of indiscernible junk. I couldn't imagine the last time someone dared to eat off it.

Gesturing toward the table, "My home office," he grandly announced, "Where I'll make my first million, Ellis." He placed his right hand on his heart.

"Yes, Sir. And at that point, you might want to have some carpet put down."

He looked at me and laughed a deep belly laugh. "In due time, little man. Have a seat."

It was easier than I expected. There were actually two chairs with enough surface to sit. I chose the one facing the high back executive chair, obviously reserved for him. You might imagine an executive chair would be out of place in a dining area, but this home existed in a land where "out of place" was in.

Gorsh walked to his side of the table and dropped his body heavily onto the executive chair, leaning back with a sigh. "I'm getting old, Ellis. This job's killing me."

"Yes. I can see how sitting behind your desk could kill you. But, please sir, only die on my day off?" I asked without missing a beat. "I don't want to get stuck with the paperwork."

He snorted. "It'd be good for you. Do something right for once, instead of all that college shit, you selfish bastard." He leaned forward, "All you actors are faggots, did you know that?"

I clutched my chest as though injured, "Argh. Clichés always wound the deepest. Shows how much time you spent on the insult. I deserve better."

"So, what's happening on graveyard?" he asked, ignoring my critique.

Returning back to a normal seated position, I said, "Police work. Why? What's happening on third shift?"

This stopped his rhythm. He stared at me for a moment, as if rolling my answer around in his mind.

"We're planting daisies, Ellis. Fucking daisies," he said measured. "Want a glass of water?" I nodded and he exited into what I hoped was the kitchen. It dawned on me that I was beginning to feel a bit uncomfortable.

He kept calling to me, asking questions about other supervisors and detectives and other street cops. I felt he pressed for information I shouldn't really be giving up. What made it even weirder was that we weren't even in the same room during the interrogation.

I kept my responses light. My fellow officers were stand up guys, good cops anyway, but I wouldn't say the same about a few members of management. Rather than give him the straight dope on that, I kept it to myself. I'd grown smarter than to just trust anyone. Wearing a badge had certainly taught me that.

What made him forget we didn't dish dirt on each other? We had each other's backs. Sometimes "we" were all there was between us and a horrible fate. It was a bond for life. Nothing could break that.

Gorsh re-entered the room and lowered himself into the chair. "Okay, Ellis, you got to keep this quiet. Don't even tell your wife. You hear me? I'm not kidding." He paused dramatically, taking in my facial expression and body language, which was blank, almost rigid.

"Barnett contacted me. Called me at home. He wants to get input on the state of the PD from someone *other* than the chief. Says it'll be confidential. He may be talking to others. He's gonna be a strong city manager." He started to squirm unconsciously in his seat, appearing conflicted. I didn't think he wanted to share this with me as much as he wanted to just get the thoughts out.

"I got a meeting with him Thursday night. Got a lot to tell him." Gorsh looked at me, deadpan. "Starting with our crappy chief...."

"Isn't that violating the chain of command? Dangerous thing to do without the chief's knowledge," I guessed. "This doesn't sound good. What if this is a *setup,* and the chief's testing your loyalty? Either one of them could be doing that. You'll be working Retail Hall dances with me."

Those dances were mayhem. Fist fights, knife fights, gang fights and other violence ruled the night. Especially when Mick Jagger's voice loudly pronounced '*I can't get no sat-is-fac-tion*'—it was an amazing trigger for violence in young men. It never failed. I probably received ten years' worth of crises training simply from working those dances on Friday nights.

Gorsh pondered a moment, drumming his fingers on the tiny circle of the table that wasn't cluttered with crap.

"And all those assholes that have laughed at me over the years. Ha. We'll see who's laughing last when I show Barnett what's going on around here," he continued, blowing past my question.

"So, what *is* going on? Does he not like Sedley?" I asked, undeterred. Something didn't feel right.

Gorsh looked at me for a long time. "Not when I'm finished, he won't." He continued to stare at me, ruminating on the words.

19

MONTHS LATER...THEATER CALLS

Through my new acting agent, I learned I'd been cast for a role in *The Fantasticks*, which had been running for the past three years at the Hollywood Center Theater. I was feeling like a big deal, as if I was really starting to get somewhere in acting. We performed Wednesday through Saturday nights, which worked great with school and work. I was on cloud nine. Another step of my plan completed.

In a matter of three intense days, I learned lines, choreography, and songs, and did a walk-through of the blocking. I didn't even get a chance to meet the other cast members until just before the performance. It couldn't have been more last minute, but I didn't care.

I was thrilled at any chance to professionally get on the stage in the middle of Hollywood. I didn't get paid a whole lot more than *gas money*...but, I was a professional. I worked in Hollywood. Who knew who might see me perform at that theater? This could be the open door into an entirely new world for myself, and I was hungry for more. This was my dream coming true.

Arriving at the backstage door at about 6:30pm on Wednesday, I was riled with adrenaline. My nerves crackled at the thought of messing up a line, but the pre-show anxiety always had a great effect on me. It forced me to really perform like my life depended on it.

You didn't even get to do a single run through. The timing could be all off, I thought, but I quickly pushed it all out of my mind. Worst case scenario, I bomb. *So what? Everyone does.*

Heading for the dressing room, I entered through the set area. In the dressing room, I came face to face with the other actors. A group of five nudged each other in front of the large cosmetic mirrors, trying to put the finishing touches on their foundation make-up.

The rest of the cast were either squirming into their costumes, muttering lines under their breath, or stopping everything entirely to turn and look at me. Most didn't, though. They were already expecting a new guy.

I detected conflict on the faces of those who made eye contact with me. They wanted the show to go well, which automatically made them wary of me. I could be a one-man shit show, for all they knew. Actors tend to be narcissistic and territorial about pretty much everything, right down to their spot in the dressing room. Some of them looked one wrong step away from pissing on their corner to mark it as theirs. I stepped inside and closed the door gingerly, exchanging a few tight smiles and wondering when someone would actually speak to me.

I turned to my little section and bent down to get my shoes from the bottom of the "closet," hanging costumes brushing the top of my shoulders in the process.

"Wow, take a look at that ass! Ohhh, honey," a man cooed behind me. I turned around, face-to-face with who I'd soon learn to be Flynn Parry. No one ever had to drag that queen out of the closet, and he was proud of it. He introduced himself with a dramatic flourish, as if actors weren't dramatic enough. Bonus points if he made the receiver of his lurid comments uncomfortable.

Flynn smirked at his colleagues as he stood before me with his hands on his hips. I could read it on his face: he was getting ready to give my ass a little smack, and titillated at the chance to be both the lifeline to the new guy and the center of attention. Suddenly his face froze and all the humor in his voice evaporated. "Oh, my God. He's wearing a gun."

I looked around the room to find the few eyes that weren't on me before, definitely were now. The entire cast was watching me, horrified. Nothing shuts up a group of theater geeks quicker than a loaded gun.

"No. No. Look, I promise I'm harmless," I chuckled a little and held up my hands by my chest in the universal sign for peace. The faces remained wary. "I moonlight as a cop—look," I Pulled out my badge to prove it. "I meant to leave it in the car, which I'll certainly do next time." I put my badge away, "It's my *job* until I make it. You all have one, I'm sure."

A collective sigh circled the room as the cast understood and began to talk again, still barely acknowledging me, but letting out nervous laughs of relief.

Flynn touched his palm to his face in mock adoration, "And you don't even *know* what I was about to do to that fanny of yours."

"Enlighten me," I joked, thrusting said fanny his way.

He threw his head back and let out a roar of laughter, then recovered, wiping his eyes a bit and patting me on the shoulder. "Wish I had, now. You'd probably have pistol whipped me, and I usually have to shell out big bucks for that," he said with a wink.

A couple of the other actors joined in on Flynn's and my laughter, and just like that I was part of the cast, badge and all. That's the other thing about actors, as narcissistic and territorial as they can be, they always welcome you like family as long as you can take their crazy shit. You just have to prove you can be as big as they can when you need to be.

But, more importantly, as long as you can really bring it onstage and make the audience feel something, make them believe you, and accept your strange peers as seriously as anything, then you're always welcome, no matter where you came from or how you got there.

The show that night was a complete success. I felt better about my potential as an actor, picturing myself in a tuxedo accepting awards in my dreams. I imagined a bright future under the lights and on the stage—I felt so alive. Finally, I had some solid experience under my belt, and there was no telling how successful I could be.

2 0

itting at my desk, eyes boring holes into the papers in front of me, I was doing everything I could to stay focused. Sarah drove the girls to the park, so I could study for finals in peace, and studying my notes was taking everything. I hadn't slept more than a total of five hours in the last three days.

I'd been working graveyard shift lately, and the still, yet unpredictable quiet of the streets was enough to make me hallucinate on more than a few occasions. Shadows darted in front of my car—either a person, an animal, or a result of my sleep-deprived mind. But sleep was something I just didn't have the time for, and I guess...safety.

I hunched over the papers and gazed at my own handwriting, determined to give my full attention to school, but my tired mind drifted off, and I found myself fixating on the issues at the police department.

Since the beginning, I'd gotten on well with colleagues and detectives. However, the more attention I'd been getting from the chief and the press, the less the *supervisors* liked me. This dynamic didn't make sense to me at that age. I figured since Chief Sedley was pleased with my high-profile community performance, the other leaders would be too. At least that was my logic. But, this same type of misunderstanding would follow me for many years. People are very strange.

Generally speaking, other officers and weak police managers do not like to see one publicly succeed. It's sort of an unspoken rule—one I never learned. Sometimes I just had to go through things to understand them. I had to experience these wacko reactions to comprehend that they existed, and experience the pain with the joy to realize the spectrum, perhaps.

Lt. Hanson, Sgt. Baker, and my good friend, Sgt. McKinley combined seemed like they didn't know what to do with me. They always seemed to be angry or irritated with me. Police work demanded that you be outspoken and aggressive with fellow officers, or you'd get eaten. Knowing this, I should have also learned to shut my mouth when around *supervisors*, but I couldn't always help myself. I loved that part of the job, sometimes more than the job itself.

Mute had never worked well for me.

One day downstairs in the locker room, officer Pat Brown told me, "You're going to be chief one day, Ellis, I guarantee it," as he took a long drag from his cigarette, studying me. "If that's what you want." Brown was known as a very serious and dedicated cop, so hearing this from him was surreal. It also made me think about some of the sergeants who might be looking over their shoulder at me.

The ringing phone brought me back to reality. I deserted my post at the kitchen table and made my way to the wall phone, moving mechanical as a robot. "Hello?"

That deep voice I hadn't heard much from lately boomed through the speaker, "Ellis, it's Gorsh." Like he needed an introduction. I'd know that voice in a hurricane. It was a bit surprising. He didn't usually like to use the phone. Paranoid in that Gorsh way of his, he thought every one of them was bugged. It impressed on me that was a good way to proceed with phones.

"This thing with Barnett is getting serious. So, we have to back away a while until it works out."

"Serious? In what way?" I lowered my voice, a ridiculous impulse I suddenly realized I'd also picked up from Gorsh.

"You don't need to know. Just be careful and keep your nose clean."

His tone reeked of conspiracy.

"I always keep my nose clean. What the hell does that mean?" I asked.

"Nothing, really." He paused slightly and then threw in, "I got to go haunt a house. Talk to you later. Just remember what I said."

I could hear him fumbling around trying to hang up the phone, then as an afterthought, "Don't call me, I'll call you. I'll fill you in, then."

The phone call hung up abruptly, and I was left sitting with an eerie silence.

The determination in his voice lingered in the air, and so did my uneasiness.

21

Two months later, I was driving home following a Friday night performance. It was 2 a.m., and I had the road almost to myself. It struck me as I crossed the line from Los Angeles into Orange County that the difference between them was so great, the transition was visceral.

I grew up in Los Angeles County, oblivious to the cultural and ideological differences between the two counties, but now I was teased in L.A. with the fact that I lived behind the *Orange Curtain*. When we moved to Orange County in 1962, I was very liberal—you know, tentatively "Fuck The Man" and all of that. I was surrounded by theater people from Los Angeles and college students. I couldn't be further removed. *Orange County is just where I sleep*, I'd think.

As I went from Los Angeles to Orange County, I could feel myself tense up a bit. I exited the 5 freeway onto Artesia Blvd., making a last-minute decision to drive by the PD and see what was happening. Wide awake from the performance and in no mood to go to bed, my veins were rivulets of energy. I was more in the mood to hang with a couple of random fellow cops, maybe make them laugh a little. It was always a good time, and I knew it would help me to wind down.

I entered the police department parking lot with a sense of belonging. That familiar feeling washed over me every time I set foot on the property. I parked my '57 Chevy station wagon among the personal cars of other officers, took my black badge case out of the glove compartment, and while sliding it into my pocket, ensured my 4" .357 Colt Python was secure in the covert holster.

As I climbed out of the car, I couldn't help but think back on my beginning here as a fresh-faced rookie compared to now. It was nice to finally feel like I knew what I was doing: badge, gun, more assertiveness than socially acceptable (for normal people at least), protector of people and property. By now there wasn't much I hadn't seen. Yet, I felt strangely nostalgic for the past. I missed being innocent. I missed not knowing how terrible—no, horrific–my fellow man could be. I came to this profession thinking people were intrinsically good, but it turned out I was very naive. Man was horribly flawed.

Although many of my experiences were terrible, I also had a lot of fun ones. They'd taught me well, and there was no way I could deny that. I loved the code-three runs: the "unknown trouble" calls. At this point, it was autonomic. Life in whatever state was under my control, I felt.

Oh, and I really wasn't complaining about the unusual amount of interest attractive females had when I was in uniform. I had accumulated cop stories to amuse and alarm.

I walked around the brick building, feeling it raise its eyebrow at me. I walked in through the rear glass doors, right in the middle of it all, to normal activity for a Saturday morning shift. Several officers were flying back and forth, buzzing on the adrenaline I had come to live for. The new dispatcher, Gilbert, manned the dispatch center under guidance of Sal, the veteran. Two female police clerks were attacking their typewriters with flying fingers. Across the room, Gorsh was leaning against a counter, casually chatting with Sgt. Pense.

I stood out among the sea of tan uniforms, dressed in my Cal State Fullerton windbreaker, a white tee-shirt and faded Levi's. There was a little smear of beige-colored stage makeup on the collar of my tee-shirt. Perhaps that's what caught his attention, but I suddenly noticed Gorsh looking at me quizzically.

I started to give him a smile, when he suddenly changed the direction of his gaze, straightened up, and acted like he hadn't just looked directly into my eyes. *Subtle.*

Recently, the entire department seemed to act strangely, and that's *really* saying something when you're talking about Gorsh and his group. Rumors about Chief Sedley had been circling with increasing speed, and most thought Captain Lenny Branson was getting ready to take over.

Gorsh walked past me to leave through the station rear door, still acting like I wasn't there. "Ellis, what's going on?" He barely moved his mouth to get the words out, not even glancing in my direction.

"On my way home from my show. Thought I'd drop by for a couple of minutes," I spoke carefully. I was searching for an answer to a question I wasn't quite sure about. But, I never got it. Gorsh disappeared through the door without missing a step, conversation over.

Sally noticed me and walked over to the counter I was leaning against. As she approached her mouth broke into a smile. "Can't you get enough of this place?" she teased, poking me in the ribs.

"Not with you here," I winked, catching her poke in both hands.

Sally was about forty years old, basically a dinosaur in my young eyes, but she was fun to be around, like one of the guys. We all trusted and liked her.

"Your best friend, Pense, is on tonight," she teased.

I shook my head. "He's not so bad. Hell, I'll take one Pense over five McKinleys any day."

"Think so?" she mused with an easy grin.

She loved to talk cop-talk. Always eager to hear about calls, and any police gossip.

"And, I'll take Keaton over both of them together. When I need backup, he's the guy I want," my voice got serious.

"Really?" she responded slowly. She wasn't quite sure where I was going with this, but she knew me well enough by now to figure she should pay attention.

"Yeah, really. If I'm out there and get a flat tire, Keaton could sling me *and* my cruiser over his shoulder like potato sacks and carry us back to the station."

She laughed in appreciation, taking the moment to picture Jim's muscular body and sighing a bit. He always had that effect on the ladies. He was really popular around the department in general. He'd made a good impression on me from the get-go.

My very first day with the department, I walked downstairs to the locker room and right in on Keaton doing pushups, while standing on his hands. My jaw had dropped open—I thought that was only possible in movies in those days. Over six feet tall and 230 pounds, and he was holding all that up in the air with his hands. I remember being both alarmed and impressed, thinking, *Wow, if this is the bar...I have no chance.*

Of course, I'd want him as a follow-up. Nothing was taking that guy down.

Unlike most of my other superiors, Jim actually appreciated the humor I slipped into my police reports. Most other supervisors saw it like I was some wise guy who didn't take anything seriously. But Jim saw that I was just trying to have a little fun amidst all the seriousness around us at all times. "Your reports crack me up. I've never ever seen anyone ever put humor in a police report, and keep it accurate and complete. Yet, you do. I love it."

Keaton may have loved it, but some supervisors didn't see any place for humor in police reports. This was tough for me, because I saw a place for humor, in well, everything. Looking back, I was a writer before I even knew I was a writer—ever defensive of the work. *That was my report and my voice, and screw 'em if they don't like it.*

My reports forced sergeants and lieutenants to open a dictionary, which really appeased the collegiate arrogance living in me. I actively expanded my vocabulary at their expense...they always say to learn by doing. I was stretching my intellect in practical ways. They saw it as an annoyance and a burden. I saw it as free education for them. We couldn't always agree on everything. (Maybe sometimes, I overdid it.)

Just then the other clerk, Darlene, interrupted us with her voice bellowing to Pense, "Sergeant. I have a call you need to take *right now!*"

Pense hurried into his glass-walled office, visible as he sat down at his desk and picked up the phone. He quickly grabbed a pad of paper, bending over it to scribble down some notes.

Darlene hurried over to Sally and me. "Wow." Her voice was low for ultimate covertness, but she couldn't hide the excitement in her eyes. "I think that caller's giving a tip on a double homicide. Pense is talking with him."

We watched Pense as his pen flew across his pad, taking down information from the mysterious caller. He slammed the phone into the receiver a few minutes later, visibly concerned with whatever it was about. He leaned back in his chair and stared at the piece of paper with his handwriting, as if he was trying to decipher a code.

"These words. What...do they...mean?" I cracked out of the corner of my mouth with a Peter Lorre voice, keeping my eyes on Pense with a solemn face. Darlene and Sally both swatted me on the arm and bit back laughter.

After a moment, he looked up and noticed us three staring in his direction. Both women blushed and quickly turned away, but I couldn't help keeping my eyes on him. Pense rose from his desk and bellowed across the room to the dispatcher, "Hey, Gilbert. Where'd Gorsh go?"

As Darlene and Sally scurried back to their work stations with ears perked, Gilbert called back, "Don't know Sergeant, he's code seven (meal break). Didn't say where."

It dawned on Pense he already knew this, and he didn't seem very happy about it. "Oh, shit." He saw the other two officers in the building and began motioning with his hand for them to come over.

"Guys. Stop what you're doing and come into my office right now. Gilbert, keep all units away from *Jerry's Bar-b-que*. We got something going down. I repeat. No units in the area until I say otherwise."

Both Fry and Hansel jogged over to the Sgt.'s office. I was only a counter away and leaning with curiosity. Pense still hadn't really acknowledged me, so I moved a little closer to the office. After a few seconds of enduring my body twitching with impatience, I approached the doorway, giving it a light knock. "May I join in, Sergeant?"

He stopped his shallow breathing long enough to take in that I was standing before him. He looked me up and down, which reminded me that I was dressed in civilian clothes. I suddenly felt a little self-conscious.

He pondered a second. "Yeah. Come on in."

Fry and Hansel took the two visitor chairs and I leaned against the doorway. Pense now standing behind the desk. "Close the door, Ellis." I stepped inside and did as he said, leaning against the door once I'd shut it.

Pense spoke quietly, but intensely. "Okay, guys. Listen up. You all know about the Gaslight robbery and double murder. We talked about it earlier this week? Here's a sketch of the suspects." He laid a composite sketch of both suspects on his desk, spreading them out with his large firm hands.

"Very attractive men, I must say, Sergeant." said Fry in his sardonic way. I let out a small, involuntary chuckle. Hansel bit back a smile.

"We just got a phone tip they may be at *Jerry's Bar-b-que* right now," Pense snapped, ignoring Fry's comment. "Of course, because of their MO, we can't go storming in there with black and whites."

Hansel leaned forward with a furrowed brow and rested his elbows on his knees. "What are you going to do?"

I remembered the briefing accounts of the Gaslight robbery in Stanton. It was only a week ago. These guys coldly executed two customers of the bar. Their fingerprints were all over three other robberies, too. The violence had escalated with each surprise appearance. Now including double murder.

"Sergeant, they could actually be in there casing the place out right now. That's what they did in the other robberies. They come in, have a drink of whatever, and look around. Then they leave and come back five minutes later, with guns drawn. Boom!" Pense looked up at me, dropping his mouth open a bit. "Shit, Ellis, that's right. And they hit those other places about this time," he said, staring off into space. He suddenly snapped back, his mind racing. "We got to get in there."

Hansel and Fry nodded in agreement, everyone in the room knew we needed to go in quickly. But the burning question was, how? If the robbers were armed and someone walked in there in uniform, there was no telling how it would go down. Just that someone would probably get hurt.

I looked down at my T-shirt and pants. *What the hell?* I thought. *I could go in there.* I sure didn't look like a cop right now. If anything, I could pass for an off-duty drag queen with the makeup stains ringing the collar of my tee-shirt.

"Sergeant, why don't we use me? I can go in first and check things out. Look at me," I said, holding out my hands.

"You're not even on duty," he said distractedly, but I could tell he was giving it thought. He knew there were few options right then, and we needed to get these guys and, of course, stop a robbery.

Fry sucked his teeth, "With due respect, Sergeant, I think it looks pretty good. This could be our best move. Just have him clock in. No big deal."

Hansel looked at me with a wide grin, nodding his head in approval. "He's the shooter, isn't he? You've seen his scores. Send him in."

Pense picked up the phone and hurriedly punched in a number. I could see Gilbert picking up his phone across the lobby in the dispatch room.

Pense spoke, "You hear from Gorsh yet?" There was a slight pause as he closed his eyes. He seemed to be more upset about Gorsh himself than his absence.

"Make sure to let me know if he calls in." Pense hung up the telephone, leaned back in the chair and took a deep breath. He held it a few seconds before releasing it from custody, momentarily looking at Hansel and Fry. Both officers were leaning forward, eager to get this moving.

"Okay. We'll talk our way through it." He turned his attention to me. "What're you carrying?"

".357 Colt Python," I offered, patting my holster. "Four inches."

"Would that be hard or flaccid?" Fry couldn't help himself.

Pense ignored him once again and stood, commanding all eyes to be on him. "I want input from everyone. But first, let me tell you what I need right now."

He talked for about five minutes, getting our thoughts on a plan we then hastily put together. Police officers were usually meticulous when it came to planning and making sure all conceivable scenarios were figured out, but we were anxious to hit the street.

Fry and Hansel jumped into action, moving out to take up their positions. Pense was stationed at "command center" in the PD dispatch room, directing backup when necessary.

Meanwhile, I got in my station wagon and headed directly to *Jerry's Bar-b-que.*

22

It was quiet on the streets as I drove toward *Jerry's*, feeling like Gary Cooper in *High Noon*. Was this a gun fight in the making? I almost expected to see a massive tumbleweed roll across the desolate road. There was not a human being in sight.

Perhaps for the comfort of a strong and familiar friend, I put my right hand under my windbreaker and felt the butt of my .357. *Hello, there.*

As I passed, I noticed a black and white hiding in the darkness at Holder and Artesia, in position. *Guess this is really happening*, nodded to myself, and by now I felt ready.

Two minutes later, I pulled into the parking lot and picked a spot right in front of the restaurant windows. I wanted as many patrons inside as possible to see my family station wagon. Maybe I was from Barstow. Meanwhile, I took the time to scan the inside of the restaurant as thoroughly as possible, so I could plan my approach. *Do I zig and zag or do I walk straight in?*

I stepped out of the car slowly and continued to stretch. A big stretch here, a smaller stretch there, like an Olympic gymnast getting ready for my damn floor routine. Besides, the stretching was sort of calming my nerves. This was not my first time entering a scene without the comfort and command of my uniform and badge, but I felt a little uneasy.

I entered the restaurant and paused, gazing around briefly as if trying to figure out where I wanted to sit. The *Bar-b-que* was pretty busy at 2:30 a.m., at least for Orange County, where most folks were in bed by ten. Three or four waitresses bustled around the room, shouldering plates of food, topping off beverages, and jotting down orders in their pocket-sized notebooks filled with scribbles. About twenty-five people in total sat scattered around at tables and the counter in various pairings. *Potentially a lot of collateral damage. Be precise.*

An indiscernible rock and roll song playing faintly in the background.

The waitress behind the right counter paused to pour some more coffee into a customer's cup as she made her way up and down giving refills. She had a cute figure and a pretty but weathered face. She wore a tan dress with a peach-colored apron. *Bet she has an entire closet full of them,* I thought. I couldn't imagine her in anything else.

"Just take a seat at the counter anywhere, Hon…" she said at me without looking up from pouring, something you would think muscle-memory could handle.

"Unless you want to wait for a table. We'll be right with you."

I wasn't a person to her, as much as a presence. She kept pouring that damn coffee. No eye contact. My hair could have been on fire. I wondered how long she'd been working here.

The only two people at the left counter seemed to be in a friendly, quiet conversation. But while one talked, the other one appeared to be scanning the room. I figured either these were my guys, or this person was incredibly lacking in social skills.

I sat down two stools away from the men, settling my weight into the red faux leather.

Since one of the men was clearly still scanning for anything or anyone suspicious or challenging, I put my hands on the counter as I sat, palms down. I picked up a laminated menu and held it up in front of me, casually considering my dining options. *Let me see….*

The same waitress from before walked up, pulled her little notepad out of her apron pocket and clicked open a pen. "Coffee, Hon?" *She remembered my name.*

"Yeah, thanks," my eyes remained on the menu, "and, I'd like a couple of minutes...."

She placed a mug in front of me and poured the coffee. Meanwhile, I was studying that menu like my college notes, taking my sweet time. It helped that it was multiple pages. Gave me time to really get a closer look at these two men from behind my shield. Each guy had an elbow on the counter as they talked, facing each other.

I mentally retrieved the artist's sketch from earlier in Pense's office. Perched on round, swiveling stools, these guys fit the picture almost perfectly. Beer Belly and Squish Face, I mentally christened them as I took in their appearances. I eventually became very sure these were the two suspects.

Now, to assess the situation and decide if Belly and Squish were armed yet. If they appeared to be following any patterns from their previous offenses, which criminals carelessly tend to do, they were in position for a quick take down (which would explain the swiveling stools over a booth).

But, most importantly, I tried to assess if one looked crazier than the other. Where there's a crazy bad guy, there was almost always a crazier one close by. It took a few minutes to go through my mental checklist. In the meantime, I ordered a stack of pancakes with maple syrup.

I decided there was a good chance they were casing the place and planning to return for their grand finale. While Squish's eyes darted about the room, Belly visited the restroom. *Can't rob a restaurant on a full bladder.* They should've had a pretty good idea of what was happening at that restaurant by now.

If their prior pattern indicated anything, they'd leave the restaurant before the barging-back-in part, which indicated a likelihood they weren't armed yet. But, it seemed clear the robbery was likely imminent.

I walked over to the pay phone at the other end of the restaurant. Belly was still in the restroom across the way, and Squish had his handsome face pointed at the counter. Like he was talking himself up for the action. I was able to watch both him and the restroom door.

I fed a dime and dialed the police department. Darlene answered, and I randomly complained to my wife about the long trip, code for "Put me on with the Sergeant."

Pense came on the line abruptly and spit out, "What you got?" I could feel his anticipation.

I spoke quietly, leaning forehead against the wall and playing with the phone cord. My nerves were humming. "I think it's about ready to happen. Maybe five minutes before they go into action. One guy's in the head, the other is sitting at the counter. I can see both from here. I'll go back to my seat now. When the first one comes back and settles, I'll give the signal, if you're good with that. I think we best take them now."

The signal was for me to stand and raise my left arm, as if stretching (very original). I waited for a few seconds. Pense's voice was calm and quiet, the way I wanted his voice to be at this point.

"Okay. Ten-four. Be careful, but go ahead and take them. Everyone's in place now and waiting for you."

I hung up the phone and returned to my seat. I couldn't walk too fast, or that hog leg pistol might make an appearance. Tucked my arm over my jacket to be sure there was no chance of that happening.

As I sat down, Squish swiveled a bit in his seat and looked right at me for a few seconds. It was as though I hadn't been visible to him earlier. We locked eyes briefly, and I gave him a nod, as if to wish him well. I also gave him a smile. He smiled and nodded back.

So much for ceremony.

His partner returned and sat down, but sounded as though they were preparing to leave. Both wore light jackets, but it was still difficult to see if they were armed. Belly beckoned the waitress and asked her to bring the check.

"I'll be right with you, Hon," the waitress purred with exhaustion. *He's named Hon, too?*

I decided this was it. I stood and began to arch my back as if moving out some leftover soreness. Released a fatigued groan, stretching with arms remaining close to my sides, raising from my tip toes. Then leaned slightly to my right and stretched the left arm up high. Slowly finished and then moved my right arm up, knowing the troops needed time to get there. Then I moved my shoulders up and down several times, as though loosening. I picked up a pancake promotional flyer to read.

I wasn't hearing a thing. No screeching tires, no footsteps on the pavement, nothing. Absolute silence out there. Both men remain seated.

I paused reading and set the paper down, giving backup more of a chance to barge in.

In that millisecond, Squish and I locked eyes once again. His nose twitched ever so slightly. I made a decision.

I reached beneath my jacket with my right hand and felt the python waiting. I gripped it firmly, sinking back to my seat as if to better read up on the special little pancake. I withdrew that humongous gun and slammed it on the counter top, pointed at both of them.

The entire restaurant seemed to come to life, and I wanted to make sure no one missed anything. I stood up tall. My gun was big and powerful, and I was fucking in charge!

I commanded, "Put your hands on the counter or I'll kill you. I'm a police officer." My face was stone, like death. "I will shoot you in your fucking face if you move anything at all, except your hands slow-ly to the counter."

Belly and Squish had finally come to life, eyes looking like they were going to pop out of their heads. It was beneficial to both sides at this point to look as though I seriously wanted to kill them. Give them something to think about other than fight or flight.

Both men deliberately placed their shaking hands on the counter, making sure they kept them far away from their bodies in the process.

To my terrified audience of diners, I announced, "Everyone please be calm. I'm a police officer...it's okay. Help is coming."

Simultaneously, the front door to the restaurant burst open and three uniformed cops rushed in. Two more followed shortly and began to soothe the shaken-up customers, moving them to safety.

I kept my gun trained on the suspects as I slowly shook my head to dissuade them from resistance of any type. They were overwhelmed and their eyes wide, an ideal reaction.

I couldn't help but notice how calm I was. I'd become an actor in a scene. Disassociated.

We began to cuff them with no resistance on their end—they were too stunned. They sat there in silence, not even looking at one another. We led them outside. They were like zombies. Their eyes were dead, just like any hope of having a nice day.

Once we left the building, a new energy seemed to strike Belly and Squish. Both suspects were starting to show a little defiance, like they just remembered they were supposed to be criminals. Their expressions became surly. They wouldn't grant a request to search their car, where their weapons were certainly stashed. We couldn't search the car against their will until someone woke up a judge to sign a search warrant. Most judges were known to have *very* grumpy attitudes for that type of thing at this hour.

Although we all damn well *knew* these were the guys, intuition wasn't enough to arrest them or get a search. This was where police work got intellectual to me. We had to get moving before the crime even began...in order to protect lives. But in doing that, we pretty much screwed up the possibility of "probable cause" (no crime, no weapons or outstanding warrants on either man) and they had a right to protection from unreasonable search and seizure. It was interesting to me, and constitutionally appropriate.

We kept the men standing for a while, then let them sit down with three uniformed cops present. We could detain them for forty-eight hours for investigation, and no one wanted to wake up a judge without exhausting other avenues.

A call was made to the department where the Gaslight bar was located. Stanton PD dispatched an officer from the original robbery/homicide crime scene to hopefully assist with identification. The scene was moving from excitement to boredom, as a cop's life often did when not in charge.

I noticed a car racing down Artesia toward *Jerry's Bar-b-que*, red lights flashing. *What the hell? Who is this? Why the red lights when you're this late getting here?*

As the car quickly turned into the driveway, I recognized Gorsh and Pense. Suddenly, the dramatic entrance made sense: exercise any chance to use those red lights and bring a little excitement into the night. Gorsh lived for the drama. I'd guess he would have reached over Pense and turned them on himself had Pense been driving.

The car screeched to a stop. Both men got out and hurried into the restaurant to get an update. *Why do you need an update now? Why don't you just wait until the reports are written? Oh, that's right...Show Biz: The head honchos are here! Everything will be okay now.*

Several minutes later, they were informed about what had happened. Gorsh approached me outside. "Good work, Ellis. Two one eighty-seven pops. Stanton will be here in a while, but these two look good to go. You got them bought and paid for, my little man." He patted me on the shoulder.

"Thank you, I enjoyed it." And I truly did. A memory to tuck away for senior years, *did I ever tell you about the time....?*

Lowering his voice, he said, "Step over here a second. I got a few questions."

As we created distance between ourselves and others, Gorsh made small talk about the scene, asking me a few questions and making comments in his gravelly voice. As we got far enough away, he stopped and turned to me with his mile-long back to the others.

"I know you got a lot on your plate right now. This'll just take a minute." He stopped talking and just looked at me for a moment. "I'm going to tell you something in the absolute strictest confidence. If you breathe a word, I will hunt you down. Seriously." He continued to look at me with intensity for a brief moment and then burst out laughing in his *Addams Family* way.

I was frozen with curiosity, but couldn't help a sardonic chuckle...something about Lurch making himself double over always got to me.

After a few seconds, Gorsh got a grip on himself and straightened up, business again. He nodded his head toward his rear, where the other officers were. "The other guys are going to ask you what we're talking about. It's about the capture, Ellis. That's it." He turned his head around to see what was going on over there, and back.

"Sedley's either going to resign or be fired." He leaned in, "You heard nothing okay? I'm telling you this because Barnett is making me chief. That's going to happen very soon." He laid a victorious grin on me.

I was shocked. *What the hell was wrong with Sedley?* I wanted to be happy for Gorsh, but didn't like what was happening to him recently and to the entire spirit of the PD. I couldn't help but wonder who he'd been manipulating to get this done. Recently, walking into the station, I'd encountered closed doors and hushed whispers far too many times for it to just be a coincidence. Also, what was going to happen to Captain Lenny Branson, the heir apparent?

"Whoa. That's a stunner," I said, masking my conflicted feelings and keeping it professional. "Does Sedley know?"

"I don't want to talk about it anymore," Gorsh said, cutting me off. "You just don't say anything to anybody."

"I won't. I won't," I said distractedly. My head searched for meaning in all this.

"Something else, Ellis. We've got to completely cut off our friendship for a while. Completely. You know, it wouldn't look good. You're already getting enough shit about being the Golden Boy with a sharp tongue," he said gruffly. His grin had vanished.

He was right, and I knew it, but he'd never referred to that elephant in the room before. It was like we both always knew I was somehow getting myself into hot water, but I never asked and he never told. I wanted more. "What do you mean? What shit?"

Gorsh changed pace, probably aware that he'd shared more than he should have. "Don't worry about it. Listen to me. I'm serious about the friend stuff. I'm going to be chief, and I can't have the slightest possibility of anyone thinking any favoritism is going down." He widened his eyes as if anticipating any possible response.

"Yeah. I understand. I'll keep my mouth shut, and I'll tell you congratulations right now. I think you'll make a great chief. I mean that sincerely." *But, do I really?*

"No hard feelings?" he asked, raising a bushy eyebrow.

"Absolutely none. Only good feelings for you. I won't say a thing," I promised, smiling up at him. I wondered if I should do more.

His paranoia was staggering.

Gorsh extended his hand to me covertly since his gargantuan back was blocking me entirely from view. We shook hands quickly and parted. Never to be the same.

23

"I don't know. We were getting ready for the second half. I looked up at the crowd, and saw my dad, wearing his suit and watching me, his star quarterback. The recruiter from UCLA sat right beside him. He wasn't even wearing a suit. Maybe I wasn't so important." David paused to brush some imaginary dust off his lapel, ramping up the drama of his high school football recount.

"At that very minute, I knew what I had to do," nodding his head. "It had nothing to do with football or a university. And, I knew it was going to tear my dad apart. But, I thought, 'What am I even doing out here? I don't really care how this game turns out. Or the season, even. Music is my game.' That's it." He paused again, recalling the day and how his dad looked cheering from the stands.

"And I knew I had to. So, I just turned away. Turned my back to my teammates, the other team, everyone in the stands, and walked off the field into the locker room," he said with a heavy sigh.

"Coach started yelling at me. Couple of guys even came into the locker room to see what was wrong. Everyone thought I was hurt or something. Surely there was some kind of reasonable explanation for this, they thought. I just told them, 'Sorry everyone, I'm going in a different direction…and I've got to start right now.'" He threw his head back for a hearty laugh, his long hair dangled around his shoulders.

Both hands went behind his head, gathering his hair into a ponytail. "See what rock and roll did? And that's freaking that, ladies and gentlemen."

I shook my head. "I love that. Perfect job. Rock and roll, baby."

We continued playing with the image of that stunned crowd and their reactions...and then commiserating about how much this had hurt his father. It troubled him. I could hear it in his voice. He loved his Dad.

"Sometimes spontaneous honesty can cause problems," I said. "It doesn't always make everyone else feel good. Take it from me. I find that not everybody is going to love it, especially if you do well." I stared down at my police jacket with the reflecting BPPD emblem on the shoulder sitting in my lap, not coming up with anything that I could share.

After a moment he moved forward in his chair, and just like that, the seriousness had come and gone. "Okay, story time. What's happening in the cop world? Crazy calls? Funny stories? Lay 'em on me. Cheer me up, buddy."

I smiled. Updating David on the mania of mankind through the eyes of this police officer had become a ritual of ours, and an easy way to laugh until our sides felt like splitting. I thought for a minute, smiling to myself as I waded through the drama I had experienced in my time on the PD—more than many others experienced in a lifetime.

"Last night I had a hilarious call about a mother-daughter situation. Supposed to be a medical aid, the mother called an ambulance for her daughter, who's twenty-nine. She was really frantic and said the daughter was screaming. She was in terrible, unknown pain and needed help." I looked at him and widened my eyes to extend the buildup.

"So, I got the call and I raced over there, beating the ambulance and everything. When I got back to her room, I found the daughter...

was…are you ready for this? She was actually giving *birth*. Ha," I chortled. "What the hell? Her mother didn't even know she was pregnant.

"I'm talking full-term baby. I'm a midwife now, thank you very much. But, it was a healthy sized, nine-month baby, David. It's not like this was a preemie. They're living together and somehow the mother doesn't even know? Ha-ha! How does that happen? You should have seen the look on her face when I told her what was going on. Pay attention to each other, much? The baby was full-term, ma'am. I laughed and continued, enjoying the reaction of a non-cop who hadn't heard this story already.

My daily life was filled with them, and as any cop, I was always in demand to tell them, less personal details, of course. I could do a full standup routine for almost every single week on the job. Mainly dark humor, it was infused with a panoply of raw, searing emotion.

David and I spent about twenty minutes making jokes at the poor woman's expense before he seriously asked, "So, how's it going with sergeants and that lieutenant?"

"Gorsh," I nodded knowingly, weighing his words in my head. "It's getting a little tight there. On the streets, it's business as usual. But at the department, I'm feeling lots of weirdness. Things I can't talk about. Lots of whispering and spy shit. I don't like it. Gorsh and I still don't talk, which is weird enough on its own. You know how close we used to be."

David nodded his head in agreement, and I continued. "But, I know he's involved in all that's going on. I hate that crap. I didn't sign up for this drama. That's supposed to be on stage."

"You don't have that much longer. What'd you say? Five years total?"

"Maybe sooner," I mused. "I'm taking eighteen units next semester."

He narrowed his eyes, "Oh man, are you crazy? I wouldn't even do that, and I got a lot more time to fill than you. Not to mention no wife or kids."

"I've got to hurry. You know the plan." I shot back without hesitation. If anyone understood my panic to "catch up" in life, it was David.

"How about that sergeant-friend? How you getting along with him?" he teased.

"McKinley? Hell, he's one of Gorsh's helpers. Spreading chaos. Very involved. Gorsh has changed quite a bit. Makes me glad I'm not in touch with him right now. Someone's gonna get hurt. But, for what? What's going on that I can't see?"

My gaze drifted out the window into David's backyard. It was getting late and the yard was getting dimmer, like the sun was extinguishing.

"What's he want out of it?" he asked, carrying me back to reality.

I let the question sink in a moment before answering. "He wants Chief Sedley out." It felt good to release. "I don't know if the captain is in cahoots with him, or what. But, he's got more than McKinley working with him. Or, everybody is working against everybody else. I don't know anymore." I dismissed further thought with the shake of my head. "Everything is different."

"What happened with that TV coverage of *The Fantasticks*?" David asked, thankfully taking me into a different direction. He always knew just what to say, and when to say it.

It perked me up. "It was great. I told Lt. Armstrong last week that part of the show was coming on TV. So that night, we had briefing in the break room, and he told the guys what was happening and we might get a chance to see it," I said, chuckling in spite of it all.

"Half way into briefing he turns on the TV and local news is about to do the story. I'm thinking 'What a nice thing for him to do.' I felt pretty nervous to see myself on screen though, especially in front of the guys.

"As we were waiting for it to come on, freaking McKinley dramatically left to go to the restroom, so he said. But he made it obvious he was boycotting the coverage."

David looked at me, waiting for me to finish. When he realized I was done, he pressed, "So, what happened?"

"Well, we watched it." I visualized the scene. "Reaction from the guys was pretty funny. Some found it amusing, most looked bored. Cops are not really into song and dance. Armstrong posted a cartoon drawing of me singing in costume on the PD bulletin board the next morning. It was a good caricature, too. Some anonymous jokester had already written 'Fag' on it.

"So now, pretty much everyone knows I moonlight as a theater guy. It's all in fun, though I do get some confused looks. They don't really know what to think of me," I thought I'd finished. But then, "They *know* I'm not a fag, just so you know."

"Oh, damn. I was going to ask you to the prom," David laughed.

I was rambling, but I didn't really care. He was someone who let me ramble, and who I felt most comfortable rambling to; the type of friend who came along once in a lifetime.

"And, of course, the look of loathing from McKinley before he ran from the room. I'd like to kick the shit out of him. You know what he told me one time?"

"I'm dying to know."

"He told me that when he was in the service in the Philippines, he went to a whore house and hired a 'really fine-looking lady.' Says she was giving him a blow job and during the process, he reached under her skirt to 'find the golden triangle' and he found a handful of dick," I paused, trying to keep in my laughter.

"I was *expecting* him to say he beat the crap out of him, or cried out in shame for this glaring oversight. Something like that. So, I asked him, 'What did you do?' And he looked at me and went, 'Well Ellis, it was too late then. I let him finish.'"

David's eyes widened. "Whoa." His mouth opened in silent laughter as he waited for me to keep going.

"No kidding whatsoever. Then I started wondering if he was *really* surprised by it at all. And also, does his wife know about this shit? She'd probably say, 'Oh, that Jack. He's such a rascal.'"

David got up and started pretending he was McKinley's wife, flailing his arms and speaking in a high-pitched voice. We enjoyed that for quite a while, and then slowly let the conversation drift to comedy and music. Before we knew it, hours had gone by, and he was playing me his most recent work, while I shared some of my recent writing.

24

Two weeks later, as I entered the PD through the back door for my shift, I felt quite a difference in office energy. A few groups of people, with badges and without, were whispering in huddles. Budding conspiracy theories thickly floated through the air.

Fry approached me at the back counter and spoke softly, "Did you see that memo?"

"I just got here. What memo?" It felt as though I should be whispering.

"City manager just appointed Gorsh as chief," he said, his lips twitching imperceptibly with each word.

That information was almost as startling to me as it was to everyone else, even though I'd had "the discussion that never happened" and was well aware of how strange Gorsh had been acting these past several weeks. Which didn't make it any better. I somehow felt like I'd been doing something wrong just from the little he'd shared with me. My stomach knotted.

The normal replacement situation for a vacancy in the chief position at a police department in 1968 was to post the job opening on the appropriate agency bulletin boards and test, interview, and select from those applicants, or to appoint the current captain of the affected PD. Seemed logical.

City Manager John Barnett didn't do either of those protocol. He reached *around* the chain of command and appointed a quirky, perhaps unstable and certainly unpopular lieutenant to be chief of police. Something wasn't right, and everyone could feel it.

"What did it say about Captain Branson?" While making sure to sound slightly disinterested, I was trying to make sense of it all in my head.

"He now reports to everyone's least favorite lieutenant who is now chief. He is so screwed . . . us and the citizens too," said Fry, his head slowly shaking back and forth.

Looking over Fry's shoulder as he continued talking, I could see McKinley and Baker in the glassed watch-sergeant's office. You couldn't hear them, but their slimy look of glee was palpable. I expected them to break out into a happy dance at any moment.

Andy Hernandez sidled up next to us, staring into the glass office with me. "Look at those guys, man. What's making them so happy? Neither one of them ever liked Gorsh."

Suddenly Gorsh himself appeared in full uniform and both sergeants sprang to action, humbly smiling and greeting the new chief, like serfs to a conqueror. Clearly, they may not be as happy as they were good ass-kissers. No, *excellent* ass-kissers.

We all descended on the office and congratulated the new chief, shaking hands and patting him on the back. Gorsh seemed to be fighting an urge to look my way, but didn't make eye contact during the entire group talk. I felt a little strange about the whole thing, like I was somehow in on this. I didn't want any part of his game.

As he got to me, he put out his hand, and we shook as I said, "Congratulations, Chief."

He made eye contact for a millisecond and closed his right eye in a wink indiscernible to any passerby. His eyes changed directions before the wink was over, and spoke with someone else.

Later in the locker room, most of us were getting ready for shift. Earlier Gorsh left the building and now conversation flowed easier. The initial shock had settled in a bit, and we were able to really talk.

Fry said, "This is a bit on the fucked-up side."

"A bit? That's an understatement." Gunner was looking down, getting his uniform ready. He turned to us, still buttoning his shirt. He walked a little closer and lowered his voice, "This isn't over yet. Something weird went down, and I bet it's going to come out."

25

1970 - ROBBERY IN PROGRESS...

F ernando stopped suddenly in place and whipped his head back to where the armed robbery was unfolding. His instinct was to become invisible, to look for the first opportunity of escape. He decided right then was his best chance, before anything got worse.

He took two quick steps and hurled his massive body to the floor, sliding over slick linoleum, as if into second base. He made it as far as behind the ladies' underwear counter and stopped with a jolt, gritting his teeth. Although his bulk and natural clumsiness had made this action quite a disturbance, no one seemed to notice his presence.

Fernando, got off his hefty stomach, and onto his knees. Taking a deep breath, he crossed himself, muttering, "Mary, Mother of God...." Slowly he stood to a bent over, but standing position, still panting.

Separated by colorful lacy underwear and two other counters, he heard the robbers loudly giving orders to the store staff, demanding quick obedience. He ducked down. Detectable fear in the voices and cries of some employees in custody reached him. Up again, he saw more than one robber, and at least two carried arms.

Fernando began to slowly and carefully move toward the center aisle of the store, staying out of sight (always his primary concern).

Louder, more threatening voices from the robbers encouraged him to quicken his pace. Finally, Fernando reached the middle aisle. This made the front entrance much closer. His eyes widened even more. He imagined a bullet entering his back as he quickly moved toward the front entrance. He could see in the windows a reflection of the light from the manager's office, and it propelled him.

KMART PARKING LOT...

The man and woman remained in the white Volkswagen as motionless as wax figures. Several moments passed, when suddenly the man disturbed their doll-like stillness, stirring a little in his seat. He leaned forward a bit to focus; certain he saw movement in the store.

"What the hell?" Squinting his eyes, it dawned on him. "Oh, crap. It's the clean-up guy!"

The woman sat up a little straighter and placed a hand on the man's forearm, gasping without meaning to. Her eyebrows had shot up in surprise.

The man watched as Fernando picked up the pace, moving with a speed that only fear induced in a man that fat. The man briefly considered starting the car, driving to the entrance and stopping Fernando's escape, but it was impossible at this point. All he could do was watch in horror as Fernando ran next door to Vons Market.

26

FILM ROLLING...

"**S**o, I had to let you know before they did," said Sue over the telephone. Her voice was calm and professional as always, but the buildup was making me feel nervous. Gripping the phone at the other end of the line at home, my knees were about ready to buckle. I stretched the wall phone's cord to its farthest extent, so I could sink into a seat at the table.

"Yeah?" I asked, holding in my breath. My grip on the telephone was so tight the color left my knuckles.

"You did it, Bill. Congratulations. George wants you in *Pendulum*. They're going to call you today," she gushed, unable to remain calm any longer. Sue had been the one who got me the first audition for a motion picture. She was someone who believed in me and pushed for me from the start. She'd directed me in one production and now worked at Columbia Pictures.

Director George Schaefer was an icon in Hollywood—famous for the five Emmys and twenty nominations resting under his belt. I read lines for him at Columbia: an outstanding opportunity. It felt like an out-of-body experience.

"Oh, Sue. That is so great. I can't believe it." This was the first day of the rest of my life, or so I thought. My voice began to tremble, so I stopped to collect myself.

We exchanged a few more sentences, and I hung up the phone, pumping my fist into the air and letting out a holler. "It's happened. It's finally starting." I smiled at no one in particular and whirled around, ready to tell Sarah and the girls.

This was what I'd been waiting—no, *slaving* for!

Later that night, Sarah and I sat alone on the couch in the living room. I thought about the movie role and what it may mean. Years of hard work were beginning to pay off, and I was on cloud nine.

This can actually happen, I was thinking. *As long as I can steer clear of the bullshit happening at the PD, the rest will work itself out.*

"I'm really happy you got the part, babe. But, I don't see how you're going to do it right now." Sarah tried to keep a good face, but the statement had profound implications, and it became clear to me that she wasn't as excited as me about this dream fulfillment of mine.

I was taken aback. I never expected anything but continuous support after all I'd worked through. I'd only ever seen the supportive love of my mother—it was how I expected my wife to be too. What about all the promises made…?

"What do you mean? I'm just going to do it, that's all. I *have* to do this." I was almost on my tiptoes with enthusiasm, confused she could have entertained such a doubtful thought. I wanted my wife to believe in me no matter what. If she didn't after what she'd seen, then who would?

"How are you even going to get there and back for three days? You can't ride the Yamaha on the freeway. You know that, and we can't get the car fixed right now." Sarah said. "That's all the way into Hollywood. Why don't you think about maybe next time?"

Next time? I was dumbfounded. I sighed, pulling my arm from the back of the couch. Calmly, quietly, "Are you out of your mind? I can't believe this."

The struggles in our relationship had been growing, but at this moment I became forced to confront them entirely. We weren't seeing eye-to-eye, and it had been that way for a while now. I stared at her: wondering if she still wanted the same things I did, wondering if she ever really did, wondering if she was going to become an obstacle.

I'd become obsessed with this struggle.

"Here's what's definitely going to happen. I can probably work on it and get a ride, both ways. But, if I have to, I'll walk in there, stay at a motel those two days, and if necessary, walk back. Understand? I'm going to make this happen!"

27

Although I was determined to keep out of the PD's BS, tension continued to grow between certain supervisors and myself. I was consistently in the news media for being a police officer with "other" pursuits, and many at the PD didn't seem to be too keen on it. I still didn't fully understand their attitude, and wasn't taking any time to slow down and familiarize myself with it. I was on the defensive.

Chief Sedley originally said, "Human interest stories on cops are beneficial for everyone." The public would begin to relate to cops on a more personal level. They'd begin talking "with" you rather than "at" you. "Could be a common-ground starting point."

Anyway, I thought I was doing my part for the department. Bringing a human dimension into police optics. But, curiously enough, few else seemed to think so.

In addition, the shift in power and alliances were jerky and of concern to many. Very few knew where they stood under this new regime. Whispering and murmuring became common.

I tried not to let management's passive-aggressive comments bother me too much. But, part of me just wanted to go at it head-on, which was another reason why they didn't like me. That, and the fact that I was never shy about voicing my opinion. After being exposed to some of their worst sides, I didn't have much respect left.

I was beginning to identify beyond McKinley, to Sgt. Baker, Lt. Hanson, maybe even Pense, as a clique of people that formed with the one common denominator: having a problem with me.

I was scheduled to take the sergeant's exam shortly. The clique had an obvious fear: I might pass both tests with a high rating and (gulp) become Sergeant Ellis. *Uh, Yeah. Very possible.*

I imagined them waking up in the middle of the night with the sweats, seeing me as a peer. It was a stretch, but made me smile. It wasn't my original intention to be insubordinate, but some situations almost demanded it. The number one offender, time and again, was McKinley.

Sgt. McKinley—anytime I looked at him, I saw the image of him on the side of that road staring off into space, while his brothers were in the middle of a rollicking bar fight and in need of help. My relationship with him looked like me being disgusted and him being oblivious, although not entirely so.

It was hard to admit that someone had so much power over my calm, but just picturing his stupid twitching face while he disrespected a subordinate officer (which he loved to do) made me want to punch him in the face and watch him cry, the tears filling up and overflowing his pock marks. So many tears that his facial tics would cause waves. And then, to pull his pants down and spank his ass until it turned bright red in front of everyone. Then, make him apologize for being such a coward.

Sgt. Baker—my beef with him came from the fact that he was a pathological liar. Everyone with any common sense on the PD knew this. He lied anytime his mouth opened. [In future years, he would be sent to prison for falsifying evidence (falsified fingerprints) to *send innocent people to prison.* He did this only for the praise and attention at the PD. That's it. That's how far his pathology went.] This man had severe mental problems, but there he was, fat and happy in sergeant stripes.

Did I say fat? He didn't even stand a chance at an obstacle course test. Sometimes I wondered how he ever became a cop with that gut in the way. He looked like an egg wearing a gun.

Lt. Hanson—was a curiosity to me. He didn't care about anything we street cops did or said. I thought he was convinced we were all idiots. He was an administrative-type guy with large black rimmed glasses that swallowed up his serious face. He had a severe flattop and wore grumpiness like a badge of honor.

His office remained separated from the action area. He actively disliked me from the day he called me into his office to speak to me about a word I'd placed in my crime report. *What?*

I stood before his desk curiously waiting for him to acknowledge my presence when he dramatically spun around and slammed *Miriam Webster* on his desk. Then he tossed my written report on the desk and proclaimed, "I looked up that word, *leviathan*, Ellis. Another big-ass word you want to use in a police report, right?" As he took a seat, his eyes never left mine, like I was a criminal.

I feigned innocence, but I'm not sure how successful I was.

"According to that dictionary, the word you used is wrong," he spat. "Leviathan means a *sea monster.*"

He paused, leaning back and waiting for my distress to come. When it didn't right away, he tried poking the bear again. "Here you're trying to be such a big college fuck and you use the wrong big word. Ha. How does that feel, professor?"

I let him bask for several seconds. Then I asked to take a quick look at his *Merriam Webster.* He smiled sarcastically and tossed the book to me.

I didn't sit because he hadn't asked me to. Standing, I opened the thickly-bound book to "leviathan," and turned the open dictionary toward him. I pointed to the word with my right index finger. "No disrespect, Lieutenant, but maybe you didn't read far enough. See here? I used the tertiary definition, which is *formidable.* Which would be *exactly* the correct word to use in this situation, this police report. And correct means not even close to being wrong, sir."

He didn't ask me what tertiary meant, but I knew he wanted to.

As he glanced over the definition, I added, "So, I guess I *am* a big college fuck, sir." I chuckled to lighten things up a bit—I had gone a little too far. I wasn't sure that I cared.

He raised his eyes to mine slowly, his face red as a beet. I wasn't sure if it was anger or embarrassment (or both), but he didn't look happy. Snaky blue veins popped out of his nose. I felt the urge to take a step back, so instead I stepped forward a bit.

"The key here is to read beyond the first thing you come to." *Just like police work,* I flashed. "I like to use curiously good words in reports, so you'll get used to it, Captain." I chuckled good-naturedly again…but still alone. I told him I'd try to tone it down. He told me to get the hell out of his office.

What a rush.

Finally, Sergeant Pense—I didn't think he was a bad person like the others. Just that he was envious of anyone who received any positive recognition from senior management, and constantly fearful that someone else might get treated better than him.

He was wary of me. He continually probed me on my relationship with Gorsh and my opinion of Gorsh. I was starting to wonder if it was Gorsh who was looking for these answers and Pense was merely the vessel.

I dealt with all of this in my own little way, or at least tried to. They say hobbies keep one sane. I had enough going on in my outside life to keep anyone on the straight and narrow, which was where I'd heard sanity resides.

Sarah became pregnant again with baby number four. This should have made me happy, but it really just felt like another distraction. I loved having all of our kids, but it was hard not to feel a bit suffocated knowing I'll have yet another mouth to feed. I still struggled just to right the ship, which had grown from a canoe into a cruise liner.

The other thing was, it wasn't planned. I knew Sarah almost better than I knew myself at this point, which meant I knew she'd *gone out of her way* to render our birth control methods moot. This was the second such *surprise* I'd received from her. I wasn't thrilled about it, as it felt like a betrayal. Planning seemed to be the right thing to do, and the only thing that made sense.

"Ellis," Pense snapped, bringing me out of my head. "Gorsh wants to see you."

Suddenly, Gorsh's massive body exited his office and began walking down the hallway, glancing in my general direction just long enough to say, "Hey, Ellis."

He suddenly stopped in his tracks as he seemed to remember something and snapped his fingers, turning to the secretary's desk. "Grace, give Ellis a copy of that memo. You know which one." She nodded and reached into her desk. "Read it, Ellis, and I'll be right back."

Without another word, he turned and continued walking. His stilt-like legs moved awkwardly as he tried to pick up the pace.

Grace walked over to me and shyly offered the slip of paper, giving me a small smile.

"Thanks." I lowered myself into the visitor's chair and looked down at the paper in my hands, unfolding it and scanning the type. The memo announced that Larry Mendoza and I had been selected as the very first community relations officers for the police department.

I was instinctively touched by the assignment. It was history in the making, and it felt like such an honor. Even though it meant no extra money (just extra work), it felt important. Something else to offer up on the resume for the sergeants' oral board.

As I finished reading, Gorsh re-appeared. He came and stood rigidly next to where I was seated and said nothing, but made it clear I wasn't invited into his office.

"What do you think, Ellis?" He finally said, half of his face creasing into a smile.

I stood up, "I'm honored, sir. Thank you very much. I'm up for it." *Because as crappy as you've been lately, I'm still devoted to this place.*

"You're getting a high profile," he lowered his voice, "which doesn't thrill everyone." Quick smile then like a switch, his voice was back to normal level, "So it'll be great. You even spoke to some groups for Sedley, but we won't hold that against you." He ripped out that big laugh I hadn't heard in a while. But, this time it sounded mechanical. "You'll represent the PD and speak to all civic clubs and other organizations. And, Mendoza will back you up and speak to the Hispanics. You'll represent the city well, Ellis. Congratulations." He extended his hand and I shook it. At that moment, I felt good.

28

POLICE BRUTALITY

You couldn't write this any better, I was thinking bitterly as I sat waiting for the Chief two weeks later. It was my first opportunity as community relations officer, and I was responding to a citizen's complaint of police brutality that had been filed.

Unfortunately, it was against me. Not the best start.

I couldn't help thinking back to that pre-hire interview where they grilled me on police brutality. Man, how little I knew. If only I could tell my past self that it was all well and good until dealing with a child abuser. The man brutally beat his child, and I was supposed to treat him like an average human being? I looked at the frightened four-year-old with welts on her back and legs. She was cold and shaking. The traumatized wife sat there, staring blankly ahead as the detective questioned her. Afraid to look at her own child, afraid to look at her husband.

I thought of my four daughters, and then I stopped thinking.

"Fuck you. I'll handle my family. You stay the hell out."

The suspect then tried to "flee the scene," almost yanking the little girl's arm right out of its socket in the process. Her loud cry made him drop the hand, and he began running down the hall toward the front lobby. I quickly realized I had to stop him. Dropping everything, I took chase.

From there, it was basically open season. Cops always wanted a piece of the action—especially when it was on their home turf, *especially* with a child abuser.

At first, I was concerned about the complaint. But, there were a lot of witnesses, and everyone knew I wasn't guilty and had written supplemental reports attesting to that. So, by now, I was feeling okay. I waited for Gorsh's obligatory slap on the wrist, while having my usual back and forth with his secretary, Grace.

"You should have access to the reports by now. 'Course, you'll miss the *best* parts—the parts not in the report, all the really juicy details." I shook my head slowly and clicked my tongue, having fun taunting her.

"Why don't you just tell me?" pleaded Grace, with slight desperation on her face.

"Can't," I leaned back in the visitor's chair. "You're *administration* now. Sorry." I shook my head again. "Too bad, so sad."

She shook her fist in my face, scrunching up her nose at me. "You'd better tell me, Ellis, you little rat."

Dilbert Gorsh had a big nose. It led him through the office door, giving me enough time to adjust my focus before the rest of his body arrived. Once he'd cleared the doorway, he glanced in my direction. "Ellis. Got a couple of questions about the brawl last night." He turned back into his office, waving me in with his right paw. "Come on in for a minute."

I was allowed into Gorsh's den.

He led into his large office with those same damn flags. *Guess they weren't Sedley's to keep,* I thought. Funny—I pictured him rolling them up sentimentally and putting them all in a special box or something on his last day. Maybe shedding a cop-tear. Gorsh didn't take a seat. He was clearly determined to maintain the aura of discomfort.

I stood awkwardly, watching as he leafed through several reports of the arrest. They rested on his desk in a manila folder with some identifiably Gorsh scribbles and scrawls throughout.

One quick glance around the office told me Gorsh didn't feel completely comfortable in his new environment. Flags aside, it sort of looked like he was living in Sedley's shell, like he just brought in all the crap from his kitchen table and dumped it here. I expected him to have Gorsh-grams posted up—adorning his walls and all marked up with his red felt pen. He needed to de-clutter his room.

Maybe he had further plans of vengeance and didn't think he should get too cozy in one spot. I couldn't imagine who was left for him to go after. Captain Branson was already gone.

Gorsh stood behind his desk and looked at me, "What about this?" he asked, pointing at the reports. "Did it go down like the reports say?" He had an indiscernible grin, the type some cops wore when they conspired to cover up something. That "we're in this together, buddy" smile. Like "throw-away" weapons. *That* grin.

Taken aback that Gorsh would try to approach me with a "we're in this together" mindset, I considering how he and I hadn't been in anything "together" for months now. But if he wanted to act like nothing was wrong, I could play along.

"Yes, it did, sir. Do you have all the reports?" I asked gazing over his papers, well aware five different police officers had already filed.

His eyes returned to his copies, "Yeah. I do. But I got a phone call telling me this might turn into a police brutality claim against you. So, I want to be sure everything is covered."

"Brutality? That's not correct." I protested with a set jaw and inched forward by taking a few reluctant steps, making it clear I wanted to keep my stay short to keep him as comfortable as possible.

"The only actions I made were to stop a brutal child beater as he tried to flee Detective Harper's office, sir—and to take him into custody. He resisted quite a bit, as you may have seen in the reports. I overcame his resistance and defended myself. Other officers assisted."

I glanced at the report closest to me, reliving the fight in my head.

I remembered chasing the suspect down the hallway from the detective's office to the lobby. As he turned for the final time before entering the lobby (made mostly of glass), I nailed his ass in a beautiful tackle. Not too bad for a guy who only got as far as one season on the high school B-football team before finding Shakespeare.

We wound up in combat on the lobby floor. All the time, my motivation was picturing him beating his four-year-old daughter with a belt and forcing her to sit on the toilet for seven full hours because she had an accident in her pants. You know, when he wasn't busy beating his wife.

All I had to see was the fear in the mother's eyes and the welt marks on that child's back and legs. This scumbag walked into the office and loudly demanded, "Give me my damn kid, you piece of shit cop. Keep out of my family," and proceeded to yank the child's arm so hard I thought he was going to pull it out of the socket.

His head soon became familiar with the lobby floor.

That's when I learned an important lesson about Mace spray: it can bounce back. This came to an unhappy realization when I gave him a full Mace delivery to the face, and it came right back to me.

It was then Sgt. Marks leapt over the top of the counter, easily hoisting himself over. Simultaneously, Bob Casey burst through the dispatcher's booth, arms at a full pump. More guys just kept coming from every conceivable inch of the PD, it seemed. It definitely taught the guy a lesson about starting a fight with a cop… in the middle of a police department lobby. You'd think that logic would be intuitive.

Maybe he wasn't used to his victims being able to fight back.

We took Mr. Scumbag to a booking cell with him kicking and screaming the whole way. When we finally got him back to the booking area, he bellowed in Mark's face, "I'll kill your whole family. I'll follow you, and I'll come to your house. I'll kill your kids, you fucker."

Gorsh studied my face for a few moments, allowing me to relive this in my head. Then he reached down to the folder, still refusing to take a seat, and retrieved two Polaroid photos of the arrestee. He tossed them on the desk toward me. I leaned in, taking a good look at the waste of human flesh. His face looked almost as bad as his daughter's back and legs did. His left eye was black, a split above his right eyebrow, fat lip and other bruises crowded into his face. *Karma's a bitch,* I thought. *Immediate justice.*

Gorsh's eyes had not left my face. "If all these reports are correct, how do they match with his face in these pictures? I mean, if all you did was tackle him and take him to booking, how did his face get like that?" He watched me.

I studied the photographs for a few minutes and began to nod mechanically as he watched.

"I don't know for sure, sir," I said, a look of perplexity on my face. "But, it *looks* like he brutally attacked the cell door with his face." I sucked my cheeks in, forcing them between my teeth.

"That your answer?" He didn't wait for me to finish, but leaned against his sumptuous chair and smiled grandly. "Okay, we're good. Don't worry about it. Everything's documented. I'll have Mark write a supplemental for the photos."

He continued, "Look, the asshole had it coming, Ellis. I get that. Just don't do it so publicly next time. What's with you and public? You damn actors." He laughed at his joke.

All of a sudden, he seemed to become hyper-aware that he was still standing up and how awkward that was. "Of course, I didn't say any of this."

orm Lawson's Nordic-blonde crewcut rippled in small waves as his eyebrows wiggled up and down during conversation. He had these full cherubic cheeks and a childlike curiosity about life. Standing in front of a class of half-awake Fullerton College students, he used his entire body to teach biology. He seemed oblivious to how little everyone cared—the lesson was for him and him alone. A few months ago, I was one of those bored, barely-awake students.

Since then, we'd become friends. Not too common between professor and student, but we had a connection. He became fascinated by my police and theater stories and wanted to know more about my point of view. This was how our friendship originally developed: after class, I'd sometimes stick around and share my stories of triumph, horror and endless comedy...no matter how dark. He loved it. We decided to stay in touch even after I passed the class, occasionally socializing with our wives in tow.

"I promised to teach a night class, so I have to make this quick. Sorry. It's a last minute save-a-colleague kind of thing." He looked apologetic; so much sadder to see on a cherub.

"But, I couldn't wait any longer to tell you my news and to talk to you about something."

I stayed silent, waiting for him to continue. I could feel my pulse in my feet.

"I've accepted an offer to be Dean of Cypress College. I start next month." His excitement broke up his face, crewcut undulating in sync. His eyes danced.

"Wow. That's fantastic, Norm," I said, unable to stop my wide grin. I grabbed his hand and pumped it up and down in congratulations. "You'll be a great dean."

Norm took a deep breath and slowly released it. "Thanks," he smiled. "So, I'm putting together classes for the fall semester, and I want to offer a police science class. I think you'd be a great fit for that. You present a whole different face to police work, not just a big tough-guy following orders like most of these kids think cops are like. You're bright, cultured and compassionate, opposite of the stereotype".

At this point, my mouth had dropped open. I couldn't believe what I was hearing, but I was getting more excited with each word he spoke.

"I know about many of your experiences, and I know about you. You're part of a new generation of cops. You may not know it, but you are, and I want you to use your experiential voice to teach law enforcement at Cypress. I think it would be great."

He stared at me, waiting for a reaction.

Experiential voice? I'd been a cop for little more than three years, and I was being offered a teaching position on a college level? Part of my list of goals included being a college professor, and now it felt within my grasp. Maybe that meant everything on my list could happen.

"Wow," I managed to get out, "what an opportunity." I was so taken aback that my body didn't know what to do; I wasn't sure if I should shake his hand or hug him. "But, I haven't quite graduated yet. How could I teach?" I was beginning to feel anxious.

Norm explained to me I qualified for a designated teaching credential, which would allow me to be an instructor without actually having a degree.

I tried to take a deep breath to simmer down. But I couldn't, not all the way. "I'm trying to take this all in. I only have three and a half years of experience on the PD."

"I know all that," nodded Norm with a calm smile. "I know a lot about what you've been through as a cop and how you handle yourself with people. Hell, you won the state speaking championships. You're a natural in front of a crowded room of people. It's what you want to do, you want to teach, and I want you to accept this offer." He looked at me for a few seconds. "Think of what this can lead to, for your goals, for your family...."

For the first time since this whole madness started, I felt like I could actually see my destination at the end of this grueling road. *This could be the perfect position for me.*

"Yes. Yes. Thank you so much. I'm really touched by your faith in me," I said, close to choking up.

At the end of a swing shift a couple of weeks later, Keaton leaned back in his chair in the watch commander's office, reading a police report. He began to chuckle. "What the hell?" he coughed out.

In the midst of his laughter, McKinley entered the office to take over shift duties. He caught Jim's smile. "What's funny?" McKinley asked, eager to join in.

Keaton glanced up, the grin still on his face. "Oh, nothing. I just read one of Ellis's reports. He cracks me up." He tossed the report on the desk and folded his hands, swiveling in his chair. "I already approved it, but you might want to read it. Pretty entertaining."

McKinley's hopeful smile faded upon hearing my name. "No, I don't think so. I think he's a smart-ass."

Realizing it was time for shift change, Keaton arose from the desk. "Maybe you just don't get his sense of humor," he said with a wry smile.

"Humor doesn't fucking belong in a police report," McKinley barked, turning the casual conversation up a notch.

Keaton's eyebrows rose, slightly taken aback. "Hey, it always flows within the report. It's accurate. It's not like he's making shit up, and it sure makes it easier to read. I don't see anything wrong with the way he does it." He spat the last sentence out, starting to get offended at McKinley's tone. Little did Keaton know, it wasn't directed toward him at all.

He began putting his jacket on, never breaking eye contact with the top of McKinley's head as he nervously fidgeted with the pens and paper clips on the desk. Arranging, re-arranging, again and again. McKinley glanced up as if to check if Keaton still watched him. He averted his eyes almost as quickly as they met Jim's, and his tongue nervously darted about his lips.

Keaton lowered his chiseled body into the chair facing McKinley, patiently waiting until McKinley had arranged everything on the shared desk just so.

"You think there might be a little jealousy thing going on there?" Keaton teased, but truth dripped in his voice.

McKinley stared at his fingernails.

Keaton prodded, "You hear he's going to teach at Cypress College this next semester?"

McKinley leaned back in his chair. His eyes still wouldn't meet Keaton's. "How the fuck did that happen? Three years on the streets, and he's gonna teach a class? Give me a fucking break." His eyes briefly looked into a distance not there, doing anything to avoid his companion's gaze. "I got to tell you. I don't like that asshole. Thinks he's so damn smart."

Keaton chuckled. "Yeah? What's wrong with knowing you're smart, Mac? Seriously, I don't get it. I really don't see where your animosity comes from."

McKinley's eyes finally met Keaton's. "It's not right, that's all. I didn't even get asked. A lot of guys here with ten to fifteen years on the PD, and I'm sure none of them got asked. Did you?" He prodded, voice filled with a quiet intensity.

"No, I didn't. But, why the hell should I have? I'm not qualified to teach a college level class. Are you? He's the college man. What the hell do we know about that? The school offered him the position, so they must have wanted him. End of story. This has nothing to do with us.

"Ellis knows his stuff, and he's good in front of a room of people. I've seen it. I don't think that position is based on police seniority. I think *teaching skills* may have a bit to do with it as well," Keaton said, eager to bring the conversation to an end. "Just be happy for him and let it go, man."

"I'm not the only one that doesn't like him," added McKinley, practically spitting with passion. "He pisses people off." Like his hair was on fire.

Keaton's face wrinkled up. "What people? And, why? 'Cause of what they say in the newspapers? 'Cause he's outspoken? 'Cause he's been offered a teaching job? Huh?" Keaton watched McKinley continue down his list like he couldn't hear him, and he realized in fact those were exactly the reasons why.

30

"**D**o either of you think Bill's job has anything to do with this?" Harry asked in his soothing tone.

Sarah and I looked at each other for what seemed like an eternity.

Breaking the silence, Sarah turned to Harry and affirmed, "I think it has almost *everything* to do with it. That and everything else he's doing. It's getting to be too much. He's driving himself into the ground."

For the next seventeen minutes, she rambled on about what a problem I am, while I tried to look concerned. *No one said it was going to be easy.*

My sister had turned us onto Harry Karman, marriage counselor extraordinaire. Harry was about fifty years old, and usually wore some variation of a pastel sweater with a collared white shirt and dark jeans. Today he topped the outfit off with a beige colored corduroy jacket with suede elbow patches, like a professor. Probably to let us know he knew his shit, but he was still cool. *Yeah, sure.*

With three and a half years on the PD, I was suspicious of most everyone not fundamental. It had taken me the first hour just to get less defensive about being a cop, which I got the sense Harry regarded pretty negatively; most people did in the late sixties.

I guess it was no surprise whose idea this session was. Sarah continued with her soliloquy, captivating two-thirds of the room.

Harry watched her, expressionless but listening carefully. *What a rock,* I thought. *How much of this crap does he have to listen to each day?*

I noticed a ray of sunlight coming in from an unclean window. It reflected on her and brightened her full, flowing hair. There was no denying she was as radiantly beautiful as ever. But we just weren't connecting how we used to. Police work alone played hell with relationships.

"Blah...blah...blah," she droned on. After all these years, I'd given listening a fair shot. It had gotten us nowhere. All night talk sessions always left me feeling numb. Now it was Harry's turn. I settled back in the chair, only occasionally masking my drifting thoughts.

As per usual, I couldn't stop thinking about what was going on at the PD. Most recently, Sergeant Keaton abruptly resigned, which seemed unlike him. I didn't even get a chance to say goodbye. He was a good cop, a great supervisor to the end, yet disappeared quicker than you could say his name. Totally unexplained. Another good cop gone. *Three down—how many more to go?*

The police department brought in a "consultant" for management. Don Copper was a civilian who'd been assigned to work *within* the police department and reported directly to the City Manager. Maybe Chief Gorsh was too busy rampaging through the ranks of anyone who may have glanced at him wrong, ever, and needed help with operations.

But, that consultant situation was worth taking a closer look at. Did Gorsh feel anyone looking over his shoulder? He should, but didn't he always? It felt like there was more to come, and something about it wasn't right.

I tuned back in just in time to hear Harry respond to Sarah's rant, which had somehow come to an end. "It'd probably be a good idea if I started seeing you two separately." He looked at me pointedly. "So, Bill," he smiled gently, "anything you want to add?"

I shook my head. "Nope. I think I said what I need to say for today."

Harry watched me, clearly disappointed.

31

"**T**he son of a bitch is actually denying my request of changing shifts with someone, so I can attend my graduation," I ranted the following week. "*My own graduation*—can you believe that? A couple of guys have even agreed to cover the shift for me, and he won't let them."

Harry watched and listened carefully. If he was at all surprised by my dramatic change in participation, it didn't show.

"Why don't you tell me exactly what happened?" Smooth as butter.

I fidgeted in my seat, figuratively trying to get a hold of my emotions before I took him through my frustrations. I took a deep breath.

"It started when I put in a written request to trade shifts with Bud Fry, something that's done regularly. It's *always* approved." I felt the anger building up again and decided to just let it take over as I continued, thinking maybe I'd feel better afterward.

I raged through a monologue of my discontent, said I wasn't at all concerned about getting the request to swap approved. So, I was stunned the next day to find my request returned to me by the captain. The word "Denied" written across it in big, blaring red letters. You could almost detect the loud mad clown laughter in the word—"Denied."

I went to his office directly to ask for an explanation. I stood there as respectfully as possible, but seething as Hanson seemed to barely acknowledge me. He was eager to get me out of his office.

150

"Whatever you want, make it quick," he'd snapped, glancing at his watch. "I have a meeting."

"I don't understand why you denied my request. It's for my graduation. It won't cause any problems, sir, I have the shift covered," I'd said, careful to maintain respect. It humbles one to have to beg for something, well-aware that the person in power has a strong dislike for you and is aware of their upper hand.

"Yeah. Well, I've talked to a few people who'd much rather you worked your shift." He looked past me, with a mocking smirk. "So, sorry. Denied."

I stared at him, dumbfounded. "But, I've never had, or even seen or heard of a request like this denied. It's my *college graduation*, sir. I've worked hard for this." *My whole family is coming.* My stomach was flipping, making itself known.

"You said that, Ellis. In your request, and about thirty seconds ago. You need to leave now."

He turned back to his desk dismissively.

A vague realization met clarity. "You're doing this just because it's graduation, aren't you?" I stuttered. I couldn't really believe "leviathan" had anything to do with this.

"Don't worry about it. They'll *mail* the degree to you. They probably do it all the time. Not everyone makes it to their graduation, you know," he said, smirking maliciously. "It's not like we're asking you to give up your degree. Ask for a day next week and I'll give it to you. You'll be okay."

"So, if I just want to stay home drinking beer and sitting on my butt watching TV, it'd be no problem getting time off. But my graduation ceremony—that's out of the question?" My voice was trembling in the retelling almost as much as it did when I was in front of the captain himself.

"And that was that," I said, looking at Harry in wonderment. "He practically threw me out of his office. I've even been told by a couple of supervisors I should think about looking for another career. *Another career?* For what? Am I failing at this one? I don't think so. Last I checked I was *excelling.* What the fuck is the matter with these people?"

Harry interjected my anger with his soothing voice, "Well, think about this, now. That doesn't have to mean failure. Maybe you just don't *belong* there. And guess what? That's okay. You've got a lot more going on for you than just being a cop."

I shook my head, my body straightening. "Not yet. I don't have a choice yet." I really didn't think I did.

32

THE WARNING...

"You'd better watch out. You got some sneaky bastards mad at you. You're quite obviously pissing them off." Ernie chuckled. His fingers pattered against the dashboard in fashion of piano playing, something he did on the side of police work.

I liked talking to Ernie. He was the only cop who understood a man's need to hold a firearm while still wanting to sing and dance a little.

I began nodding my head for no one in particular. "You know, fuck 'em, Ernie. I'm not into that shit. I'm doing my job. Everything else isn't their damn business."

I was sitting in my police car, the driver's side window peeled to match Ernie's, who was parked exactly parallel to me, bumpers pointed in opposite directions. We chatted away on one of our classic ten eighty-seven meetings.

"Maybe, but you can't stop it. Like at briefing when you *sincerely* explained to Baker why Lenny Bruce was a ground-breaking comedian. Just after he'd finished pounding him for being foul-mouthed on stage. The look of disgust on Baker's face as you talked? They remember that shit, Ellis. It adds up." His face brightened as he recalled, "Oh yeah. And last week when you brought that queen into the briefing room? Are you crazy?" He laughed again.

A few days ago, I had brought Lynn to rehearse a few scenes with me in the PD basement, normally used for briefings. I truly didn't think it was a problem. I was off duty and had permission from Lt. Armstrong to use the space, but, okay. Guess I'd be a liar if I'd said I didn't think it would raise any eyebrows. I mean, Lynn was over-the-top flamboyant, and I loved it. But I was pretty sure my colleagues wouldn't. I knew they would be aghast.

"I got permission ahead of time," I reminded him.

"Not everyone knew the details." He shook his head, still wearing his helmet. "Man, that got around. You and your gay boy rehearsing up a storm."

"Well, fuck 'em again, if they don't like it. That's show biz." I pointed my chin toward the window frame, defiantly. "Would broadening their horizons just a bit really be the worst thing? I'd make them less boring, that's for sure."

We sat quietly for a moment. Then, Ernie asked, "How'd your class go?"

"Great. I loved it. Going to do two this next semester. I seriously think I've found nirvana. It's part of my forever future, you know." It was ecstasy to talk about it.

"How'd Palermo do? He was kind of pissed at you. Said you barely gave him a C," Ernie smiled, reveling in the PD gossip.

Stu Palermo, a fellow officer, friend and student in my class, had become surly with me since grades came out. But I'd warned him about the class before he signed up. I was very clear that I wouldn't be going easy on him just because he was a brother in blue.

"I want to make sure you know ahead of time. This is the very first class I've taught, and I want this to be part of my future career. Your time on the PD and our friendship won't have a bearing on your grade. I've got to do this right. I hope you understand. Your grades will get the same objective evaluation as everyone else. I promise you, Stu. I'm not kidding."

Guess he'd thought I was kidding.

33

CODE ALEX A

My police radio crackled and blared, "All units, this is Control One. Stand-by." Every cop in range looked at their radio, expecting to find the answer.

Control One commanded all radio communications for Orange County when there was a major emergency. Any time Control One took over the radio, everyone dropped what they were doing and listened. All incessant police chattering immediately ceased, waiting for the voice to continue. I could feel the silence spread out over the county from the privacy of my cruiser.

"All units proceed to 'Code Alex A' locations in North County immediately. More to follow. Repeat, proceed to Code Alex A *now.*" Code Alex A created a virtual sealing off the county main arteries to contain fleeing dangerous suspects. They'd dropped the net. *Something fascinating is happening,* I thought. *Something big.* Officers began hauling ass to their predetermined stake-out locations, amped up by Control One's commanding essence.

"All units, we have a possible double one-eighty-seven (murder). Shooting on Katella, Anaheim involving drug dealers . . . . Fleeing unit is a stolen, late-model, white van with rear windows shot out. Two to possibly three suspects, described as white, early twenties. Considered armed and very dangerous."

I hightailed it toward Beach and Artesia, my assigned spot. But as I was driving, my intuition loudly spoke up. I'd acquired a sort of sixth sense when it came to stolen vehicles, which was a story unto itself. Some cops had it for dope, some for stolen goods. Stolen vehicles were mine. I didn't know how it happened, but if there was a stolen vehicle in my view, I would intuitively get alerted to it. This happened several times and *always* accurately.

Letting that intuition take control, I drove past my assigned area and headed toward the 5 Freeway onramp, about half a mile away.

I reasoned with the voice in my head, coming up with the following: *if I'm a criminal who just shot and killed two people, I'd be hauling ass to get out of Orange County ASAP. And, if I was on Katella in Anaheim, the best route would be north on Knott Avenue to the 5. They should be coming into this intersection about now.*

Doubt wasn't found anywhere in me; I knew what was going on. I could feel their flight pattern in my veins. Pulling at me, tempting me to leave my assigned area. I began to sweat with anxiety.

Part of me was shocked when I looked up and saw a white van approaching the intersection with two young men in the front seats, but a deeper part of me had been expecting them. *Knew it.*

I smiled inwardly. I parked in the right place.

The van made a casual, controlled and safe left turn onto Telegraph, an adjoining road to the freeway. However, this turn was made a bit too quickly and placed them on the wrong side of the freeway to allow entry. Of course, it was always possible they were locals out for an evening drive, wrapped up in conversation and not paying attention to their turn.

Or, maybe they saw my black and white, and turned left on a knee-jerk reaction to being up to no good—fleeing suspects from a double murder.

I drove into the intersection and turned right to get behind the van, also casually. I couldn't help but wonder how I'd explain myself if I had to call for backup. At this point, I was miles away from my assigned spot. *Shit, I'm not wearing my helmet, either.* In the past I wouldn't have thought twice, but the way things had been going of late, I had a feeling Gorsh and other superiors would love the chance to catch me doing *anything* out of line. *Why am I worrying about this right now?*

As I tucked in behind the van, I noticed something certainly unusual for a casual night drive. The rear windows appeared to have been shot out; glass fragments on the rear bumper easily confessed it.

Both the van and my police unit were driving at normal speeds. The suspects obviously didn't know that I knew anything about their crime, and my bet was they were hoping to God I didn't find out.

Meanwhile, I was still racking my brain for a reasonable explanation to feed the backup for my even being there. Unable to wait any longer for an epiphany of reason, I picked up my radio, settling on, "Twenty-three eleven, I have emergency traffic. I am behind the suspects right now."

Once again, all the chatter ceased.

Control One asked for our location, and I was advised to wait for backup before stopping the van. Several units were assigned for backup.

The radio started going crazy. It was like every cop and dispatcher in North Orange County was trying to speak at once, like a group of happy ten-year olds just released for recess.

Control One soon established over the radio (without waiting to hear my opinion) that I would take the suspects down when other units arrived at Valley View, by Denny's Restaurant. Through the cacophony of police chatter, it occurred to me how busy Denny's would be at this time of night. I continued to follow the van as I considered the situation and determined it to be a Control One decision not based on the reality around me.

These were two (at least) suspected fresh murderers. The take down would probably be dicey, and was it really the best idea to have that going down in the midst of a bunch of civilians trying to have a late-night snack? The sirens alone would cause an uproar.

So, I concluded Control One's idea wouldn't fucking work out, and I would take them down right now, before backup arrived. I felt good about it, and that's about all I considered before calmly making up my mind.

I attempted to get radio time, but it was useless trying to talk over everyone else. Things were moving faster by the second, and I finally gave up trying, barking to anyone that might hear, "Twenty-three eleven. I need to stop the van now. I'll be out of the unit with suspects."

There. Couldn't say I didn't warn them. I wasn't waiting for Denny's.

I put on the overhead lights, and the van immediately changed pace, slowly pulling over to the right side of the road. I squinted, making out the two figures from earlier. There was no guarantee another person wasn't hiding in the cargo area, ready to pop up and shoot my ass through the back window. Freeway populated vehicles were loudly whizzing by.

I pulled my car over to the side, put my spotlight on the rear window, and quickly took out my twelve-gauge shotgun. I got out of my unit and turned my body toward the van, pointing the twelve gauge directly at the driver.

"Turn off your engine and throw out your keys. Both of you get out of the van, NOW," I loudly demanded. I glanced again at the rear window. "Do everything I say or I will shoot your fucking ass. I promise you. I will not hesitate."

I found myself alone with these (possibly armed) suspects of murder and drug dealing, and a part of me felt like I should be at least a little scared. But I wasn't. I coped with it in the same way I always did; I was just playing a cop in a movie. Just another day on set. And, if they messed with me, it wouldn't end well for them.

I remained behind my open door, using it as a partial shield.

Something didn't feel right. One of my costars got out of the van and stared at me for a moment. We locked eyes, and I waited for him to make a move. Instead, he quickly got back in the van and shut the door. A few seconds went by. I couldn't tell what was happening and was starting to get concerned. My silver screen illusion was slipping. He got out of the van again and watched me for a few chilling moments. My mouth sprang to action first, shouting threats of death in their general direction, doing my best to persuade him to come all the way out of the van and stay out, which he did.

The other suspect started coming out of the van, but moved very slowly, almost theatrically slow. Not at all like suspects pulled over by a cop with a twelve-gauge shotgun pointed at them.

I started to feel as though they were trying to misdirect me. *There could easily be a third suspect still hidden.* With my free hand, I carefully drew and aimed my .357 magnum pistol. It was powerful enough to blow through any door if necessary and kill the person behind it, as well as the person behind that guy, if I aimed right.

I kept my eye on the suspects while cocking my head to hear the radio traffic screaming from the car speaker. No one on the radio seemed close to figuring out where I was. And I didn't feel comfortable enough to put down a gun and reach for the car mic.

Slowly, I lowered the pistol back into the holster. The driver watched me, bewildered. I continued shouting at both to comply, but they weren't even responding. It felt like I was underwater, slow motion, going backwards.

They continued to stare at me with strange looks on their faces. *What the hell is going on here?* I felt vulnerable, facing these two men standing on opposite sides of a van with the growing possibility of a third hiding inside.

Thinking I should *shoot the fucking driver*, I used my free hand to help lift up my shotgun, chamber parallel with his chest. I didn't feel there was much choice if I wanted to stay alive.

My finger was in the process of pulling the trigger, when it suddenly hit me, and I stopped. These guys couldn't understand what I was saying because of the loud freeway noise. My threats were drowned out by truck traffic. That's why they weren't complying. They were compliant, but confused. The driver had the facial expression of Harpo Marx, and I was in the process of shooting him. *Oh, my God. I could have shot Harpo!*

I exhaled deeply, shifting my shotgun back to the rear window as I moved forward, shouting louder for them to drop to their knees and put their hands behind their necks. They seemed to be relieved to find no one else was going to die, especially themselves.

Backup arrived in a dramatic rush and all at once. I took both into custody while others searched the van for the possible hidden third suspect. The street looked like a used police car lot, with a plethora of flashing lights freaking out the freeway traffic.

A short time later, Gorsh arrived with Sgt. Baker, and approached the still active scene. I could tell they were impressed with the turnout. Lots of cops from various agencies peppered with onlookers. Few sights were such a thrill. More lights than the Academy Awards.

Gorsh sought me out after the suspects were cuffed and securely in the caged backseat of two cars. He pulled me aside, "Good job, Ellis. Great arrest."

"Thanks, Chief. But, to be honest, the whole time I was worrying you were going to write me up for not wearing my helmet." I spoke tentatively.

One of his newest rules was that officers must be wearing helmets, <u>at</u> <u>all</u> <u>times</u>. He was maniacal about it, as with most things.

Gorsh laughed for the audience as though that was the silliest thing he'd ever heard. Even though no one else could hear what I said.

"No Ellis, I don't think so. Sincerely, great arrest. I heard everything on the radio. I'm proud of you." He patted me on my shoulder.

I got a tinge of nostalgia. For a moment, I thought I saw it in his eyes, too.

Baker asked, "Hey Ellis, how'd you even happen to be here in the first place? You were assigned to Beat One." He smiled darkly. He wanted me to answer in front of the chief. I was sure he expected me to do what he did best.

Before I could answer, he snapped, "You were told by Control One to wait for backup. Why didn't you do that?" Smugness and nastiness melded horrifically on his fat face.

Shortly after the call, Baker and Gorsh sat at Denny's in front of two steaming cups of coffee.

"Who the fuck does he think he is?" Baker scoffed. "What if those guys showed up where he was supposed to be instead of where he was? Whole different story. Different ending. Oh, but he's the golden boy. Fucking intuition, my ass."

Gorsh responded, "Hey, he played his hunch. He took a chance. It worked for him. *Again*. It was a damn good arrest, and I'm not going to fault him for it."

Baker leaned back and took an exaggerated drag off his cigarette, shaking his head at Gorsh. "We're going to the college on Tuesday. I've got an appointment with the genius dean who hired him. We need to clear things up. Mac is going. Maybe Hanson, too."

Gorsh took a drink from his coffee, studying Baker. "You guys are fucking nuts with this. Don't involve me." Meanwhile, his expression was passive.

34

"I don't know, she just said Norm wants you to call him as soon as possible, and to use a pay phone, not the home or work phone," Sarah's voice cut through the line, tinged with confusion and worry.

"Okay, thanks." I was at a loss for what this could be about. I instantly felt uneasy. The sudden request didn't make sense, and my mind was already racing with possibilities.

After shift's end, I drove out of the city to Fullerton to make the call from a pay phone.

"Hello?"

"Norm? It's Bill Ellis."

I heard Norm's quiet breathing for just a moment before he put the phone down and moved to close the office door. I heard it click shut, and he was back on the line.

"Jesus, Bill. I can't believe this. It was like the damn mafia in here yesterday."

"Who? What are you talking about?" I asked, confused and sick from the putrid mixture of stale beer and cigarettes trapped in the phone booth with me of callers past.

"I had three Buena Park cops in my office yesterday. Scaring the shit out of me," Norm said evenly with tense undertones.

"Why? What were they doing there?"

"It was about you, Bill. These people have a giant hard-on for you. They don't want you teaching here. No question about it. They made sure I understood. I'm telling you." He paused, "I'm not supposed to be talking about this."

He sounded hesitant to continue.

I searched my head for a response, but all I could think of was, "What the hell?"

"They're pissed that you're teaching law enforcement at this college; asked me why I hadn't spoken with more senior members of the force. They said you don't have enough experience to teach. They seemed jealous and spiteful.

"They really don't like you. I told them I *knew* of your experience when I offered you the position, and I liked your style. My hires are always weighed heavily by my personal assessment. My judgment. Seniority, I told them, is only part of my consideration. I told them people with fifteen years of experience sometimes only have one year's experience, repeated fifteen times. That pissed them off even more. They were like bullies on a playground."

I could picture Norm saying this in person, speaking with animated eyes and jittery movements. His fear and uneasiness were palpable. For the first time, I felt ashamed of the PD.

"What were their names?"

"I didn't get them all. Frankly, they scared the crap out of me. They were all in uniform with guns and they all had either stripes or bars, I can tell you that."

"One of them named McKinley?" I already knew the answer.

"Yeah, I think so."

I continued, "Was one of them a fat ass?"

"I got to be honest with you. I don't feel comfortable even talking about these guys or what they said. They told me they could make life hell for me any time I go through Buena Park. I go through it twice a day. They know that. They told me." He sighed heavily. His voice sounded distant, tinny.

"Bill, how did they know that?"

"They just didn't like the fact that I'm teaching?" I asked, ignoring his question. I was still trying to piece this together. There had to be something I was missing. I felt as though someone had kicked me in the stomach.

"Bill, I'm so sorry. But, Sue and I talked about it last night. I can't be in the middle of this. I can't take that kind of pressure. I'm a glorified biology teacher with the chance to run a college. I'm not someone who gets in the middle of a police fight. Jesus. I'm not that guy; not at all.

"I think I'm going to step away from the college offering law enforcement classes for a while. Take a pause. Let things settle." His voice was thickly apologetic.

Settle? I fought a strong urge to rip the damn phone out of its socket. I leaned my forehead against the dirty booth and closed my eyes, letting the phone swing next to my knees. I could hear his voice, "Bill, Bill? Bill, are you there?"

All this shit had been a precursor, and I just got fucked. Perhaps a complete career lost.

The goal I'd been working my ass off for, taken away from me in a moment. Because of jealousy? *What do you do with something like that?*

I noticed my mouth had dropped open, and I was silent.

I pledged to Norm I wouldn't discuss our conversation with anyone at the PD. Not that there was much I could do, anyway, but my initial shock wasn't going away—especially since none of these men had ever given me a clue they'd had difficulties with me teaching. I knew they were having issues with me getting all the news media attention, but this too?

It didn't even make sense to me. Big bad police officers, sneaking around like a bunch of passive-aggressive little bitches. The resentment was swarming inside of me, and so was the rage. My dreams became images of me beating them senseless. Every day weighed heavier and heavier, my stomach in constant knots over this subtle negative tension.

There was no justice in law enforcement.

I decided to limit my interaction with those three, just to be on the safe side. I didn't completely trust myself to temper my reaction. Funny though, I thought that was what I'd been doing the whole time.

35

ENTER THE PHANTOM...

I t became increasingly difficult for me to hide my frustration and anger. I tried to be the bigger person since I needed the job, but this had me permanently locked into livid. I analyzed the situation...what they had done would set my goals back several years at the very best. I couldn't wrap my arms around that much pettiness, from my brothers in blue nonetheless. Well, not my *real* brothers in blue, to be fair.

Weak fucking management.

The only question now was, who will I get the opportunity to pay back first? I considered it a necessary counterpunch. There had to be consequences. They'd attacked my family and I wouldn't stand for that. Complaining or trying to talk about it clearly wasn't going to cut it, either. How could they possibly be expected to tell the truth? This was their game.

Coincidentally, there was a lieutenant's exam to replace the vacancy left by Gorsh taking place in three weeks. It'd been posted on the briefing bulletin board for over two months. So, I considered it a good place to begin. It provided a wonderful landscape.

Sgt. McKinley had been studying since the first day the date of the exam was posted. He studied very hard, to the point of sweating. That sounded ridiculous perhaps, but I'd actually seen it. He was also a real ham about studying. When McKinley cracked a book, the entire PD damn sure knew about it. He moaned and groaned, stretched his arms out every fifteen minutes, rolled his neck around, and shook out his shoulders with bravado. There was no doubt what he was up to.

The thought of him as a lieutenant was as frightening as it was disgusting to me. In fact, I couldn't comprehend why he would even be trying, or why anyone around him would *encourage* that. What made anyone think the worst sergeant ever would even be an adequate lieutenant? I just couldn't see it. I'd spent a week in Tijuana, Mexico, working with their infamously corrupt police, state and federal, and all of them were better sergeants than McKinley.

Why was he even there? I didn't know of a single street cop who trusted him as a supervisor or as backup. The way I saw it, messing this up for him would be a sort of public service, in addition to my own private little payback. He was "selected" as sergeant before they began giving exams . . . probably blew the chief.

The closer the exam date approached, the longer the list of McKinley's facial tics became. Most of the guys joked about his potential failure with each other (as if he wasn't paranoid enough when no one was talking about him), and he picked up on it.

Enter *The Phantom*, the new PD Superhero. An all-knowing, anonymous figure who called it like it was, but in a mysterious, calculated, invisible way—a fighter for justice.

A few weeks went by without much going on out of the ordinary, until one day McKinley found the following poem scrawled on a piece of plain paper and taped to his downstairs locker for everyone to see.

"ROSES ARE RED
VIOLETS ARE BLUE
IF YOU'RE TRYING TO MAKE LIEUTENANT

WELL, TEN TWENTY-TWO"
(Code numbers meaning disregard, forget about it.)
SIGNED: *THE PHANTOM*

Cute, right?

Instead of seeing humor in it, McKinley was, of course, deeply offended and intensely pissed off. What minuscule bit of self-esteem he harbored was in jeopardy. The moment he saw the note and heard the muffled snickers around him, he ripped it off with a cherry-red face.

Four other officers and I happened to be in the room, getting ready to go on duty. Conversations muted and eye contact danced around McKinley. He may have ripped it off his locker, but it was very obvious everyone had already seen it.

He tore the poem into little bits and pieces, staring at us while the veins in his forehead pulsated in quick rhythm. "Someone thinks he's very fucking funny, I guess. Look, I'm not laughing." He pointed at his angry face, so we'd get his point.

Three tics in a row erupted on his face. "This is *not* something you do to a sergeant."

Everyone froze. I answered, "I don't think anyone in here even read it, Sergeant. We all came down from the break room together, and it was already there. Hell, I thought someone was leaving you a note or something."

Fry straight faced, "Yeah, I thought it was a note."

"What did it say anyway?" I asked innocently.

Everyone was able to hold their laughter, but McKinley obviously *knew* that everyone had read it, and that made him even more nervous. Easier than I thought.

I could tell he knew it was me, which I was more than very fine with. In fact, I *encouraged* it. It fed this new need I had: to show them I knew what they had done to me, to drag it back into their line of sight and make them pay. I longed for the confrontation I hoped it would bring, ready to swing on him if necessary, hoping it would be necessary.

I sat through the entire thirty-minute briefing that night with a large, knowing smile pointed toward him, a sharp contrast to the deep, burgundy flushed on his face. But, he said nothing to me. I wanted to do a Snoopy dance on his prostrate body.

I still had Sgt. Baker and Hanson to deal with, but there was time. This was feeling pretty good, so far. But then again, it was all I had.

Word of *The Phantom* spread like wildfire through the department. Most everyone knew it was me, but no one could prove it, which of course made it that much better. The game they didn't know they'd bargained for.

Most of the guys thought it was just a good-humored prank—just some more of Ellis' quirky sense of humor. They didn't understand the deep malice behind it, the message I was eager to get across. The fury it expressed for me.

With each passing day, *The Phantom* acquired new silent fans.

Harry laughed delightedly. "You're fucking certifiable. They're going to get your ass. You can't fight these people."

"I think I can fight them," I contested, folding my hands against the nape of my neck. "In fact, I think that's what I'm already doing. They need to pay. Don't forget what they did. And those fucks need to pay out in the open."

I considered for a moment. "McKinley knows it's me. He's feeling it. Well, fuck him. Word gets around fast in there. Nearly everyone is laughing about it, and that makes things *wonderful*," I spat out.

Rather than this being an outlet to help me feel better, it fueled my anger. I could feel the discontent churning and bubbling inside of me, begging to take things even further.

"You're fighting back, I understand that." Harry responded, nodding. "But, do you think you might be getting a bit too feisty?" He looked at me, hoping I'd come up with the right answer. The one he had.

Wrong. I rolled my eyes and exhaled loudly. "They took my career, Harry. What are we talking here? Manslaughter? No. Just a cute little poem with an annoying effect. An effect that satisfies me and irks the people who deserve to be irked.

"Isn't that what art's all about? Expression? And, no one can prove where it came from." I smiled and leaned forward with a wink, "They taught me that."

Harry watched me with an unchanging face. "How's this affecting Sarah? What does she say about it?" he asked slowly.

I shrugged. "She doesn't want me there anymore, anyway."

"Does that tell you anything?" He leaned forward. "Bill, you're young and bright. You've got so much going for you." He looked at me, as if expecting me to come to some sort of revelation right there, right then.

"You know what, Harry? It doesn't really tell me shit. Because even with all this, I still love the work. What can I say? If I'm sergeant in eight months, like it looks, I may never leave. Sometimes things just work out. If those fools can be cops . . . I can be everything they are . . . and more."

36

"Hi Camille. Chief in?"

"Depends," she answered with a coy smile, "What do you need?"

"I want to introduce him to our new reserve officer, Bud Ledbetter here."

A month ago, I'd been surprisingly appointed assistant reserve commander by Lt. Houser, and Bud was my first choice as a new reserve officer.

Camille smiled at Bud and reached for her phone. "Chief? Excuse me, Officer Ellis is here to see you."

His voice boomed through her earpiece, "He is? Well, give me thirty seconds and send him in."

Camille hung up and repeated what he'd said, either completely unaware I could hear his voice a mile away, or too polite to assume.

We waited just beyond the requisite thirty seconds. Then I walked to the door and eased it open to let Bud and myself in. I didn't see the chief anywhere in the office. Bud and I glanced at each other, our body language a shrug and raised eyebrows.

Suddenly, the chief's hand popped over the edge of his desk and flailed around like a fish out of water.

His voice growled, "Where the hell are they? My marbles. I know I lost them around here, somewhere." His hand continued to grasp at the air, searching the desk. All I could do was stare in wonderment.

He suddenly popped to his full height with a ridiculous vaude-villian grin and loudly pronounced, "Ellis, I've finally lost my marbles. Can you—" his voice stopped short when he noticed Bud.

"Oh," his voice dropped twenty decibels, eyes lowered to the ground as he cleared his throat. "I didn't know you had someone with you. Just joking around."

I glanced at Bud. He looked a bit bewildered. Meeting Frankenstein for the first time was probably unnerving, especially with him on his hands and knees in full character.

Genuinely surprised, I wondered how Gorsh could think it perfectly okay for him and me to joke around at this point. Our relationship had shifted so drastically. But, I'd had enough taken away from me as it was, so I forced a smile that didn't mean anything. "That was very funny, Chief. Great visual."

Bud stood by, without changing expressions, as though nothing outrageously out of the mainstream had just happened, which is why he was my first choice.

* * *

Two weeks went by, and I could hardly keep my composure. I noticed McKinley watching me every single day, the tics on his face increasing and astonishing me with their innovation.

"That sounds like you, Ellis. Something you would do. Come on. You can tell me," Baker said the other day, trying to butter me up for a confession. "I know you don't like McKinley. Who does? He's an asshole. I won't tell anyone, promise," raising his right hand as if to swear an oath. "I just think it's funny. Three cheers for *The Phantom*."

It didn't quite work for Baker to be "one of the boys." *You look like a mischievous egg, wearing a gun and helmet,* I was thinking, *but actually you're just a lying, back-biting coward.*

The Phantom's profile was rising along with the risk. The personal rewards were growing just as quickly. My anger wasn't really diminishing, but it was becoming manageable.

By this point, other officers and I spent hours laughing over McKinley and the look on his face as he read my now infamous sonnet "Ten twenty-two." *The Phantom* was quickly becoming a cop cult hero.

But, now's not the time to rest on my laurels, I reasoned. I had more to do.

I became even more driven as I discovered how far his habit of hiding rather than backing up, had gone. And, he at least in part, destroyed my career at the college. I still felt a strong compulsion to punish him and the others. It was for my fellow cops, for my family, and most importantly, for myself, so I could look myself in the mirror.

I waited a while until my normal days off, and arrived at the station an hour ahead of the other cops on my shift. I entered from the rear doors and snuck downstairs to the basement locker room. I pulled out a fresh piece *The Phantom* had typed up for the occasion and taped it to McKinley's locker for everyone to feast on, musing his reaction.

"ROSES ARE RED
VIOLETS ARE BLUE
YOUR WIFE SUCKS COCKS
AND YOU DO, TOO.
SIGNED: *THE PHANTOM*"

I was aware of the absurdity of what I was doing, but only enough to laugh about it. Not enough to stop. I chuckled and howled all the way to school, relishing in the look expected to take over his face. Even had to pull over once, I was laughing so hard. Who knew hatred and humor were so closely related? Must be the adrenaline of it all.

I'd thought it through, making sure to do this on a night when I had class, a proper alibi. But, it was difficult to concentrate on class work; I felt so happy with the process thus far.

I spent the entire class fantasizing about other ways my alter ego could torture McKinley. Enough to get him to put his hands on me. That way, I could do my real revenge on him, while looking like self-defense.

Maximum damage in minimum time. Guaranteed.

The next day, I telephoned Fry at his home and casually asked, "Anything happen last night, Bud? I just heard somewhere *The Phantom* might have been in town."

"Ellis, you're crazy, man. You're going to get yourself in deep trouble. He was insane when he saw it. I never seen him like that."

"Serves his ass right. Bastard. Did he cry?" I was hungry for any sordid details of McKinley's humiliation. I smiled with teeth.

"No. But, I'm telling you he waited until Hanson came in and showed everything to him. I think they're going to have an official investigation."

"Official investigation? What? Over a poem? No one investigates the damn *Phantom*," I said, firmly. I remained indignant.

"I gotta go. I'm going to light a candle for you, Ellis."

"Take that lit candle and fire it up McKinley's ass. I'm sure he'd like it. Especially the burning part." I cackled.

"I'm going to stop talking to you. They'll tap my phone."

"Oh, you big puss. Everybody loves this. It's good for morale. It's been great for my morale." Even though we were on the phone, I swaggered.

"Wait a minute, I've got to go, too. I think *The Phantom's* at my front door." I hung up the phone, chuckling at the dark fun and vaguely hoping I knew where it was leading.

It was time for a shooting workout. I unloaded my .357, 6" Smith and Wesson and tied twine around the very end of the blue steel barrel. Then, I fixed the twine to a sock half-filled with sand and tied it to the barrel of my gun.

I turned on the TV and stood, aiming the revolver at various people on television, dry-firing single action and double action for several minutes. I kept my arm straight out. The additional weight on the end of the barrel was good exercise for shooting. It steadied the hands. I did this with both arms.

I'd been made fun of for my consistent practice, but they didn't call me one of the best shots on the police department for nothing. Being number one in shooting gave me an edge that no one else could match. As a cop, it was a pretty big deal. I was medaled a "Distinguished Expert."

Annie walked into the room and watched my exercise with wonder in her eyes, boning up for when she became a cop, just like her daddy.

After *The Phantom* situation marinated a couple of weeks, I was approached by Roy Stern, who also knew I was *The Phantom*.

Hell, by this time, even the chief knew, just as I wanted. *Tribal humiliation.*

"Ellis, this is pretty fucking funny. That weenie McKinley's all over the PD, crying about this. It's driving him loony with the lieutenant exams coming up. So, I'm thinking I got a good idea. I'll join you for one time only, if you want. Just between the two of us."

Then he offered me an intriguing proposition.

Roy somehow had a combination lock that *exactly* matched McKinley's lock, down to scratches and marks. His idea was to use his personal bolt cutter so we could cut McKinley's lock and switch it without his knowledge.

When he tried to open the combination and couldn't figure out why it wasn't working, it would send him over the edge, exactly what I was looking for. Prime time entertainment.

Two nights later, Roy and I made it downstairs to McKinley's locker. Roy brought his bolt-cutter and I carefully guarded the door as he cut off McKinley's lock and replaced it with the identical-looking lock. I taped up another note from *The Phantom*:

ROSES ARE RED
YOU HAVE A TWITCH
I'M HAVING FUN
PAYBACK'S A BITCH
YOUR FRIEND, *THE PHANTOM*

We left the PD using different exits, so we wouldn't be seen together, even by surprise.

Five hours later, I came back for the beginning of shift. When we got ready as usual in the locker room. No one was aware of the lock situation at all. However, most had seen the note, looking my way as they did. I ignored all eyes, fidgeting around with items in my locker as they muttered and glanced.

It was down to only five of us when McKinley himself sauntered in, putting on his suave and confident façade. But, it was peppered with facial twitches, which always gave him away.

I controlled the urge to smile, biting the inside of my cheeks. Pain shot down my face.

Getting my gear together, I could see McKinley glancing at everyone to gauge their reaction to his coolness. *Hello? I'm cool. Look, please.*

Nothing. His somber reaction to their lack of reaction would have been almost sad if it hadn't been him. But, he was him, and so it was delicious to me.

McKinley turned and sat on the bench in front of his locker, finally coming in sight with the note. He read it quickly (for him), and tore it off with a heavy sigh. "This is ridiculous. Somebody's going to get their ass in a sling over this. Asshole. What's so fucking funny, Fry?" he barked.

Fry's smile evaporated. "Nothing Sergeant. Sorry. Just in a good mood." Fry never said anything that wasn't sarcastic.

McKinley sat again and took his combination lock in hand. His breath was jagged as his thoughts riled. He spun the dial quickly as he hunched over it, forever paranoid one of us would somehow pick out his combination.

He reached to tug the lock open. Nothing. No give.

Brow furrowed, studying the lock closely. He began grinding his teeth, as beads of sweat formed on his forehead. He tried again, this run a bit slower.

As if this would give the combination time to understand his input.

Again, much to his dismay, the lock did not open. He even tugged three times, very hard. Realizing he was perhaps, yet again being fucked with, his eyes darted about the room to see if anything was going on, to see if anyone focused on him any differently. Maybe he didn't realize someone usually did.

Fry asked, "Something wrong, Sergeant?"

"Forget about it," grumbled McKinley. He stood, stretched and walked to the water fountain, appearing as though he wanted to start screaming. He drank much longer than necessary as he tried to gather himself.

It started to get rather awkward, when it became obvious he wasn't still drinking any water, but he'd remained hunched over the fountain. After a bit more fake-drinking, he seemed to steel himself and straightened up for the return walk to his locker. *If only Stern could be here*, I smiled inside.

McKinley returned to the bench and sat heavily. He looked at the locker, stroking his chin and perhaps extrapolating his options:

He was in his street clothes with his gun and uniform in the locker. It was close to midnight.

He was dumbfounded.

Slowly, he sat up straight and took a final, determined stress-filled run at the lock. Now he was *sure* everyone was looking at him. This time, he was right. He painstakingly tried the combination sequence. Then he firmly gave the lock a single, hard tug. It didn't open and defeat showed in his face and body. Misery oozed out of his pores. He stood and tugged two more times, as if the change in angle might improve his chances of success.

With his face, red with anger, he kicked at the lock. This caused him a loss of balance, and he fell onto the bench, almost falling off, and onto the concrete floor in the process. His expression morphed into embarrassment.

He was also panting, clearly in pain from landing ass-first on unforgiving hardwood. He stood again and whirled on his heels to glare at us—his eyes wild and his face covered in sweat.

No one moved, except me. I smiled, or maybe smirked. Only slightly, stretching both arms over my head to catch his attention so he wouldn't miss it.

His eyes locked with mine for a moment. His anger increasing in an instant, reflected in his pupils. "Fuck this," he suddenly roared, breaking the pin-drop silence. "I'm outta here!" He spun again on his heels and stormed out of the room, almost running into the wall on his way out. *Wish he had.*

Everyone watched him with bewilderment, wondering what could have happened with his lock to make him so pissed off. We continued readying for shift.

McKinley walked directly to his car and drove home without another word. He remained on sick leave for five days. Five whole days.

Meantime, *The Phantom* was ready for his own television show. Everyone talked about McKinley, and how he was falling apart.

Partial payback was achieved. I'd take emotional pain, for now. Future steps would be considered after the sting from this one subsided.

Photographs were taken of the "crime scene," fingerprints were even lifted where possible. Ironically, Roy Stern's bolt-cutters were used to remove the odd lock that would no longer open. I really couldn't make this stuff up.

A formal investigation was opened. Rumors were that a covert video camera had been installed to monitor the area around McKinley's locker in case *The Phantom* were to re-appear.

No one in supervision ever spoke with me of the incident.

＊ ＊ ＊

A month later, I requested a transfer into the detective bureau. Lt. Burns called me into his office to discuss my request. He started out by taking time to compliment my performance as a cop. "But," he told me, "There's no way in hell you're gonna get into dicks (detective bureau)."

"Why? What do you mean?" I sincerely asked, taken back by his blunt words. *This couldn't be a consequence, could it?*

"You know why, Ellis," Burns said, dryly. "Everyone here knows you're the damn *Phantom*. We just can't prove it, yet. But we will." He leaned back in his chair.

Looking directly into my eyes and smiling slightly, "you're pissing off the wrong people. I don't know why you're doing this *Phantom* shit."

He threw my request for transfer on the desk with a sigh of dismissal.

"That's not true, sir. I'm not *The Phantom*."

Since *we all knew* that wasn't true, *The Phantom* had served his purpose. He'd thoroughly and publicly bludgeoned McKinley, and so *The Phantom* retired, undefeated.

The investigation would die, and I would be the killer.
I was in control, not them.
I was slightly bummed, but hugely elated as I left Burns' office.
Checkmate, McKinley.
Bite me.

37

Several weeks later, I turned my police car into the grassy Knott's Berry Farm parking lot off La Palma and Western. Entering the parking area, I quickly recognized Palermo's vehicle, parked and waiting for our arranged ten eighty-seven.

His car honked in acknowledgement. I headed in his direction.

I wanted to become friends again after the awkwardness that fell over us when he took my class at the college.

As I said, he didn't get the grade he thought he deserved simply because we worked together. He was surprised, displeased and he made it obvious. I stood by the decision I'd made *clear* to him beforehand, but that didn't stop me from feeling uneasy about the whole thing.

So, what better time for a bit of burlesque humor? *The broad stuff sells to this crowd. Laughter heals and all that shit.* I turned my helmet around backwards, not yet sure where I was going with this. My chinstrap was sticking out the side. I contorted my body the best I could without getting out of the car, and fixed my expressive actor face with a look only a mother could love.

I accelerated, heading directly at Stu; hopefully giving the appearance of a cartoonish mad man.

The closer my vehicle got to his, the smaller his smile became until it slowly widened with abject horror. A flutter of emotions hit Stu's face as he realized my car was about to ram straight into his.

I pressed down on the brakes, intending to slightly turn the wheel at the last minute and pull up right next to him. But, the grass was unusually slick that morning, and the car surprisingly became airborne. Something knotted up in my chest. I felt my body go slack with shock and locked my hands onto the steering wheel tightly, knuckles white like snow. I tried to push the brake pedal through the floorboard. I tried to *will it* to stop!

Stu and I locked eyes, me in the air and him in his parked car. Synonymously ringing through our heads was surely the drawn-out word, *Shiiit.* Something in the back of my mind told me I should be doing something, anything, but what?

Time moved in slow motion from that point on. I remember staring at Stu's lifted eyebrows, like that would change anything. I allowed myself to be fascinated by how largely his mouth had opened. I'd become an audience. Everything else was out of my control.

I wondered if it would hurt.

The morning quiet became greatly disturbed by the loud collision. It seemed to echo…but, maybe that was just me reliving it.

Everything in the near area seemed to stop. Ours were the only two cars on the lot. The air seemed so still, so peaceful.

I glanced down at myself, sort of expecting a severed limb. Nothing. I gazed back up at Stu. He appeared unharmed and stared back at me with astonishment. His eyes were the size of saucers, and his mouth still hung wide open.

For some crazy reason my mind wandered to what nearby pedestrians would be thinking right now. They must have heard the loud crash, but couldn't see us or our cars. What could they be thinking?

It was kind of bizarre, and I bit my cheek to keep from smiling. Now wasn't the time. It wasn't that I saw the damages to police equipment funny; I didn't. I just suffered from a sort of Tourette's syndrome for laughing inappropriately; it haunted me throughout my life.

We both exited and Stu gave me a wondrous look, opened his arms wide, as if to say "What the fuck?" and then he put his hands on his knees and cocked his head, "What the fuck?" in a voice hauntingly close to a whisper.

"Oh, man. I am *so sorry*," I managed to get out quietly. "When I hit the brakes, the car took flight." I put my palms out and shrugged. "You don't really expect that to happen with brakes, right? Look at how wet the damn grass is. I lost control." I looked at the damaged vehicles incredulously.

"Yeah, Ellis. They call that hydroplaning," he said slowly, enunciating each word as he glared at me. "You'd better call this in. I'm not going anywhere near it." He slowly shook his head. "I can't believe this."

"I will." I couldn't help but think again, *this is the sort of thing the public should see. Cop as human.*

"Stu, think how funny this is." I reached for him to see it my way, to agree, to what, reassure me? "Two police cars have a head-on collision, and they're the only two cars in the entire parking lot," I said, spreading out my hands like it was a headline. I laughed nervously. "You could do a standup on this, for crying out loud."

I was expecting Stu to join in at any moment now. I looked over, surprised he hadn't made a noise. We needed some comic relief.

He wasn't smiling.

"Enjoy the moment, Stu," I suggested, my tone suddenly serious. "You've got to save the unusual memories like this for later, when you're old and alone."

I moved toward my car to report the accident. Using a police radio is like having a party line. The guys on the radio found it much more hilarious than Stu and responded by cackling anonymously from their cars. I was desperate for anyone to distract me from how little humor I knew the high-ups would see in this skit. I mean, my employment *was* kind of tenuous.

Responding supervision arrived rather quickly, but also didn't share my vision, as I had expected. He quickly became cantankerous about everything.

More arrived to survey the scene. The fact that so many cops had taken time out of their day to come see this made for a funny scene, if you were an outsider. Especially an outsider with an attitude.

I remained stoic though, professional, but the other cops kept furtively glancing at me. Probably wondering if this might be some extension of *The Phantom*.

Or perhaps they were expecting to see me sobbing on the ground and wailing, "Oh the horror! How could I have done such a thing?"

They seemed a little taken aback that I wasn't.

"Wait, wait. You two have to calm down, for crying out loud. You're talking over each other. Anyone able to find anything, yet?" Gorsh asked.

McKinley stood, too much hatred running through his veins to sit. He sighed, frustrated to have to change momentum. "No. No prints or anything. But, I *know* he did it. He smirks at me almost like he's setting a trap. And you know what? I think he knows about our visit, too."

"Well, if he does, that's your problem." Gorsh shook his head slowly as a reminder to all that he did not approve of what they did at Cypress College. He fleetingly reminisced on the times Ellis would talk about his goals, making note about how that would have completely shattered at least one of them. Almost as soon as the thought entered his mind, he discarded it.

"I think what we're getting at is, he could be a danger when he becomes sergeant. That's about six months out. He really could. You know what he's like," Hanson threw in.

Gorsh stared at the wall behind them. It was clear that Baker and McKinley were concerned with Ellis being a sergeant. For Hanson, it was only now becoming clear.

Hanson continued, "I'm sorry, Chief. I know you two used to be friends, but I think he's got to go. It's not going to be easy, because it hasn't been so far."

Gorsh sighed in submission to the idea that was probably his in the first place, "You're going to have to build a good case against him. And his personnel file shows you've got only positives right now to turn negative. Just get me grains of sand. I'll do what needs to be done."

A reel of their talks flashed through his mind—Bill talking about goals, his family, everything he wanted for himself. Gorsh quickly disregarded it again.

Hanson rubbed his hands together and grinned. "I was hoping you'd say that." He picked up a manila folder no one had noticed yet. "I got your number one negative, your first piece of sand right here. Happened this morning." He grandly displayed an accident report.

"What are you talking about?" Gorsh leaned in to get a closer look.

"Ellis had a head-on collision with a second police car in Knott's parking lot. They were the only two cars in the entire lot, and the other car was parked," he paused for effect, "with the motor off."

Gorsh greedily stuck his paw out for the report, watching Hanson's eyes. "You kidding me? Anyone hurt?"

Baker chimed in, "No. But, both cars were pretty damaged in the front. Ellis said it was too bad the public couldn't have seen it."

He shook his head in disgust, looking to see if Gorsh noticed his disgust, and wondering if he should change his look to something else.

"Who was the other officer?" Gorsh asked almost to himself as he glazed over the report. "Oh, wait. I see. Palermo. Wait." He tapped his index finger on the report. "Isn't he the accident investigator today?

He looked up as Hanson nodded his head, "Ironic."

"I drove out to the scene," Hanson interjected. "And I'm with Jack, Chief. Almost felt like Ellis was happy, but you couldn't put your finger on anything. It's that fucking attitude, lately. And, you know what else?"

He stopped until all looked his way, "Reynolds told me 'off the record' that Ellis is writing an anti-police management article he's going to submit. He says Ellis mentioned *Playboy*."

Gorsh chuckled, "Oh, please. He's just jerking Reynolds around."

"No, I believe it. That's something *Playboy* would eat up," Baker said, as he spoke his headline. "*Rebel Cop Gives Inside Scoop*. Think about it."

Hanson offered, "Yeah, that's pretty far-fetched. Even so, it's a bad idea for that to be floating out there right now."

Gorsh sat straight up. "Remember, he was just in a movie. Probably in with that Hollyweird crowd, now. They'd love him." He pondered, "He'll eventually know someone who knows someone. Mac, you tell Reynolds to get as much info as he can about the article, or pretend-article."

"Oh, it's real," McKinley confirmed with shouts of joy in his heart. "Reynold's *heard* parts. Ellis read some of it to him."

"See what you can get, hear me? I'm going to look into it, but I don't think we're allowed to do that without prior city approval. You know, publish?"

Hanson grinned like the Cheshire Cat. "You mean you don't know?"

"Never had a reason before, wise ass. Leave the report with me and I'll come up with a response. And, beyond that," said Gorsh, slowly tilting his head up toward Hanson, "just leave."

Weeks later, Harry gently closed the door and turned to Sarah and me as we sat on his couch. After months of separate counseling, he'd asked us to return to his office together.

As he found his seat, he heaved a sigh of contentment that all shrinks are partial to and smiled at us both. "How've you guys been?"

"Fine," we said simultaneously, yet not together.

He leaned back, clasping his hands around his stomach, studying us carefully. "How's the marriage coming?"

I glanced at Sarah, waiting for her to jump on the opportunity to speak. When she didn't, I masked my surprise and quietly began. "We're working on it. Talking out a lot of stuff. Mostly useless, I might add. But, we're talking it out."

Harry looked puzzled, "What useless stuff?" he asked. Sarcasm wasn't exactly his strong suit.

As Sarah and Bill sat upstairs, Burns and Hanson were surreptitiously just outside the building on the first level of the two-story complex. Hanson squinted up, trying to see through the blaring sun, without looking like that's what he was doing.

"Suite 2D. Write that down." He covertly dictated. Burns complied, glancing about before scribbling in a small notebook.

"It says, 'Los Angeles Women's Free Clinic' on the door." Hanson turned to Burns with a curious smile, waiting for him to finish writing.

"What the hell is that about? Does his wife have female issues?"

"Who knows? Thought they all did. We just got to keep looking. I'll check this out when we get back. Don't worry about it."

38

It was *Judgment at Nuremberg* in Buena Park. Gorsh hit me with a three-day suspension with no pay for the head-on collision, which I appealed, bringing us here. It felt good to stand up for myself at the time, but now it felt like it had become my duty to fight against every supervisor that disliked me.

Not that there was this huge mob, or anything, only five or six. But, it was beginning to feel like I was in the middle of a circle, with my back exposed.

Sgt. Marks and Captain Hanson were "co-prosecutors" presenting for the PD at the appeal hearing. I sat as the only person on my side. *Truth only needs one person.* At least that would be my attitude moving forward.

The arbitrator in the appeal was John Barnett, the city manager, with a thinly-veiled bias to a certain government organization, and a low tolerance for boat rocking.

It felt weird knowing I was my own attorney, and that my client was *guilty.* It brought a little extra tension to the party. I was determined to fight them tooth and nail for absolution, but I wouldn't bet my vacation money on it. I just wanted them to look bad in any way possible.

I felt it was all part of the fabric of distrust and understated anger that now flowed between us like a river: them versus me. They wanted to get me in any way they could; this was just a skirmish in the battle. The Cypress College debacle remained fresh in my mind. *As it should.*

The appeal hearing lasted over two hours. Marks and Hanson were busting out all kinds of diagrams and reports they'd put together, presenting each one with a dramatic flair. I pictured them in line at the Xerox machine, sweating with the anticipation of taking me down.

They'd also made the court listen to their "expert" opinions, in other words, pretty much repeating exactly what was on the charts and diagrams . . . but now in monotone. *This is why you lose cases, you simple fucks.*

I presented my side as planned with enthusiasm. But, things weren't exactly going the way I wanted them to. I didn't have any charts or diagrams. Just a flair for drama and the strange ability to use it in the courtroom. But, isn't *everything* theater, after all?

I wanted to win just to show them I could, to rub their noses in something. In front of important people. But at that point, it wasn't looking good. I needed to fight offensively, and win using their facts. They had so many. I was sure they wouldn't mind.

When it was time for closing arguments, Marks stood up to present to the court. The diagrams were displayed again for a reminder.

"Mr. Barnett, Ellis' own testimony that you heard…was that the Knott's parking lawn had been watered very heavily that morning." He stopped and looked directly at me.

"And he didn't notice this in time to stop safely. He said he was only going 20 miles per hour, which we, of course, dispute," Marks said, looking at me stonily.

"Nonetheless, Ellis has been through pursuit training and has participated in many high-speed pursuits, including a pursuit at over 95 miles per hour…in the rain, for which he received that letter of commendation. It's in front of you, sir."

He slowed his speech, "So, he *knows* about cohesive factors. And the factor for grass is such that even going '20 miles per hour' as he stated…that's still fast enough to lose control of the car." He stood there with his arms shrugged, palms up as if to say, "What else do we need? Take him away." Time to zip it up.

Barnett took off his glasses and massaged his eyes. When finished, he planned to end the hearing and take it under consideration for three days. He couldn't wait to get out of there and into a warm bath. It had been a long day, and he was beginning to smell himself.

He reluctantly opened his eyes to find me seated silently with my hand raised high. "Yes? You wanted to say something more?" he asked wearily, probably thinking to himself, *What the hell now?*

"Yes, sir," I began, lowering my hand and glancing over at Marks. I'd suddenly become inspired, realizing I would have the very last closing statement.

"I just wanted to respond to what Sgt. Marks finished with." I could tell Barnett might not want to allow this, based on how badly he obviously wanted to leave, so I didn't wait for permission before continuing.

"You see, he told me about this *theory,*" I bent my fingers into air-quotes, "a few days ago. I thought it sounded incorrect at the time and told him that, sir." Now I was looking at both Marks and Hanson. Neither seemed to have any clue where I was going with this.

"So, I took a vehicle that *exactly* matches the vehicle I was driving that day. And I
   tested in reality the theory he's resting his case on."

Marks shifted his weight, looking uncomfortable. He still couldn't tell where I was going, and he wasn't used to being confronted like that. *I brought all these charts and diagrams in, what the hell?* He was probably thinking. He glared at me, almost daring me to continue.

I continued, "Sooo, in testing this 'theory' five separate times, I drove on wet grass *faster* than 20 miles per hour and slammed on the brakes all five times. Once, I drove 28 miles per hour before braking. On every single occasion, the car stopped quickly, without a problem." I paused for dramatic effect. "So, my practical testing shows his 'theory' is totally incorrect."

Marks and Hopkins stared at me with no response. They'd stuck their collective dick out, and I'd stepped on it. I was Raymond Burr, and that was worth at least a notch for me.

One week later, Barnett issued his decision. The accident was declared unavoidable, and my three-day suspension was reversed. Negative reporting would be expunged from my file.

Whoa, I won. I was guilty, let me be straight on that . . . and pretty much everyone knew it. But, I beat them up and rubbed their noses in it, like *The Phantom*. Except this time, they *saw* me. They met my eyes as I took them down. It was a rush!

I really didn't give a shit anymore. I was enjoying myself.

It was the talk of the department. Everyone wanted to get their two cents in, wanted to feel the vibration. Fighting police management was practically unheard of, let alone successful. Especially, when it included damaging two police vehicles. I was a damn celebrity, and they'd taken a beating.

Lots of guys came up to me and asked how I'd possibly won. Deadpan, I'd go into detail about Sgt. Mark's theory and how I tested his theory, all this stuff that got me off, with faux sincerity. I tried not to let on how I really felt. No one really knew the anger within me.

I smiled to myself each time I was asked to retell it, which was often. Somehow, no one questioned my testing. No one came forward to say they'd never seen or heard of me taking out a car to try things out. I guess no one was curious enough to make the move.

A couple of the guys asked me if I was worried management would retaliate. I couldn't deny that it'd crossed my mind, and I was feeling somewhat expectant. Yeah, I did humiliate those guys, a couple of times. They were more than unhappy.

But at the moment, I basked in my success.

One more salty victory made its way to me, the ultimate victory in this case. Chief Gorsh had been instructed to read Barnett's final decision aloud to me. If I had it my way, he'd announce it to the entire PD. But, I now sat outside his office.

There seemed no coming back from this. But I felt defiant, and still deeply betrayed.

"Ellis, the Chief would like you to go in," said Camille, careful not to look me right in the eyes. She was obviously feeling uncomfortable about the whole situation. I made sure to give her a big smile.

Gorsh's door opened and Marks stepped forward, a pleasant looking smile painted on his face. He looked like he was wearing a Halloween mask. "Come on in . . . Ellis," he invited. The scowl was in his voice.

As I entered the office, Gorsh remained seated behind his desk with Hanson in a chair directly in front of the State of California flag. Marks closed the door behind me and took a seat. Gorsh bent over the document, carefully reading in his methodical way.

I stood in front of the desk waiting for him to acknowledge me, feeling as though I was in an underground bunker and this may or may not be war.

Gorsh looked up, lifted the paper he was reading, and stood behind his desk. "Okay, I have to read this to you, Ellis," he said gruffly. He looked incredibly uncomfortable, squirming around a little bit. His eyes remained on the paper.

He cited the reversal of suspension robotically, never meeting my eyes in the process. I stood there staring straight ahead as he read, careful to hide any positive feelings.

When Gorsh finished, he paused shortly, and I took the opportunity to say, "Thank you, sir."

"You can leave now," Gorsh said, voice low.

Only then did he look at me. His intense eyes bellowed, *We're not finished!*

As I turned to leave, Marks stood and put out his hand to stop me. "Wait. I do have one question that's bothering me, Ellis."

That stopped me. I turned to him, "Yes, sir?"

"Your closing statement about the tests at that hearing kind of knocked me off balance. What you claimed about your testing process didn't seem possible to me." He shook his head slightly and grimaced. He glanced at the others. "So, Pense and I took the exact same vehicle you had, and we repeated your tests on dry grass." His voice was beginning to rise.

"I drove at 25 miles per hour on five different runs, and you know what happened? I lost control of the car every single damn time. Every time, Ellis. Dry grass, too. Not wet grass." Now his face was slightly flushing.

He searched for a reaction. "Based on what we found and your closing statement, I just wonder what you have to say about that."

I looked him in the eyes, smiled and shrugged. "I don't know, sir. Maybe I'm just a better driver than you."

39

Six police cruisers parked tightly together as seven of us stood in a circle waiting for Bob Casey to speak. It was pitch dark; I could barely make out the man standing next to me. We definitely weren't visible to passing traffic.

Each officer had the stoniest visage he could muster—probably to impress Cooper, who was very oddly present. No one knew what to think of him and his strange position within the department. He was not a cop, he was a "management consultant." He started to be around us more and more.

With Gorsh all over the place and in a constant state of paranoia, Cooper began to assimilate within the ranks of the PD. Like he wanted to be one of the guys. He joked around with us as often as he could, laughing at quips he couldn't have really understood. Many times, we spoke in numbers, not words—Penal Code, not dictionary.

No disrespect, Cooper seemed like a good person. But, he could never be one of the guys; not until he'd worked a couple of suicides or fatal accidents or bar fights. He couldn't even begin to imagine the kind of shit we'd been through. When you are a firsthand witness to life leaving someone's body, you have to learn to cope in ways that only someone else who'd been through it understood.

Had there been a chief capable of communicating this unusual appearance clearly to his subordinates, and they to their subordinates, we'd probably have felt at least a semblance of comfort in our jobs. But we certainly weren't getting it now.

When Cooper looked in my direction, he did a double-take that was too innate to be subtle. I was suddenly positive he knew about *The Phantom*...and the beating I gave management during the collision suspension appeal hearing. I watched him out of the corner of my eye, focusing on the present moment with the thought in the back of my mind.

Stu and Ernie were there along with two plainclothes detectives, one of which I'd trained when he joined the PD, Don Harriman. He was an amazing physical specimen, looming high above anyone else on the PD. But, with all six feet, two hundred and forty pounds of him, he still laughed like a little girl. I couldn't get enough of it, and I found myself making him laugh every chance I could. We'd spent a lot of off-duty hours together, feeding off each other's energy.

We smiled at each other and nodded. Our bond was strong and would remain for decades, no matter what lay ahead of us, and there was plenty.

Sgt. Pense was present, but he'd instructed Casey to handle the situation while he attended to Cooper, to ensure Cooper stayed safe, to throw his body in front of any bullet or fist headed for good old Cooper. Or at least, to make it seem like he would.

There were five of us in uniform as we gathered together, including Cooper of course. Dressed in *his* usual uniform: a business suit and tie.

"Okay men, listen up," Casey barked. Everyone stopped the small talk and looked in his direction, which made him bristle up with delight at being the center of attention.

"Here's the situation. We've got three escapees from the Indiana State Pen. They're supposedly holed up at the Pioneer Motel, room number nine," he postured. The motel was about a thousand yards from us; you could almost see it.

"Couple of units are watching it from a distance right now. We have this: somehow one of them supposedly got accidently shot, by one of the other two guys…in the fucking motel room. Which no one heard? I don't think so." He shook his head, taking off his helmet. His hair was sweaty, and short strands stuck to his forehead.

"So, they freak out, take the guy shot in the shoulder to Beach Community and drop him off. Course we get the call and respond. Injured guy was okay with talking to us. He says they got a lot of guns in that room. Said they say, there's 'no way' they're going back. Said he wouldn't either, except, he got shot." He spoke quickly, making eye contact with each of us.

"He seem sincere?" Fry smirked, looking around to see if anyone else had heard him.

"We ran their plates, and they come back stolen from Nevada," Pense relayed.

Don let out a Betty Boop, "What are we waiting for? Let's go get their asses."

Cooper looked startled at Don's assertiveness; the rest of us loved it. In times like these, we needed someone to plunge headfirst into the fight. It riled us up, prepared us for what we had to do. A clatter of testosterone-fueled chatter erupted. Some howling. Chest pounding. But it began to look as though Cooper would rather head on back to the station. You know, sit at a comfortable desk somewhere. Consult.

The knowledge of this would stick with me for the rest of my life, regardless of being a policeman. No matter where I found myself, I would learn again and again that once you are faced with violence or gunfire, there are just two ways to respond. You can either howl in its face, or head back to the station. I was a howler through and through, and that's not something you ever un-know.

"That's what we're *gonna do*. So, listen up, okay?" Casey looked at Don, a feeble attempt to establish his authority in front of Cooper.

Don let out another giggle, "Okay, you're in charge, just trying to get things moving." He put his hands up in surrender and glanced around the circle with a smile.

Truth be told, he could ruin Casey's entire life with one hand tied behind his back. I think when you were as tough as Don, it was much easier to show humility. You knew you had the power to change lives at the drop of a hat.

Bob pulled out a piece of white paper with his crudely penciled rendition of the Pioneer Motel layout, the building clearly in an "L" shape.

"Okay, you can see the building is pretty simple." Pointing his excited finger to the middle of the upside-down L, "Room nine is about here. I want you three to position over here to the southwest of the door." He looked at them like he was General Patton himself. Readying for battle. They nodded, almost in unison.

He looked at two other officers, "You two position southeast of the door with me." He gave them the same once over, evaluating their manliness.

"Don't anyone let your presence be known or make a move until I give the sign. Get in place quietly. Don't be seen from their room. Ellis, you and Ernie cover the back," he said in a throwaway manner.

I worked to hide my shock, but couldn't stop my immediate thoughts from boomeranging. *Why would you put your best shooter in the back of the building?*

"Everybody go radio silent until you hear me." He was looking toward Pense and Cooper, in case he'd said anything wrong, as was often the case.

I looked at Ernie, "Come on. I'll ride in your unit, and we'll set up in back."

He turned to walk away, muttering, "I'd rather be playing the piano," out of the corner of his mouth.

As I caught up with him, he continued, "I don't like it when they can shoot back, man."

"Then quit," I said as he entered his vehicle. "What did you think you signed up for, crossing guard?" I reached into my car and retrieved my 12-gauge sawed off shotgun from its locked position.

"Ha-ha. Very funny. Come on, let's go," he said through his window as I got in. He applied the gas, and we moved quickly out of the parking lot along with other clusters of cops and cars. All heading for a possible shootout. Adrenaline flowed from every vehicle.

Except maybe Cooper's.

A few moments later, Ernie parked his black and white on an adjacent residential street, and we exited silently, me with my 12-gauge and him with his nervous quips.

"Great fucking planning," I vented. "They got twenty cops in front, you and me in back? Yeah, that's gonna go well." His face didn't move much as we approached the rear of the motel, north side. He was very serious—I silently wondered if he had even heard me.

"How the fuck do we know which room it is?"

"Casey said room nine is in the middle of the building, about there." I pointed toward the window where I expected a quick exit might soon take place. I silently hoped for it. Ernie didn't move and seemed to be hoping for the opposite.

"Let's get closer to the building and take cover the best we can," I said as I moved straight toward the building, ensuring that I wasn't visible from the open window of any motel room. A cluster of small trees and bushes would have to work for cover.

"I'm moving over here," said Ernie. He moved further away from the window, taking what appeared to be a more *indirect* approach to the situation.

Sometimes it's better to take shit head-on. That's what Don would be doing right now, and that's what I wanted as I moved a bit closer to the window.

We maintained position, with Ernie staring at me for a few minutes. It was getting awkward. Finally, we heard Casey's macho voice sling through a megaphone, "Attention in room nine! This is the Buena Park Police! We know who you are, and we know you're in there. You've got no chance to escape. You got one minute to come out with your hands up, or we're coming in!"

"What the hell is the matter with him?" I stage-whispered to Ernie. "They're going to be coming out *this* way. He didn't tell them anyone was in the back."

Ernie's eyes turned into saucers as he realized. He remained perfectly still, staring at me. *He'd rather be playing the piano.*

Suddenly, a bathroom light in the center of the building ignited, bathing us in exposure.

"You've got forty-five seconds to come out, or we're coming in," Casey warned the world. I could hear in his voice that he was more excited to hear himself speak in such a high-stakes situation than whatever would actually follow.

The bathroom light turned back off as the sliding window of the bathroom creaked open. Out popped the crown of a man's head, snaking around to check if the coast was clear.

"No one's there," he exclaimed, turning around to face an anonymous someone.

Before either Ernie or I could make a move, the man was falling, ass-over-tea-kettle onto the ground. We watched as his body tried to fight gravity, but failed irrevocably. He'd had a handgun in his right hand coming out of the window, and I watched as it flew several feet into the darkness. His surroundings were now damp grass (the kind I was used to crashing police cars on). He wasn't able to hear the thumping sound coming from my ribcage.

"Go. Go. Run." A voice from the bathroom urged in a frantic, sharp hiss.

So, ass-over-tea-kettle-man got up and began to run. He took three steps before falling again, so eager to escape, he couldn't get his body to synchronize. He stumbled forward on baby giraffe legs, struggling to straighten them out.

As soon as he found his footing, Ernie jumped on him and pinned him to the ground in perfect timing. I ran toward the pile of limbs to make sure Ernie was in control, and the man had no other weapons.

Pinning his head to the ground as Ernie handcuffed him, I noticed he wasn't saying much. Maybe the rebel had leaked out of him.

"You've got fifteen seconds now, come out with your hands away from your body, or we're coming in." The booming voice ricocheted off every perceivable surface.

There was a pounding of frantic footsteps as the other escapee began running westbound behind the motel. He galloped over a medium-sized brick fence, not even turning to look back.

I ran toward the wall. Impossible to see if the man was armed, it was safe to assume he had a weapon. I decided not to ask. In my mind, he was an escaped and fleeing felon, likely armed and ready to die before being taken back.

He moved quickly, and there was no stopping this man. He headed into a single-family home residential area that held a lot of possibilities for a hostage. I acted instinctively.

I quickly aimed my shotgun at his upper body, slowed my breathing and pulled the trigger. I held all of my strength in that finger—it felt like it weighed fifty pounds.

Click.

"Five seconds and we're coming in."

"Click?" I said incredulously. No chance to think further. I racked in another round and aimed again, pulling the trigger with haste, and now a surprising ease. *Click.*

A jolt went straight up my spine. *What the fuck?* I threw the shotgun to the ground in frustrated disgust, suddenly hyper-aware of my vulnerability.

My eyes remained on the fleeing escapee as I jumped over the fence and began running after him. I wasn't closing the gap quickly enough to deter him from entering any home at random. Once inside, who knew what horrors could consume a quiet family.

I drew my 6" Smith and Wesson .357 magnum and aimed, but at the last moment, I saw a man and a boy returning from an evening walk. They were completely unaware of our drama. The peace surrounding their gentle smiles and easy conversation was in sharp contrast to the inner turmoil I was experiencing. It was arresting to watch.

I holstered my weapon and continued running after this bastard. There was no opportunity to tell him his time was up. Meanwhile, back at the ranch, Casey and the boys would be "coming in" by now.

The escapee rushed directly toward the enclosure of the nearest residence. I continued to run, but managed to pull my weapon just as he reached the fence.

As he climbed to the top, I quickly aimed and fired. It sounded like a cannon. The instant release of adrenaline worked its way through my body in seconds, settling my eyes back into focus. My bullet had pierced a leg, and a small pool of blood quickly formed.

There was a long silence. All I could hear was the ringing in my ears.

The escapee seemed frozen in time. He looked at me as if to ask *why*; his eyes pleaded with me. He resumed in his fall over the fence, grunting harshly as his body smacked into the ground on the other side. He disappeared into the residential backyard, leaving a trail of blood on the fence.

Still not knowing whether or not he was armed, but certain he wasn't dead, I proceeded toward the fence in a defensive posture.

The side lawn of the home was dry, but well taken care of. Flowers bloomed and a huge willow tree swayed slightly in the wind. Everything was quiet in the backyard.

Suddenly, I heard police sirens as Casey and his gang raced toward the gunfire. However, no streets from their direction came through to this neighborhood, so they had to drive around the block, and the sirens went silent.

If I could hear them coming, so could my bleeding, hidden escapee. No sound of breathing or anything implied that a human was on the other side of the fence. I stood very still against the fence with my gun drawn—the one that worked.

Scrunching up my face, I put my ear on the fence to listen closer.

Still nothing. I reckoned he was desperate to get away, determined to not be taken back to prison. He didn't look like the type who did well in there.

This situation was unlike any other in my career. While it was bound to happen, part of me wondered if it ever actually would. I was very conscious of the people around us—people who considered themselves to be safe at home. No one had come out to see what was going on, which I found strange after such a loud takedown.

I decided the convict was no longer just on the other side of the fence waiting to shoot the first cop he saw. He had resumed running. I got up and ran around the other side of the house, hoping to surprise him one way or another.

Suddenly, I heard Don shouting as he ran full speed toward me. Don hadn't waited for any sort of signal. He heard a shot and immediately began running toward the fire, toward his buddy.

"Ellis, Ellis, you okay?" he hollered as he barreled toward me. He never failed to be a wonderful sight, with his arms pumping up and down at his sides and his legs flying beneath him. His face determined, jaw set.

"Barely. The fucking shotgun wouldn't fire. I hit him, but he's somewhere on the other side of the fence, probably running like hell." I looked into Don's face for a fleeting second and saw the experience he'd acquired the past year as an undercover narc. "Ernie probably needs help. He's got a suspect cuffed."

"It's okay, backup is there. You were going around the back, right? I'll go over the fence. Let's do this." Without hesitation, Don began sprinting toward the fence. I didn't have any hesitation either as I continued to make my way around the house.

Coming up the driveway, into the backyard, I met with Don. Obvious by a path of small blood drops leading to the next fence, Mr. Escapee remained on the move, still resisting.

Don signaled to me that he was going over the next fence. I turned to run around the house to confront anyone he may flush out. As I ran toward the street, several police cars arrived, screeched to a halt and revealed an army of officers getting out and fanning through the neighborhood. I indicated where Don was with a hand wave and directed manpower to where I'd been going.

Sgt. Pence and Cooper pulled up in a plainclothes car. Pence pointed me to the car with a frantic wave. I holstered my weapon again and ran to the car.

"He's gone over the fence and Don's back there. Someone has to go around here to catch him if he flushes him out. I don't know if he's armed, or not," I rushed. "I've got to get my shotgun. It's back next to the fence, on the ground."

"What?" Pense asked. "Why is that?"

"Because the damn gun misfired on me, Sergeant! Twice! I could have been freaking killed."

40

Three hours had passed, and I'd called Sarah to tell her I'd be very late, without any details. It didn't feel like something I should casually drop over the phone.

I'd taken copious notes after the incident and turned in the failed shotgun into the Watch Commander for an internal investigation. Two officers were dispatched to the original scene of the shotgun disappointment to search for any evidence of what may have happened.

By now, the lone escapee had been found cowering in someone's vegetable garden and taken to the hospital with non-life-threatening injuries. Sgt. Pense called the station and advised me to not follow-up at the hospital, even though I needed intake information for my reports. I was puzzled, and just staring at my notes, when Don walked into the report room.

"Hey, Ellis. Good fucking shot. Went through his thigh and the wood fence behind him. Was that a .357 load?" He was grinning from ear to ear. "I don't know if they've figured that out, yet," he said, indicating management.

"They won't. Cooper wouldn't want to get his hands messy and Pence has his nose up Cooper's ass. Can't see much from there." It was departmental policy that officers could carry .357 magnum revolvers, but could only shoot .38 bullets. But .38 bullets didn't have any real penetration power, and that just never made any sense to me. I figured shooting at someone successfully would require... *extreme* penetration.

"What kind of report are you writing?" Don asked as he glanced at the notes in front of me.

"Damned if I know. Watch Commander told me to hold off for a bit. I don't like the sound of it. They seem to be looking at the shotgun as a crime scene unto itself." I stood and stretched out my aching body as Don continued glancing at my notes.

Suddenly, Sgt. Pense and Cooper filled the doorway. Don turned to face them.

"Excuse us for a minute, will you? We've got to have a private pow-wow with Ellis, here." Don nodded and left the room as both Pense and Cooper took seats facing me.

Pence craned his neck a bit to see my notes as Cooper asked, "How are you feeling? It was pretty tense out there."

I gave a flat smile and nodded my head, "Yes, sir. Especially when my equipment didn't work. I could have stopped him way before he climbed into that backyard. That could have turned real ugly."

Pence stopped straining to see the notes. "You did good, Ellis. No one got hurt except an escaped convict. Hell, with your shooting, you don't need a stinking shotgun." He tried to feign a laugh. I wasn't buying it.

Cooper persisted, still interested, "That the first time you ever shot anyone?"

"Yes, sir. Unless you want to count the time I shot my youngest daughter, you know, because she's so damn fidgety." He looked at me quizzically. "I was aiming at the apple she was holding on her head." I shrugged my shoulders.

I chuckled along with Pense. Cooper was startled by cop humor, but I felt good breaking him in. Often, it was the only way we could cope. With humor and emotional distance. I was getting very good at both.

"What I need to know, Sergeant, is who is going to cover the crime report? Are mine supplemental to the crime report or to the arrest report?"

Pence looked at me with a thin, half-smile while Cooper smoothed the crease in his pants.

"I've organized myself for the purpose of writing two reports, under whatever heading. One outlines the 'Officer involved shooting' from start to finish . . . and the other outlines the cause for an investigation into the malfunctioned weapon."

Cooper straightened, "Who advised you to do this?"

"I think it would be my training, sir. Nothing else makes sense to me." I looked at Pence.

Pence cleared his throat and swallowed hard, "Damn coffee is going to kill me." He looked at me, "Ellis, if you feel you need to write two reports, go ahead."

"I will. Each one will be a supplement to the other and to the original crime and arrest reports. Do you have anything to add?"

Cooper smiled, "You have everything well covered, don't you?" He looked impressed.

"Okay. I'll be out in the field. Call me when you finish," Pence dismissed as he stood up.

Cooper followed, but stopped short to add, "I know how you feel about that shotgun issue, and we're going to find out what happened. I'll keep you up to date." Then he left.

I sat there alone for several moments. Things didn't seem right to me. *Why the sudden interest from Cooper? Didn't he have a chief to consult? Why did the shotgun misfire twice?*

As I wrote the reports, I began to piece things together. I eventually discovered the rounds that I'd racked were "wadcutters." They were only meant to perforate paper targets at target practice, and never used as real ammunition. Except this once, of course.

So, who put those in my shotgun?

Time passed without much mention of that night, until Officer John Taligate approached me to apologize for the shotgun misfire. "Hey, I'm really sorry, man. I never thought anything like this would happen. I was the one who changed out the shells with the wadcutters, so I could use them at home." His eyes didn't meet mine except fleetingly.

"Fuck, John, I can't believe you did that. Someone could have been killed. I mean, when the hell were you going to change them back?" This seemed almost preposterous.

"I don't know. I wasn't thinking, I swear. I'll work a shift for you, or something, man. I'm really sorry." He still appeared close to guilty tears.

"So, what happened in the investigation?"

He shrugged, "I humbly confessed, and they gave me a written reprimand."

I was stunned. "Tell me you're shitting me. I was given a three-day suspension for denting two fenders, and you get a written reprimand for putting my life in danger?"

John backed up a step and put his palms up, "I don't know, man. I don't want to talk about it anymore." He turned to walk away, "Again, I'm sorry. You got a free shift vacation from me when you ask. It's what I can do."

As I watched him walk off, I thought, *He's right, it's what he can do.*

41

Norm still wasn't returning my calls from his office at the college. I'd left a few messages, but each time the tightness I felt in my chest over both my loss and the limitations I was under, told me to call it at three tries.

Both Sarah and Harry kept trying to convince me to stray from the PD and all that was going on, certain it had become the source of all evil for me. Somehow, they were united on that thought.

At this point, I was starting to let their words sink in a bit. I'd spoken with Keaton on the side, and he admitted that he'd caught officers following him on a couple of different occasions. He couldn't imagine why, but he also couldn't help but notice. He hadn't worked at the PD in almost a year, now.

I became a little paranoid for myself. I still worked for them, after all. If they were willing to tail someone who had no connection to the PD anymore, what were they willing to do to an active officer they obviously couldn't stand?

I constantly glanced over my shoulder, and thoughts raced through my head, wondering if they were tapping my phone or talking to someone close to me to try and squeeze out some dirt. Any dirt.

Sorry, no dirt.

I couldn't help thinking back on the day I graduated from the academy. I felt excited to be a part of something bigger, my brothers in blue. My only *brothers* were on the streets with me. Most of management represented the invisible enemy.

Just before Christmas, Bob Burns sat in front of Gorsh's desk, wearing his detective suit, dark brown sports jacket with tan slacks. A bold fashion statement. He ran the fingers of his right hand through what was left of his fine hair.

"But is that enough?" Gorsh asked, shaking his head in doubt. "Have you interviewed any neighbors?"

"We thought it'd be counterproductive at this point. After all, they're his neighbors," Burns answered dryly.

"What else you got?" Gorsh said, practically salivating in anticipation.

"I'm thinking we can send Gutierrez in to question Ellis' house-keeper when they're gone. She doesn't speak English."

"Housekeeper? Wait a minute. Have you checked his finances?" Gorsh asked, his eyebrows drawing together.

"They're cheap, from Mexico," Burns answered, smacking his gum. "Anyway, if they hold true to pattern, they should be going to that L.A. Clinic this next Tuesday. And, they should be gone two and a half hours. Gutierrez can go in and find out what we need in thirty minutes, tops, save us six months of dicking around."

"I *know* I've been followed. I'm sure I have. It's like they want to see where I'm going, or what I'm doing, at all times, and I can't figure it out. This whole thing gives me such a creepy feeling, Bill. I can't take it anymore," Sarah told me with a shaky voice. It was 12:08 a.m. on January 1, 1969. She began to cry with quivering lips, so I held her, trying to calm her down enough to continue the story. The first time in months I'd actually wanted her to keep talking.

"You're probably not being followed, but just feeling like you are is enough. I'm sorry," I assured, patting her softly. I distractedly thought of Keaton.

She aggressively broke loose from my arms and stepped back, dragging a palm against her teary right cheek. "You said you were going to quit if they didn't stop. You told me that in front of Harry," she said, raising her voice and now pointing her finger at me.

"It's not that easy," I whispered, not wanting to wake the girls.

"Here's something that's easy. Do you love me? Do you love your daughters? Then *choose* us. Quit," she snapped, hands flying to her hips. Her lower lip trembled slightly. "That's easy."

I shook my head at her incredulously. "Darling, we're in no position for that. How much money you think we've got saved? Fifty bucks? I love you and the girls very much. That's why I'm staying until there's an alternative that gets us where we have to be. Or did you forget?"

"You'll find another job. I'll work if I have to," she pleaded.

"Yeah, I don't think so." I couldn't duplicate this schedule and income, necessary to finishing the education and developing my career in acting . . . and, I still had it in my blood. Nothing had changed there.

Sarah flailed her arms at me, a wild look in her eyes like she wanted to start swinging. "What's the matter with you?" she cried. "Can't you see what's happening?"

I took a couple steps forward and held her arms down with a hug. "Okay, okay." I stared at her, waiting for her breathing to slow. I brushed a few stray hairs out of her face.

"Look, I have to be the one to make the decision about my work. It's my life, not just this job. Not just being a cop. Give me some time to think."

We spent the next several hours talking about our marriage and everything that irked us in life with each other. We laughed, we cried and we made passionate love. It was a strange cycle, but it was one that I was used to by now.

Arriving home after a visit with Harry several days later, we encountered our housekeeper frantically packing her bags, muttering to herself in rapid Spanish.

Noticing us, she stopped and her hand moved to her chest. She rushed to Sarah and gushed, "Oh, so very sorry, *mija. Pero .. .* have to go now. My cousin coming to pick me up." Her normally pleasant face contorted in anxiety.

She turned her attention to me, "The *policia* came, Mr. Bill. He ask many questions about you and your *familia*. 'What you do? Where you go? Do he drink? Do she drink?' He stayed long time .. . at least *treinta minutos* . . . uh...*como se dice* . . . thirty?"

"Yes, thirty. Did you get the officer's name?" I asked her calmly; meanwhile my mind was racing.

"Gutierrez maybe . . . I no remember. I can't stay here. I have to go back. My . . . cousin will be here soon," she repeated, on the verge of tears.

The next day, I was approached in the break room by McKinley, who told me to submit to him a memo explaining why I wasn't at work the day before.

"I don't think putting 'the flu' down would be a good idea either. I guess you were up and moving about," he was leaning in toward me, hungry for a reaction. "Coming from above me," he motioned his thumb upwards.

"I'll fill it out in a couple minutes and put it on your desk." My face was placid.

"Don't forget," he turned and walked away with a smug bitch smile.

Two days later in the evening, Harry called and asked me to call him back on a pay phone.

"Free clinic, may I help you?" Harry's voice.

"What's happening?" The phone booth felt a little steamy. I kept the door open.

"You're not going to believe this. Scratch that, you probably will believe this. Today, a Lt. Burns and some other detective came to my office . . . without an appointment, mind you," Harry said, voice dryer than a bone.

"What the hell did he want?" I bit down on my tongue—otherwise, I would have shouted into the receiver. I felt my face flushing with anger. *They're fucking closing in on me.*

"Don't know yet, besides wanting to see your files and talk about you. I told him I wouldn't even have a conversation without your consent, so he said they'd be back. Told me to keep it confidential and left," Harry answered.

"I imagine I'm going to see him again. What do you want me to do?"

I closed my eyes. Several seconds later I opened them with a sad clarity of what I had to do. The only option that made sense anymore. Anything else was killing me.

I wanted to be alone. Could they take *everything* from me? My future that I'd worked so diligently on? Wasn't the teaching job enough?

They had both barrels pointed at me.

We talked for a while longer, and then I went home and spoke with Sarah. I felt like leaving the PD would save our relationship, and with three daughters that seemed like what I really needed. What I hadn't had the time to consider was the profound sadness and sense of loss I was being thrust into. I still loved what I did.

A couple of gut-wrenching days went by, and I regretfully resigned from the PD with a one-week notice. A sense of indignation seemed to overtake the tears within that week.

They may have driven two other guys out of careers, but I wasn't them, and this wasn't over by a long shot.

42

THE PURCHASE

"You're sure you want to do this?" David had taken the last four years to let his hair grow longer than ever. It hung below his shoulders; the tips slightly golden from all his time spent in the sun.

If the clean-cut cop and his hippie friend didn't attract enough attention before, now they really did. Usually we relished in the startled looks we received, but today we were aiming for discreetness.

"Yeah. I'm sure," I nodded. "I want to do it tonight. You said I should try this, didn't you?" I asked him, waggling my eyebrows lightheartedly to ease his hesitation.

"I did. I did. But you must admit this is sudden, Bill. You're not setting me up, are you?" David's eyes comically widened, and he slowly backed away from me, looking left and right before blowing his act by cracking up.

"Come on," leading me to his van. "Only the best for you. I got two already rolled up for you."

I grinned and threw my arm around him as we walked, playfully punching him in the arm. "You're a good buddy, you know that?"

Later that night, Sarah and I huddled together on the couch, with our eyes frantically darting around and our ears attuned for any sign of little pattering feet on the floorboards. The girls had left for their granny's house hours ago, but we had to be sure.

Convinced we were alone, Sarah nervously turned to me, curiously watching my hands as I took a match to our very first marijuana joint.

"Here's another finger to you, Gorsh." I proclaimed to his theoretical presence. It seemed to follow me everywhere I went these days.

"What did you say David called this?" Although we were alone, Sarah's voice was barely a whisper. *Who knows who could be standing on the porch nowadays?*

"Acapulco Gold. He also said to only smoke half . . . *no matter what*." I stared at her for a while, my face completely deadpan, before we both burst into laughter.

We began to pass the joint back and forth, coughing a little less with each toke. Halfway into the joint, I was convinced David had underestimated me. I felt nice and relaxed, but also like I could smoke a lot more. Nothing was as I had expected, but I also didn't know what to expect.

We sat there looking at each other, searching for signs of being high . . . and finding none. Everything seemed totally normal. We were disappointed. Were we supposed to wait? This was supposed to be our big "happening" event, finally joining our peers and dipping our toes into the sixties. Maybe we'd even pay more attention to The Beatles.

After a few more minutes of unfulfilled anticipation, I suggested we finish off the joint. Maybe we were smoking it wrong?

A couple minutes later, the joint was toast. Impatient for any sort of result, I looked at Sarah. "Fuck it, let's do the second one. This isn't working worth a crap."

This is what they'd been talking about all those years? Where was the Reefer Madness?

We were both coughing quite a bit now. Deep coughs, like bits of my stomach were going to come up. I started to wonder how laboring a rebellious act was supposed to be as I tried to swallow with my raw throat.

We began to hit the second joint, passing it back and forth and staring at each other curiously until finally, we collapsed into a simultaneous and hysterical laughter that didn't cease for the next two or three hours—we weren't keeping track. The kind of blissful, irrational, insane laughter produced by being completely and totally high off your ass.

I shrunk very, very tiny—or she grew to the size of a balloon in the Macy's Day Parade, I wasn't sure which. I didn't care. Everything became comical.

Colors were swirling around, and my thoughts were breaking down and being projected to me in a big intellectual and cultural way . . . or at least that's how it felt to me.

But above all else, everything stayed uproarious. In the hilarity, we found profoundness. So, we tripped, and we laughed, and we tripped, and we laughed.

We had an intense sexual experience that surpassed anything we'd felt recently, or ever, and it went on for hours. I felt like we were traveling through different dimensions together. I drank in every inch of her body slowly and decidedly, as if it was the first time I'd ever seen her, and I may never again.

We partied all night—laughing, making love, and having what we thought was deep conversation. We talked about everything we could think of, and then thought of some more.

Some hours later, I awoke on the living room floor in a lump of pillows and blankets. A candle still burned on the coffee table. I was surprised to immediately find this was nothing like getting drunk. I had absolutely no hangover, no headache, and no apologies to make. I felt great.

Yet, it was obvious we'd smoked more than we were ready for. Sarah was still sleeping, looking more relaxed than she had in years.

But, it was now time to go to work, and I dressed in my police uniform and went, completely rejuvenated and feeling like I could take on the world. I was amazed by the experience and decided to try it again—next time with a reasonable amount.

Fuck you, Gorsh.

The week went as well as possible under the circumstances, but my attempt to find work was surprisingly unsuccessful.

I racked my brain for options, settling on getting a security management job somewhere until I could finish my master degree. Sounded easy enough, but Gorsh was eliminating my options steadily with his extremely negative input to every inquiry about me.

A few officers even overheard that he'd been making phone calls just to gush negative information about me to anyone considering hiring me.

The way police administrations cooperated regarding personnel departure issues made it difficult for an officer to move about within law enforcement without a "blessing." This process eliminated the possibility of a cop checking his options. It, of course, also provided another channel for cops to be controlled by management. Because movement for personal reasons became almost impossible. Management always had the final say.

Work performance verification was crucial in a hiring decision. When a personality conflicted with someone in management, references would become an ever-present negative.

The last day approached with none the wiser but me. Except—I was ready to go out with a personal snapshot. I enjoyed making memories, like I told Ernie.

4 3

My very last day on duty, my emotions were all over the place. I was patrolling southbound on Western Ave. from Artesia Ave. in my police car with reserve officer, Jimmy Jarrett. Jarrett had a high-profile position in business beyond the PD, but wanted to be a part of law enforcement, and put in about fifty hours a month.

He'd been under my command while I worked as Assistant Reserve Commander. We'd had a lot of very memorable times together, and had become friends.

He wore a good-looking hair piece. It was really very nice; brown and wavy and matched his smooth demeanor and Southern charm. Beneath the Southern charm lived a calculating man, carving his future. He'd eventually go on to become the mayor of Buena Park.

I pulled into the parking lot behind the Dairy Queen on Western Ave. and parked in the rear, turning off my engine.

"What are you doing?" Jimmy asked.

When I didn't answer but stared ahead, he smiled nervously. "Is this it? My surprise?" He looked around the lot. "What's going on?"

I smiled at him, but didn't speak. About that time, a silver-gray van pulled into the lot and glided toward the police car.

"Jimmy," I said grandly, "This is your surprise . . . I'm about to give you a great memory. Savor this memory. Think of it often. It'll make you laugh. You are about to witness a police officer in full uniform, get out of his black and white police car and openly buy a bag of pot in broad daylight. From a hippie. Just a little going away present from me to you. The memory. Not the pot—that's for me," I added, giving him a big Cheshire grin.

Jimmy's mouth slowly dropped open as he saw I wasn't kidding around. He glanced at the van as it pulled closer to the car, catching sight of long-haired hippie David behind the wheel.

David and I exited our vehicles at the same time, and as we approached, David extended his right hand and pumped mine up and down enthusiastically. "Good day, Officer Ellis," he bellowed in the presumed voice of a politician. "So nice to see you again." Very proper.

Traffic was very light. David stretched his arms and legs, arranging himself with a fair view of the street. He was well aware he was about to commit a felony for his friend to have a laugh. He couldn't wait to see how this played out. He'd never been through anything like this before. *Had anyone?*

"It's in the front seat, if this is still cool." He glanced at Jimmy kind of as a question, who remained seated and silent, not making eye contact with anyone.

"Yeah, it sure is," I said, trying to ease the hesitation. "Ten bucks, right?"

I pulled a ten dollar bill out of my uniform pocket and waved it enough for Jimmy to see. "This is a ten, Jimmy, if you didn't catch that," I said, grinning. "I'm buying a lid. Three fingers, he tells me. Whatever the hell that means."

David returned to the van and opened the driver side door. He reached beneath the front seat and retrieved a small baggie of marijuana. He put it under his shirt before standing upright. Then he turned and walked back to me.

"How do you want to do this?" he asked.

"Well, obviously you have to get it out from under your shirt and hand it to me as I hand you this ten dollar bill. It's part of the effect, you know," I answered, maintaining my slight grin.

He looked both ways for permission, and then slowly brought his right hand beneath his shirt. He shoved the baggie into my palm, giving me a small wink.

I casually walked over to the police car door and placed the baggie in my briefcase, fleetingly wondering if this was such a good idea.

Jimmy smiled as I climbed back in the car. He looked completely stupefied. Without making eye contact, he said, "I can't believe you just did that."

"Why? I told you I would." I said.

"Thanks again, you damn hippie," I waved to David as my black and white drove past him.

Later that day, I reluctantly pulled into the police station parking lot for what would be the last time. It was the end of my last shift ever, and I wasn't sure how to feel. Jimmy got out of the car and joined me to approach the building. It felt surreal.

"Ellis, you're crazy, but I do love it," he chuckled, slapping me lightly on the shoulder. "You weren't kidding. This is a memory I'll always have. You know it's safe with me." He chuckled again, flashing a big smile at me. "I loved it, man."

I knew I could believe him.

We entered the station and parted ways. He tipped his imaginary cap to me and strode down the hall, still muttering and chuckling to himself. I walked further down the hallway to the chief's office, prepared to pick up my final check.

My legs felt a little heavy as I realized these would be the last steps I took in this building. I paid attention to the walls, the windows, and most importantly, the people around me going about their day. *For the last time.* I was deeply sad and preemptively nostalgic.

As soon as I turned the corner and had Gorsh's office in sight, I was intercepted by Sally. "Let me get your final check, Bill. It should be on Camille's desk," she said before I could get a word in. "We sure are going to miss you here. You always kept things interesting," she chuckled. "Make sure you visit us."

"Yeah, I don't think so, Sally. I'm pretty sure I'd get accidentally shot in the ass," I smiled at her to let her know it was just a joke, and I was completely okay with how things had gone down. I figured if I let her know that, maybe it'd be true.

Sally shuffled in and around Camille's desk looking for an envelope addressed to Bill Ellis, but couldn't find one. "Gee, I don't see it here."

She searched throughout the desk and found nothing.

I was feeling uncomfortable during this. Although already nostalgic, I wanted this to be my last day at this place. This place where a cop risked his life every day, and gave everything he had to his brothers and to the entire community, and got shit on in return.

I really needed the money. One salary split six ways barely cut it as it was, and now I didn't even have that. Or the side jobs that came with it.

"Let me call Camille at home," Sally said apologetically. She dialed the phone as she sat quietly, avoiding eye contact while we waited for Camille to pick up. Eventually, she was rescued by a voice on the other end.

"Hey, Camille, sorry to bother you on a Sunday, but I can't find Bill's check," she began, waiting for any sort of help.

Silence.

Sally nodded and glanced up at me nervously. She hung up slowly. "I'm so sorry, Bill. You're going to have to come back tomorrow for the check."

I felt like I'd been slapped. What they'd put me through these past months wasn't enough? Oh, no. Now they wanted to harass me by forcing me back in there another day . . . as nothing more than a private citizen. A needy one. The optics would be great for them.

"Don't apologize. Not your fault at all," I mumbled, turning away from her.

I placed my badge and other department issued items on the desk and left the area without a verbal word to anyone. But, I stopped briefly at the report area to write a final memo to Gorsh.

Shortly after hearing the sound he'd been waiting for ever since he got in that morning, the sound of my equipment being turned in, Gorsh heaved a heavy sigh. He waited several moments, then got up to check in with Camille now that it was safe for him to leave his office.

He thought briefly that maybe he should have said something, anything to Ellis before he left for good, but at this point, there weren't really any words left. This particular resignation was different from any of the other guys. His feelings were different, almost sorry.

He'd made his way outside his office and glanced at the memo Ellis left him. The words exploded in his mind and out his mouth, "*Why, that little shit!*" He looked at the memo again, his hands shaking with rage. His feelings of hesitation had turned to blinding antipathy.

Gorsh actually *ran* down the hallway to the police station back area, where he hoped the former officer would still be. "Where's that fucking Ellis?" he roared to anyone as he got to the back door.

Someone said, "He just left," and Gorsh ran back the same hallway to the front of the station, into the lobby and out the front door. Citizens in the lobby were startled with the sight of a six-foot-seven mad man wearing a suit and running at full speed through the area.

In the distance, Gorsh squinted to make out my car driving to the front exit. He screamed out, "Ellis! Come back here! Ellis!" His right fist clenched and raised into the air.

The final sight of big old Frankenstein was barely visible in my rearview mirror.

I reluctantly returned for my check at 11:30 the next morning, having called earlier to make sure it was ready and Gorsh was gone. That wouldn't be a pleasant encounter. There was the awkwardness that Gorsh should feel and the seething anger I would feel. And the confusion, *who thought they would take The Phantom so seriously?* 'Course, my resignation was voluntary. But we all knew what was going on. The skirmish had gotten out of hand.

I entered the police station from the front. *Just like a private citizen.* Gunner was seated at the front desk. I stared at him, thinking about how he was hired the exact same day as me. He and I attended the academy together. Gunner had been there for my entire police career.

Unfortunately, we'd stopped speaking to each other about a year ago. I'd witnessed him using unnecessary excessive force on a handcuffed arrestee, and privately told him I'd report him if I saw one more incident. Either that, or arrest him myself.

Since that conversation, he'd barely glanced in my direction. Except on a call or as a backup, of course. Both of us were always there for a brother, no matter what.

Today was different. As Mike noticed me enter, he dashed around the counter, calling to me, "Ellis, wait up." Cutting through the dispatcher's area, he beelined toward me with a huge smile, and embracied me in a muscular bear hug. "I'm sorry, man," he muttered.

He moved farther away from the counter, motioning for me to do the same.

"Hey, man, whatever that was between us, I'm letting all that go. I apologize." He looked into my eyes and lowered his voice, "What you did to Gorsh yesterday, you have the biggest balls I've ever seen. You're my fucking idol. I was right here. I saw him running out of the lobby doors, screaming 'Ellis! Ellis!' Not kidding you at all. He even chased your car. I don't know what you said in that memo, but it fucking-A worked for me."

I smiled and thanked him, and also apologized for the drift, glad we'd put our differences behind us. He was a good man and a good cop. He would shortly leave for L.A. Sheriff's Office for "more action." A dedicated warrior, always looking for a war.

Camille was seated at her desk. She looked up as I entered. "Oh, Bill. Sorry about yesterday. I thought you knew," she said, shrugging her shoulders shyly.

"That's okay, Camille. I never thought it was you. Just taking orders and all that German shit." I smiled, but not really. *Just give me my check.*

Camille spread a sheet of paper and envelope on her desk. "Would you sign this? It's a receipt saying you got your check."

"A receipt that I got my check? Are you kidding me?"

I didn't even know why I was surprised at this point.

Camille kept her eyes on the document. "I know. I know. Just please read it and sign it." She handed the papers to me, still avoiding eye contact. As I began reading the document, I lowered the check into my right breast pocket. I read through it and then read again, just to be sure.

The bottom line was, my net earnings were $7.87 less than what they should have been. Things like this kind of jump out at you when it's 1969 and you've got five people to take care of and looming unemployment. A frown was forming on my face.

"Wait, a minute. What's this deduction?" I returned the form to Camille, pointing at my discovery.

She looked at the form and uncomfortably pretended to read it. She smelled of coffee.

She bit her lip, unable to put off the response much longer. "Oh, yeah. The chief says you didn't turn in your Mace. So, he told me to deduct the $7.87. It's what the Mace cost."

"Wait. Am I on *Candid Camera*, Camille?" I leaned in.

"I turned in my Mace with everything else. Right here on your desk so you would get it this morning. This is insane. I'm not going to sign your damn form. I want to see the chief."

I was suddenly livid. Now I knew why they also wanted me to come in while Gorsh was gone. He didn't want to be here when he rubbed my nose in it.

I felt backed into a corner. But no—they'd taken enough. That was my family's $7.87.

I decided to fight. I wasn't about to let them do that to me. The Mace remained missing, despite me having turned it in. I couldn't logically figure it out.

How dare they even question me in the first place? I was a cop, for crying out loud. I was going to steal $7.87 worth of equipment?

Two weeks following my separation, I attended a Buena Park City Council meeting and made a written and public demand for repayment of the $7.87. Admittedly, it was kind of a strange happening, but it was part of the "process" for them to deny my demand to set the stage for a court hearing. An annoying and time-consuming process in which I was compelled to participate to move the process forward.

The council members didn't seem too concerned with my request. They were practically napping with their eyes open. The clerk finally reminded them to 'deny,' which they did without much comprehension.

"*Gorsh vs. Ellis II,*" the rematch was held at the Anaheim municipal court house, just three weeks later. Chief Gorsh represented the city of Buena Park, and I represented my ass. It was like *David and Goliath*. Winning this case had come to mean more to me than almost anything as the weeks passed. It consumed me. It seemed symbolic of our relationship. Them prodding, me reacting.

The judge read the case declarations as we took our places. It seemed like he took the time to wonder a whole host of things about this case. *You don't normally get this kind of turnout for a seven-buck dispute. There's more than meets the eye, here.*

He double checked the $7.87 demand and looking puzzled, asked for opening statements.

As we shuffled through our papers, my mind flashed back to several days ago. I was packing our stuff in the home garage for our necessary move, when I stumbled upon the Mace canister in dispute. I was stunned. How could this have happened? Gorsh was actually correct. They didn't receive my Mace. I was outraged all those weeks for no reason.

Oh, to hell with it, I thought. *It's the principle of the thing.* I went off to court anyway, not wanting to miss a chance to screw with Gorsh. I considered it an important part of my payback. I imagined I'd do it in such grand fashion (perhaps even with a dash of music) that Gorsh would have a fatal heart seizure, and I could watch him flopping on the ground.

I'd subpoenaed two witnesses from the PD and one reserve officer. I prepared for a major presentation. Without a job, I had plenty of time and plenty of motivation. I don't know why, but it seemed even more fun now that I knew I had the Mace the entire time.

Maybe, *The Phantom* was in the courtroom.

Gorsh presented first. He stuttered, he stammered, and his suit somehow seemed huger than his body. (Had he lost weight?) Not a great public speaker, this man. No wonder they'd used me as a spokesperson while on the PD. They could have used one of the prisoners and it would have been a step up from Gorsh. A grumpy, sweaty gorilla. Not a crowd pleaser.

I watched his anger progress as I opposed him theatrically in my presentation. I paraded in my witnesses that systematically, and sometimes unknowingly, unraveled the case for the City of Buena Park.

For small claims court. It was quite an effort from both sides, but quite candidly, I could have made it a two-day trial. I had a counter for every move possible. I even wore my tap shoes.

Now, this was *playing the house.*

The judge eventually ruled in my favor, and it felt like a scene from *Inherit the Wind:* Gorsh and I were the two attorneys arguing over evolution. I received congratulations by those who attended the ignoble trial, while he slunk away in a muted huff. I almost would have felt bad, but this was the absolute best thing to happen to me in months.

I caught a glimpse of Gorsh as he was leaving. He practically salivated with what I understood to be a need for revenge. Even though he didn't know I had the can of Mace . . . yet. I pushed it to the back of my already cluttered mind and turned to leave, victorious once again.

I felt like *The Phantom* had returned . . . to stay.

44

FOUR MONTHS LATER

"Ellis, this is Armstrong. How are you doing? I hear you're still having a rough time getting work." I could hear his compassion through the phone; he was one of the good ones.

I closed my eyes for a moment, letting his voice ring through my ears, briefly memorizing every decibel. Hearing Lt. Armstrong's voice gave me a feeling of nostalgia for something only 120 days removed.

"Yeah. You could say that," I answered, sliding into a chair at the kitchen table. "I can't seem to outrun the curse of Gorsh. Maybe I shouldn't hit back."

I felt the urge to warn him to watch his own back when it came to Gorsh, but I couldn't find the right words to say it.

"Well, I don't agree with what he's doing. I'm just trying to work with it. I have to." A slight pause. "Anyway, the reason I called, I know this guy who runs security for Kmart. He's got a part-time opening now that he says will go full-time pretty soon." He paused, and we both knew why. "He won't be checking the PD for references because I'm vouching for you. Just keep that part quiet."

A few days later, Armstrong came through. Seated in the snack bar area of the Kmart store in City of Industry, I waited to be interviewed by the Regional Director of Security, Walt Morgan. This was one of those super stores that carried just about anything you could want. That was a huge deal to people back then—try and imagine a world before Costco. Before these crazed, wide-eyed folks hell-bent on finding the BEST DEALS IN TOWN had a designated place to call their own. Back then, people went to Kmart.

Kmart corporate retailers were smart. They recognized that most of their shoppers were lower-income families looking for the cheapest price, so they marketed to that bracket almost exclusively. My experience in the police department had taught me that lower-income earners tended to be more likely to dip into petty theft.

I found customers would steal anything, in remarkably creative fashions. There was, of course, the classic switching of the labels, the bounced checks, and of course the "accidental" walk-out before paying—with about ten items stashed under their purses or underneath the baby carriage. Or even disgustingly so, in their underpants. *Yeah, please put that back on the shelf.*

The good old physiological fight-or-flight was proven solid time and again as the red-handed bandits either tried to punch me square in the jaw or flee through the parking lot. Bags of Cheetos and mini lighters dropped out of their waistbands each time a foot hit the pavement.

The public was a circus.

"Mr. Ellis, please have your application ready, and I'll take you to the security office," a voice interrupted my thought. I glanced up to see a lady of about thirty years old, her body contorted slightly enough to make it look like she was leaning to the left. There was a slight moment of alarm for me as I thought she was about to fall over, but that was just how she looked. *Interesting posture.* Part of her hair stuck to her forehead; it had probably been a while since she'd seen a shower. She was wearing those black Working Woman

Dickies and an off-white shirt with her name proudly displayed, whatever it was.

I was too distracted by her lean. I still thought maybe she was about to lose her balance. She turned, lean straightening slightly as she marched ahead.

Now I was confused. I didn't know what reality was. I followed her down the hallway, keeping my eyes trained on her torso for any signs.

A hallway and two doors later, I was seated across a desk from the security director, allowing him to consider me for the position. "Yeah, I did a few training programs with Gary, good man," Walt said, taking the time to study my resume as if it were thrice as long. Walt was about six-foot-two and huge—solid as a rock. Wearing a suit and tie, an exciting combination of brown and brown. He was in his mid-fifties, retired law enforcement from the Boston area.

Walt looked up from my resume and smiled. He seemed easy-going. "Gary said good things about you. Said you'd left the PD to finish work on your master's degree?"

"Yes, sir. That's right," I said, wishing it were true. I guess it sort of was true.

"Also, you have a background in retail security, undercover? Moonlighted at both Sears and May Company. That helps. And I see you taught law enforcement at Cypress College. Very good. Why don't you tell me a little about yourself?"

We did the usual interview song-and-dance, him dangling the position in front of me like a carrot, until he finally acquiesced and handed it over. It wasn't like I expected much competition. We were talking about retail security, here. I had lots of cop stories in my arsenal to both entertain and establish credibility.

Thus, began my exposure to the dark underbelly of law enforcement: retail store security. I started working pretty quickly—I think they were too embarrassed to give a seasoned cop whatever measly training session the job typically required. They threw me right in with little to no introduction. I learned in twenty seconds I wouldn't really need one.

The job was a pretty depressing existence, even for my dispiriting life status. Most of the guys here wanted to be a cop badly, but for whatever reason, they just couldn't ever pass the entry exams. So, they turned to security work and became pretend cops with inferiority complexes.

I was reminded of that line of Paul Newman's in *Harper*, "I hear you have to flunk an IQ test to become a cop, is that right?"

45

A FEW WEEKS LATER...

Our house now consisted of bare walls and echoes. I stopped and just stood there with a fake smile and a fixed gaze, watching Sarah and the movers taking a few things from the house into a rented truck. I felt hollow inside.

Sarah came over and put her arms around me. "What you thinking about, darling?"

I stared at our home as the emptiness surrounding it just seemed to multiply, and slowly shook my head. "We could lose this. If we don't get it rented quickly, it's gone. Look at how hard we worked to get here. That's what I'm thinking about. Who knows when we'll ever get a chance to own a home, again?"

I felt my jaw clench, flashes of Gorsh and his lackeys coming before me. What I wouldn't give to smash in McKinley's face. *Look what these people have done to us, to all of us,* I thought. It was hard to think back that far, but I knew I hadn't started it.

Mary materialized, staring up at Sarah and me. I embraced her, so I could hide my angry face. "Daddy, Papaw forgot these," matter-of-factly, holding up her tennis shoes.

Dick and his male friend from work entered from the bedroom moving Mary's mattress. "Hey, you talking about me?" Dick called out to his granddaughter.

I ignored him, allowing my residual anger to morph into sarcasm. Pointedly, I addressed Mary, "Oh, no. How could he forget those? Well, it's because he's a Papaw, honey. They forget everything."

Dick laughed and continued toward the truck. Behind the laughter, he was trying to come to grips with me not being a cop anymore. He *loved* me being a cop. He relished my cop stories, bringing me around his friends as often as possible, so they could all live vicariously through me. He also loved the fact that I carried a gun wherever I went. His needs were pretty basic.

As Dick and his friend exited the doorway, Annie and Kate brushed past them with their sights set on me and Sarah. Annie appeared at my leg, grabbing onto it and beaming up at me, while her younger sister Kate hung onto my other one. I gazed down at the two blonde heads gleaming below me and forced a smile. I'd already let them down, but there was no need for them to actually know that.

"Did they finish building our room yet?" Annie asked. All the girls were excited to be living with their cousins.

"Not quite yet, babe. But we're going to move in anyway. We'll show them," I said, patting her on the head and giving that same fake smile.

Mary couldn't wait any longer. She was still holding out her tennis shoes. "So, Daddy! What should I do with these?" She was in a serious huff. It was very cute.

Exhausted, I managed to get out, "Why don't you just put them in the car, darling." I fought the urge to sob. The pain ran deep.

Later that night, Sarah and I sat out in our new "room." It was still in the process of renovation, which was a nice way of saying we had no doors yet, and our floor was concrete. Our walls were bare, unpainted drywall.

"No, little brother. You'll come stay with us," my sister Linda had said when I told her about our growing financial troubles. "Seriously, Scott and I talked about it. You can rent out your house and that way you won't lose it. We can put up walls around the patio and make two whole rooms. A room for you and Sarah and a room for the kids. It'll be easy. Scott's a pretty good carpenter. He'll build it. Your girls will love it, like a sleepover." She noticed the concern on my face and took pause, searching my eyes. "It won't be forever," she patted my hand. "You'll pay us a little rent."

It was almost midnight and the kids were fast asleep in their section of the patio. The couch we were sitting on was only about three feet from the bed, barely enough room for a dresser on the other side. The concrete made everything cold, even in Southern California. When anyone stood at the house kitchen sink, the window looked out upon our bedroom. Even the attempt at curtains did little to give us comfort.

Stu Palermo looked up as I approached his table. "Hey, Ellis." He half-smiled. He was in the snack area of Kmart, a half-eaten sandwich in front of him. He stood, wiped his mouth with a napkin and reached out to shake my hand . . . then gestured to the chair next to him.

I'd been there a month, and it felt so good to see someone from the PD. I took a seat with enthusiasm.

"Thanks for coming by, Stu. You putting on weight? What's happening with the guys?" I was talking a mile a minute, but I couldn't help myself. I realized in an instant how much I missed my brothers on the street.

Stu expelled an unintelligible sound. "It's good seeing you, as well. Too tame around the PD now without you."

He looked at me and slightly shook his head, cutting straight to the point before I had the chance to say another word. "Hey, Ellis, I came to talk to you because you've become poisonous in Buena Park, and I hate to see it. Why do you keep fucking with Gorsh? Why? This guy hates you with a passion. I'm telling you. You've taken this way too far."

There was no trace of amusement on his face, his eyes sparkled with an alertness he didn't usually have. His perspective on the situation did not even remotely align with mine.

"Excuse me, Stu," I interrupted, reliving why I'd left in a few seconds. "Back up a minute," I held up a hand, "I happen to be *reacting* to him fucking with me. What do you expect me to do? Grab my ankles? Is that what you would do? You're making me nervous, here." I leaned back into my plastic Kmart chair.

Stu pondered this for a few seconds, running the fingers of his right hand through his thick black hair and looking into his coffee cup as though the answer may be at the bottom.

He looked back up at me, ready to respond. "All I'm telling you is this: first, I can't come here anymore. If I'm seen with you, that could become a problem. And I just can't handle that right now."

I stared at him, trying to process what I was hearing. He continued, "Second..."

What the fuck's left? I thought.

"We've been told to stop you and write your ass up, if possible, and give you a ration of shit if you're caught driving through Buena Park. The chief told us this," rapping his knuckles on the tiny Kmart table during the short pause. "I think he wants you to hear about it. That's all I'm saying."

Stu's body was stiff. I realized he'd been speaking completely monotone—he sounded like a tape recording. I was beginning to wonder if this was a voluntary visit, or if Stu had become a passive-aggressive messenger.

"Don't worry. Appreciate you letting me know. I've got no reason to go anywhere near the PD. I come to work, drive to school and into Hollywood. That's it. No reason to drive through Buena Park. I don't live there anymore." I knew every inch of that city and felt a vague sense of loss in that statement.

Stu leaned back in his chair and brought his coffee to his lips, looking about fifty pounds lighter. Finally, he forced a smile. "So, what do you do around here?" He barely suppressed a laugh. To a cop, department store security was mostly comical.

"You catch shoplifters or something? You just walk around and look through those mirrors?" He cocked his head to the string of paneled mirrors extending through the rear of the store, chuckled and continued without waiting for me to answer, "You do this part time?" I nodded.

"Interesting. You still doing any acting or that stuff?"

"Nope. Just school and one acting workshop right now." I was beginning to feel worse about my position in life. My current position was only a step above prostrate.

"Is Sarah working?"

"No. She's taking a couple of classes at Cal State. You remember how curious she is about everything. She's 'learning about herself.' It's kind of New Age or whatever. She's into 'exploring her mind.' She does this whacky group therapy with my sister," I said, chuckling.

"No shit. What's that about?" Stu asked with genuine interest, a smirk forming at the corner of his mouth. *What's he expecting?*

I leaned back and flicked my eyes to the ceiling. "I don't even know, Stu. Life's going to go by just fine without me having to know that." I smiled and slowly shook my head.

"So, don't blame the guys for not calling you or anything. Everyone's kind of in a paranoid mode," Stu said without missing a beat, as though this was what we were discussing all along.

"As opposed to how relaxed it was before?" I raised a single eyebrow.

"Seriously. There's even rumors about Baker going around." Stu lowered his voice substantially. "Maybe that's why he helped push you out. There's talk about him messing with evidence."

"I remember hearing something about that," I said, thinking of a locker room conversation from several months back. "What would that have to do with me?"

"I don't know. But, you were on the list to be sergeant in a few months." Stu was staring at me, waiting for something to sink in.

Saying everything, without saying anything.

"Think about it," he continued after a pause. "Anyway, got to go. Candy's going to kill me."

He stood and shook my hand again, eyes giving the store another once-over. *Probably to make sure no one there could possibly recognize him.* But the way this was shaking out, maybe he was sent here and signaled to his partner their work here was done. And to what end?

At that point, no conspiracy was too wild for me. I tried to just return the handshake and leave it at that, but my curiosity was getting the best of me.

"So, when are they going to get rid of that piece of shit? Everybody knows he's a 'pathological liar,' Gorsh's own words. Actually, I already know why he doesn't get rid of the fat ass. But, what's that have to do with me?" I asked, watching him carefully.

Stu shook his head. "I don't want to talk about it anymore." He let go of my hand and took a few steps back. "Good luck with your situation. I'm being sincere. Say hi to Sarah and the kids, and Candy will probably call Sarah in a decade or so, and we can have dinner." We both chuckled and shook our heads.

He added, "No honestly, Ellis. I can't see you for probably a very long time."

"You were kind of boring anyway. But what about the other guys? My brothers in blue." My voice dripped sardonically. "They're not allowed either?"

"To be honest, I don't think you'll be hearing from anyone. Things are getting even weirder in there. More than just you. Everyone's acting fucked up, all the way up to and *especially* including Gorsh."

He caught himself, like maybe he'd said too much. "But, I gotta go. Gotta go." He gave me a strong hug and turned to escape before I could add anything.

I watched him amble up the aisle as Pam Ryman, a jewelry salesperson and new friend of mine, approached my table. Pam and I kept each other company with jokes and small talk during slow times at the store. She was four years my senior, an attractive lady with bright red hair and a charming smoker's cough. Made her voice sound like June Allyson.

"Hey Cowboy, want to have coffee?" She was smiling at me, waiting for me to respond.

When I didn't, her smile paled a bit. "Bill?"

46

I t was my first day off in a while. Scott and Linda were throwing a barbeque for both families and a few neighbors to kick off the summer, and maybe give us a sense of community.

Linda, Sarah, and our neighbor Donna Burns, sat at a picnic table in the backyard talking while we relaxed. Our stomachs were swollen from the big meal, and we leaned back in our seats, as satisfied as we'd been in a while. A lot of that tiring psycho-babble was being tossed back and forth. You know, the New Age-y crap that everyone was into at that time. They ate it up. I was starting to think I was at a Harry Carman workshop.

Scott leaned his torso out of the screen door and waved me down. "Hey, Bill. Why don't you come in for a few minutes? Thought we'd shoot the breeze a bit." He grinned easily.

I stood up and stretched. "Sure. Sounds good."

Sarah slowly shook her head, brow furrowed, "He looks like he's got the weight of the world on his shoulders. He's still got anger issues toward the PD, and I don't blame him. That whole thing is disgusting, and it just continues."

"How could all this be continuing if he quit? What are they doing?" Donna's brow mirrored Sarah's as she spoke.

Eager to be involved, Linda offered, "It's more like what are they *not* doing. It never stops. His ex-chief is making it impossible for him to get a decent job." She had never felt very comfortable with the two women and was making every effort to feel like part of the group—she would have said anything to agree with them.

"How so?" asked Donna. "I thought Bill was working at Kmart."

"*Very* part-time," Sarah responded, eager to take back control of doling out the information. She shot Linda a warning glance, "Like, twelve hours a week at minimum wage."

She saw Donna's consternation and added, "To apply for any real job, you have to include where you've worked on the resume. The last four years he's been with the PD. Any company considering him will always check his last employer. That chief has seen to it that all those calls go directly to him. And he knows just what to say to make sure Bill doesn't get anything better than...well, Kmart security."

"I thought they couldn't do that," said Donna, cocking her head to the side.

"I thought so, too." Sarah looked down at her hands. Her voice was suddenly soft. "But he's had at least three people tell him in person why they couldn't hire him. It always comes back to the chief."

"That's terrible," exclaimed Donna. "Can't you do anything?"

"It's kind of complicated. They used to be good friends. Then, I don't know . . . ."

"He's going to finish his master's degree in the next year, and he may have a teaching job at Fullerton College waiting—a teaching job they can't screw with. I think we'll be alright again," said more for her own benefit than anyone else's. Her posture straightened a bit.

The three men lounged about in the living room. Seated on the couch, I gazed out the rear window and looked at the patio that was our home for now. This is where I've come to, where all that hard work and asshole-and-elbows studying got me. Living on a patio somewhere in West Covina.

"So, what do you do, part-time? Look for shoplifters?" Joe asked, leaning back with his legs stretched out.

"Well, I guess that's the main focus. You know . . . and a few other things," I said with a shrug, embarrassment flushing my cheeks.

"But, this could go full time, right Bill?" Scott asked from his spot on the couch. He was relaxing there, playing with the ice in his glass. "Isn't that what they told you? Probably bump your pay a bit." He popped an ice cube in his mouth, sucking on it through his teeth as he waited for my response.

I rose to go to the restroom. "Yeah, they said that. I'm not looking for a career with Kmart, though." *Hope my trajectory is a little better than that*, I thought. "Be right back."

I pulled up the toilet seat and commenced my business, allowing my thoughts to drift as I stared at the cream-colored wall in front of me. I wanted to take advantage of being away from the others for a moment—I didn't know how much more time I could take in the hopeless hot seat. I took my time behind the closed door, staring at my reflection in the mirror. The stress I felt was visceral. I silently prayed for someone to start talking about anything other than Kmart.

No such luck.

When I returned, we went on for quite a while about my current job. I was surprised how interested these people seemed to be in undercover security, but then again, they were probably just trying to make me feel like less of a loser.

But the talk allowed me to get to know Joe better, and so far, liked what I saw. He seemed like a good neighbor, and he'd been friends with Scott and Linda for seven years. He had a decent sense of humor, which was always a good sign to me.

Over the next few weeks, visits with Joe and Scott happened often. We laughed and joked about our lives, shot the breeze about our wives, work, and friends in the neighborhood. We found it darkly hilarious that we were all getting the shitty end of the stick lately, and we seemed to cling to these commiseration sessions.

Joe's meager paycheck didn't go far enough to keep up with Donna's visions, and he couldn't seem to make her understand. Aside from handyman odd jobs here and there, Scott had been unemployed for over a year. And me, I was a part-time pretend cop playing house on my big sister's patio.

The way we saw it, we could either sit in a circle and laugh about it, or pass a knife around. Laughing was cleaner.

47

Gorsh waited on the phone for Walter to return, surrounded by the eternal clutter of his desk. He sat leaning into former Chief Sedley's old brown leather chair, which he'd never bothered to switch out. His body was rigid with tension as he thought about the spiel he had told to many others in the last several months. Perfecting it each time.

Walter's voice returned to the phone, "Okay, I'm back. Sorry about that. What can I help you with, Chief?"

"Actually, I think I may be able to help you with something, if we can be confidential?" said Gorsh, rolling the words around in his mouth, the way he did when he had something heavy on his mind. It helped shift his speech to *casual*.

"Of course, we can. What is it?"

Gorsh slightly lowered his voice as if the walls had ears or the flags were bugged.

"I was talking to a couple of my supervisors earlier, and someone said you might be creating a full-time position in your City of Industry store. Is that going to be soon?"

Walter chuckled, "Is there something I don't know? You're not applying, are you?"

"No, I'm not," Gorsh barked in the phone, defensive that someone would question his high standing. "But, I wanted to talk to you about someone who may be...."

243

"I thought about you the other day. Are you still working part time?" asked Harry, inter-lacing fingers as he leaned back in his chair. I looked at him, startled to hear him speak. I had been focused on the dim lighting of the room, wondering if it was some sort of psychological tool to help people feel more comfortable or something. It wasn't working for me.

"Yeah. They're supposed to move me to full time. But, it hasn't happened yet," I responded, staring up at the ceiling lights. I fixated on a slight, but annoying buzz accompanying the flicker.

Harry thought for a moment. "I might have something for you, if you don't mind the drive into L.A."

I returned to the room and nodded my head vigorously, hungry for any sort of lead. "I just need something to keep the wolves away long enough to get this damn master degree finished. Then we're okay," I said, repeating my mantra with a sigh. "Is something wrong with your lights in here?"

Harry ignored me, leaning forward. "Wait. Forget the lights. I might have something here for you. You could set limited hours. I'll teach you everything you need to know."

"Like what?" I perked up a bit. Sat a little straighter.

"We can talk about that later, if you're interested. But, you could make very good money for the family while you're getting everything in order. Get your own place, again. Can you imagine still living on Linda's patio a year from now?" Harry asked, raising his eyebrows knowingly. I realized he had somehow become my friend.

I scoffed instinctually. "Oh, no, no," I said, grabbing a handful of M&Ms out of a bowl on his desk.

"It sucks much worse than you could even imagine. There's no space, no privacy. It's fucking freezing on the concrete, and it's not even winter yet. The kids are getting on each other's nerves. Also, Sarah and Linda now have that damn rivalry-tension between them. But, you already know all this."

I popped a few chocolates in my mouth, chewing silently. Pensively.

"Let's talk about what's been going on with you." Harry sounded like he had an agenda.

"And that full-time position we talked about has been put on the back burner for a while," a hesitant voice iterated over the line. "I'm sorry. If you get something else going on, I completely understand if you want to leave."

"No. No. Don't worry about that. This job works perfectly for school right now. I'm happy with this arrangement if you're happy with me," I said, eagerly leaning forward in my chair as if the man could see me. Gripping the phone as if it were a life jacket thrown to a drowning man.

Walter drove to the store that same day and told me of his recent telephone conversation with Gorsh. It disturbed him, he told me, but he needed to keep a good relationship with the city because of the Kmart store at the Buena Park location.

"So please keep this confidential, like *I* was supposed to do. I'm only telling you this because you're a family man." He looked to the floor. I could feel him trying to figure out how to proceed. Soon, he looked back up.

"To put this simply, this man *really* wants to see you go down. He kept going on and on—it was incredibly unprofessional, but like he was in some sort of trance. An Ellis-hating trance. And that's why I felt compelled to tell you about it—it was creepy. Why would he be calling me about you when you've already been working here for a month?" His eyebrows arched in question.

He waited for me to respond, and then continued when I just stared back at him.

"Okay then. Well, it seems like there was an unfortunate personality conflict, to say the least. But in the end, he didn't really have much substance beyond anger, except something about a 'head-on collision' that you were exonerated for, I guess."

He shrugged his shoulders and raised his eyebrows, "Oh, and taking him to small claims court and you winning? By the way, according to him, that story made its way around the PD, and he feels cops are laughing behind his back. There's that," he smirked.

Touchdown. I hummed a few bars of "Happy Days Are Here Again" in my head.

He stopped and smiled curiously at me. I got the sense he had something else he wanted to say. He leaned forward. "Sometimes they *need* to be kicked in the ass," pausing slightly. "But, I really didn't hear anything negative when it came to performance, Bill. I called a couple of contacts I have at Buena Park PD, and they had good things to say about you. So, don't worry about your job at this store, just don't expect full-time any time soon. Sorry. Okay?"

I called Harry early the next day to see if his offer for employment still stood. I still had no idea what the job was, but I wasn't too picky at this point. Luckily, it did still exist, and he reminded me the money would be "very good."

However, he didn't want to talk about it over the phone. So, I hurried to his office to discuss the details, wondering what it could possibly be during my drive in. Perhaps facilitating group sessions? Office management? Personal security needs?

Once in Los Angeles, at Fairfax and Beverly Blvd, I parked my car across the street from CBS Studios and made my way into his office. The first person I saw was his part-time receptionist, Tina. She was twenty-three years old, wearing her usual tie-dyed top with a silk scarf around her neck, and form-fitting Levi's. Harry wasn't a stickler for professional dress.

"Hi," Tina said, greeting me with a smile. She tugged at her scarf a little bit, loosening it.

"You can go on in. I moved his next appointment so you have plenty of time. How's that?" She was so pleased with herself for making this schedule change, I felt like she was expecting me to high-five her or something.

I chose to meet somewhere in the middle. "You're the best office manager I've ever met," hoping she wouldn't ask me how many I'd met.

Harry opened his office door wearing his uniform, a sweater vest and sports coat. He smiled widely, "Mr. Ellis. Come right in and don't harass anyone, please." He winked at Tina to let her know, "This is a joke, Tina," the way unfunny people like to validate themselves.

I entered the office and sat down in the deep, leather visitor's chair. Harry closed the door and walked to his side of the desk, gently lowered himself into his chair.

"You've got me intrigued. What's this job offer about?" I asked, staring at him.

Harry sat still, right elbow on knee with his head balanced on his fist. He was smiling at me, searching my eyes.

"You know you don't have to worry about my phone being tapped anymore. That's long gone, I'm sure," I finally said when he still hadn't spoken.

Harry chuckled quietly. "No, I wasn't thinking that. What if they're tapping my phone?"

That took me by surprise. "Who?"

"Not Buena Park. It has nothing to do with them or you. You do realize the universe is a little bigger than that, don't you?" Harry asked with a twinkle in his eye.

"Oh, very funny. The guy whose job is to get me to talk about myself needs to humiliate my curiosity." I chuckled.

Harry simply smiled as he manipulated a random paper clip. "Damn, haven't heard you laugh in a while. Feel good?"

I nodded.

He tossed the paper clip into the wastebasket. "Let me tell you about my idea…."

Twenty minutes later he'd laid his secret idea on the table, years ahead of *Roe v. Wade*. I stared back at him in slight shock. At that moment, I knew I'd never be able to look at him the same way again. *Trading one evil for another. But he would never see it that way.*

I simply stood up, turned around and walked out the door.

48

1970 - ROBBERY IN PROGRESS...

I n less than two minutes after Fernando disappeared inside Vons, the first police car slowly moved into the lot. Red lights, no siren.

Then another. The speed and silence of their arrival was impressive.

Instinctively, the man in the Volkswagen hunched down in the seat of his car and motioned for the woman to do the same. She quickly followed suit.

Two more police cars without siren arrived. They continued to arrive in that manner, slowly surrounding the store with a sea of black and whites.

Most of the officers were out of their cars, some shotgun ready. But, strangely enough, they didn't make any movement toward the store . . . .

INSIDE...

With the six employees bound and under Scott's control, Joe took a short walk around the store just to make sure that damn clean-up guy wasn't wandering around somewhere. He walked past several aisles carefully looking down each one.

Approaching the center aisle, he was thrown off by a sudden vision of police cars and heavily armed cops in his peripheral vision. He stopped dead in his tracks and swiveled his head to the window; his heart threatening to pound out of his chest. He squinted, hoping the horror would have just been a bad dream that he was now waking up from. Detecting sudden movement, he focused on two of the officers approaching the store. Fully armed.

Fear seized his body. He turned and ran back to the manager's office, making sure to keep out of view of the police officers. He hurled his body through the office door, startling both Scott and the victims.

"Holy fuck, the cops are here!" He whispered it harshly and lightning-fast, as if it were one word. It played over and over in his head. *Holyfuckthecopsarehere! Holyfuckthecopsarehere! HolyfucktheCOPSAREHERE!!*

The employees tied up on the floor looked up at Joe with confusion and a glimmer of hope. Scott had immediate clarity. In the process of emptying the safe of cash, he stood up quickly, lurching forward.

"How many?" he asked with stacks of bills gripped in each hand, he looked terrified to hear the answer.

"We're fucking surrounded!" Joe's eyes were huge, big shiny white balls on his dark face.

Bob the manager looked at Christy. They locked eyes for a brief moment. *I wonder if this isn't your fault somehow,* Christy thought. *You dumb shit.*

"Watch everybody. I'll be right back," Scott said as he moved into the store area. He could hear Joe taking control already from behind him.

"Everybody, sit very still and don't talk. Don't say a word, and you won't get hurt."

Scott moved his long body like a panther through the store aisles, avoiding visual contact from the storefront. But, the emergency lights of all police cars were lighting up the night with red and white flashes. He could hear what sounded like a police radio crackling in the distance. He wondered if anyone else had been caught. His mind immediately went to his kids.

He moved closer and closer to the front of the store, feeling overtaken by a stark-raving fear. *It was that fucking clean-up man, I know it was. That stupid bastard!*

He waited for a moment to be sure the position was safe, then he peered around the aisle separator to assess the battle status. *Oh, man, we are so fucked….*

He clearly saw three officers in huddled conversation. Maybe they think it's a false alarm, he entertained hopefully. He took in as much as possible while remaining covert. In the distance, he watched the VW bug as it drove out of the parking lot.

He knew if Joe were here to see it, he'd be convinced they were being abandoned in action, but Scott knew better. All he could do was hope his leader made it out okay.

He noticed the three cops talking with enthusiasm and apparently making a decision that could impact a lot of people in this corner of the store.

Hell, in this corner of the town.

Seconds passed, and the officers still were not trying to enter the store. Scott could see a fourth officer speaking into his police car mic. Eventually, the three cops at the door moved back toward the police lights. Each one positioned himself behind his car, guns drawn ostentatiously.

Scott used this movement to his benefit and scurried back to the manager's office. He concluded the cops knew they were inside. That had to mean something. They weren't rushing the store. But why not?

He reached the manager's office and entered quickly, smelling a tension in the air that hadn't left since they got there.

When Scott entered the office, Manager Bob took this opportunity to be a leader. "Please don't hurt us. This isn't worth it," he pleaded from his spot on the floor.

His leadership was short-lived when Joe grabbed the back of his collar, "Shut the fuck up! What did I tell you?" Bob cowered at Joe's touch, instinctively curling up into a ball.

This caused Delores, the floor manager, to begin crying and peeing her pants. The stench of her urine rose in the air as the sound of the stream attracted the attention of everyone.

Joe said, "That's gross, fatso. Knock it off," and nudged her lightly with his foot. He felt as though Delores was deliberately pissing the floor as a challenge to him.

Scott gave Joe a long, exhausted look. *Freaking idiot.* He knew he needed to take charge of this circus. "Everybody, calm down. Let me fucking think."

"Hey, I've already thought," Joe fired back with wild eyes. He pointed at the victims, "These people are now hostages." His body language was pugnacious; his voice, high.

"Don't get crazy on me. Give me a minute to think. They're not coming in."

Scott began to pace in the little floor space he had, unknowingly stepping on a few toes of the victims. No one dared to protest.

As he paced, his mind wandered to the different smells in the room. The woman's urinal stench mixed in with everyone's nervous sweat, was making the whole room pretty ripe. The bad breath of fear and the body odor was distinguishingly hostage.

Joe contributed his own special brand. A sharp stench that seemed to overpower even the random cheap perfume and lilac powder. A potentially harmful stench. Scott could barely breathe. *Let's hope no one lights a match*, he chuckled to himself, while another part of him wondered how he could joke at a time like this.

Joe wiped his eyes to get the sting out, "They're not coming in...because they know we have people in here." His voice was firm, powerful.

49

A collective haze of smoke made its way to the living room ceiling. Donna had taken one for the team and stayed home with all the kids at her house, while the rest of us gathered in a circle, passing a joint around the room as we suppressed giggles.

It was the same pot I'd bought from David all those months ago. *Probably a little stale*, I supposed. *Does weed have an expiration date?* But, oh no, it still did the trick.

I'd pre-rolled twenty loose and amateurish joints just to calm myself, and get my mind off everything after that final day on the PD. Then I put everything in a baggie, threw it in the back of my sock drawer and almost forgot about it.

But somehow, the urge to try to try it again had made its way to the front of my mind. These consistent anxieties called for some relaxation and laughs. But, this time in moderation.

It didn't take too much convincing for the others to join in. They too, were hoping it'd take us away from our terrible present. At least for a few hours.

"But, you handle money too, don't you?" Joe asked, interrupting our roaring laughter at my personal account of the shoplifters I'd been dealing with at work. Although I didn't enjoy my job, I certainly enjoyed making fun of the people at my job. "You ought to rob that damn place." He threw his head back, his bloodshot eyes turning to slits as he laughed.

"That'd be quite a shoplift," I laughed.

"Oh, come on, Billy, it would be great," Linda began with her tongue in cheek. She was talking louder than she seemed to realize. "You could just act like you're in a movie. An actor doing a scripted robbery. Except, you keep the money because it's real." Her eyes had drifted to the ceiling as she spoke, desperate to keep up with the thoughts in her brain. She suddenly burst out into a laughter so abrupt, it even seemed to surprise her. She leaned forward on the couch, almost falling off.

Her laughter slowed down, and her face suddenly switched to consideration. She sat straight up, deep in thought. Scott watched her as she turned to me, "You know we laugh but, if anyone could do it it's you, little brother. You told us their security sucks." Her eyes were like bloodshot saucers.

"You actually could do that, Bill. You know you could." Scott threw in, eyes still fixed on Linda. "Shit, what if everyone in this room could pay all their bills and get their family straight?" He looked around for a reaction. Linda was nodding her head fervently.

Joe sat upright, the humor now gone from his eyes. "I could get Donna that new patio."

"Yeah. Just a *home* would be nice," Sarah whooshed out all breathy and dreamy, staring at me with hazy eyes.

I somehow got to my feet and took all of them in as I shook my head, "Well, now I know what old people are talking about when they say pot takes over your mind." Then before anyone could counter, "Oh, I know, I know. You're all simply joking. But, that's how conspiracies to commit a crime start. And that's a crime in itself, you know." My jaw locked into place.

A few more laughs and quips were exchanged: "Oh come on, we were just kidding around!"

"Yeah look at the ex-cop—can't even *joke* about doing something bad, huh little bro?" Soon the subject was dropped and changed to something forgettable, like what the room would look like if it were painted light blue, or if the new steakhouse on the corner served good Caesar salads. A commonality to soothe us.

But, as the next week passed, no one from that night ever really forgot what we'd talked about. Including me.

"I think everyone seriously wants me to do this." I said aloud in Harry's office, letting the words linger.

"Times are hard. A hundred dollars a week doesn't get it done for a family of six. And the solution's all right there," more to myself than to him. "I know it's terrible to even think about it."

I barely noticed he was in the room with me.

"We know that. It's the actual doing it that's difficult, I imagine," Harry cracked. I felt his gaze burning into my left cheek. He was doing his therapist bit, staying silent for the most part and letting me do all the talking, all the elaborating, and all the living.

"I don't want to talk about it anymore," I responded, putting my hands to my ears like a child. It was nonsensical. I was the one who'd started the conversation.

"But, I've realized it's not that difficult." My hands slowly lowered. There was a drumming in my ear that must have started in my heart. I took a deep breath and let it go.

"Rams are gonna have a good year, I think."

Harry stared at me for a few moments after I exhaled, and then slowly nodded. "Yeah, that's what I've been reading."

Later that night, Sarah and I were in our concrete room. The house was silent, and I thought I'd take the rare opportunity to try and study. She had other plans.

"So how would you do it, if you were a robber? Come on. I won't tell anyone," she prodded me with animated eyes. She was sitting up cross-legged with a straight back, highly energized with anticipation. She took on the look of a child begging for another bedtime story.

"I feel like I'm talking to Linda. Why don't you just drop it? It hasn't been funny for days." I rolled my eyes pointedly. I felt a surge of anger for her even bringing it up again. But, it may just have been guilt over the fact that I'd been thinking about it almost nonstop.

"Yeah, but it's exciting to think about it." She leaned back on the couch and threw her arms over her head, staring at the ceiling with a wistful smile. "Can you imagine, back in our own home for the kids' school year? New clothes for the girls? We're a big family. We need a home, darling." She rolled over to face me again, and rubbed her foot up against my leg.

"I know that. You've just got to be patient, and not get crazy on me. We'll work this out." I looked at her for a moment. "Meantime, why don't you get crazy on me?" I moved her hand up my leg.

She sat up and kissed me hard, with passion and then suddenly broke away. "We'd better not do anything. Kate has a cold, and we don't have doors."

I stared at her as she put on her slip-on shoes, aware she had pulled out an effective and powerful card. I waited for her to look at me. I wanted her to know that I was onto her, but she didn't do it. Her back was straight, stiff; nose in the air.

"She could walk in on us. We're still on the patio, remember?" she said quietly, her voice turned cold as ice. She looked at the floor.

The next day, Sarah left for group therapy and Scott was sleeping, so the house stayed somewhat quiet. I'd been busy studying in the bedroom when I suddenly felt the need to take a break. I headed for the kitchen, intent on finding a snack to refuel my energy.

I was surprised to find Linda leaning against the counter, silently fostering a glass of water. Her eyes moved to take me in. She didn't seem surprised to see me. It was almost as if she waited for me to walk in. "I think you should do it."

I didn't have to ask to know what she was talking about. "I really do. You know we're hurting. Maybe this isn't a joke anymore." She put her glass down and moved closer to me slowly, like I was a deer, and placed a hand on my shoulder.

I glared back at her. "We never should have joked about it in the first place."

My body leaned against the sink, unmoving and silent.

"But, in fact, you'd really be helping us out. *All* of us, ten kids and six adults," Linda drilled with a smile. She walked back to the counter and picked up her glass of water.

"Four of those kids are mine," I blurted.

"I know." She stared down at her glass, thoughtfully running her finger around the rim. "Sometimes bad things just happen." Without looking up she uttered, "Ask yourself. What's the constant in your situation?"

Before I could give it any thought, she looked up and continued. "Gorsh, right? You were doing just fine, working your ass off. A good cop. He was always screwing with you, even to this day he's doing it. Well, here's the perfect chance for retaliation. And the best type of retaliation is the type that also benefits you and your loved ones. You can accomplish two things at once," she urged.

I laughed, "Yeah, sure." But lately, I had to admit to thinking about it. Not that I would. I shook my head in dismissal.

Linda was quick to egg me on, "You know, Sarah has, too. Don't tell her I told you." She knew she'd found her talking point, her opening, and gripping onto it for dear life.

I turned to her. "What do you mean? What did she say?"

She drew back, not wanting to come on too strong. "She just wants a home for her family. It's natural. It's a good thing," Linda said softly, but her eyes still pleaded.

Sarah was not yet home, and my mind wandered back to the PD as usual. *Okay, so maybe Gorsh had one more reason to be pissed.*

I drifted slowly off to sleep with old scenes playing in my head like a movie: I was at Buena Park PD. It was all so familiar. The PD basement room, filled with the guys. But for the first time, I was at the podium facing everyone.

"So, that's the basics. You've been working a half-hour of overtime that you are not being paid for every single day since you've been here. I did it for four years. So, think about that for a moment . . . . I actually worked 560 hours without pay. How about you? How many free hours have you given?

"I ask for your support in this class action suit and offer you an opportunity to become attached as the association or as an individual, depending on what you guys decide to do. This is fair and right, and it's good for you and your families."

Silence. Stillness. I didn't expect a round of applause, but the sound of chewing gum would have been something.

The entire time I'd been speaking to the "private" Police Officers Association about an important and personal part of their lives, the chief of police and Captain Hanson were prominently seated in the back row.

Obviously watching everything and everyone. This was the only part of the scene that felt entirely familiar. There was an uncomfortable tension in the air. It was obvious to me the cops were intimidated. They weren't even allowed a secret vote, but were instead forced to vote in front of the chief. I would never have imagined this happening. Opinions and free thought were completely off limits, without that ever really being said aloud.

As the meeting drew to a close, Gorsh made sure I saw him giving a big, overly animated "victorious" grin and nod, to make sure I knew he'd won.

However, I moved on with the case, whether or not I had anyone else's support, which I viewed as a win in the long run. It was the payback that just kept giving. *Still checking them off,* I thought.

The *Santa Ana Register* arrived earlier to cover the meeting, and was denied entrance, thus ensuring a story in the newspapers.

Which was the last thing Gorsh would have wanted.

He and I had too much newspaper attention as it was.

50

"Here you are, sir," the counter girl interrupted my thoughts, making me turn to her and remember where I was. "You can have a seat. We'll bring the pizza to you."

I smiled vacantly and nodded, my palm open to receive the loose bills and coins. "Thank you very much."

I returned to our booth, and about twenty minutes later, Scott and I had eaten halfway through our pizza, while carrying on a friendly conversation.

"Think the Lakers going to make it this year?" Scott asked.

"Chamberlain, Baylor and West? Man, if they can't win it with these guys, I don't know." I was on my second slice and eyeing my third.

"We doing this for the peace and quiet?" Scott smiled as he looked around at the barren restaurant. An older couple had since placed the last of their pizza in a to-go box and left.

He shrugged, embarrassment coloring his hopeful face. This was the first time either of us had been with less than six people at a time in weeks. It was enough to make anyone hyperaware. However, he must have sensed there was another reason I'd asked him to meet me there.

"Maybe you got an idea for the Linda/Sarah tension?" he said with a playful smirk.

I waved my hand, brushing it off, "That's all menstrual."

We laughed a little more. A woman had just walked in the door and glared in our general direction. Maybe she thought we were talking about her.

Shakey's Pizza also offered fried and barbecued chicken, pairing perfectly with the pizza. I was lost in my food. Scott took the opportunity to occasionally glance at me, letting me know he had something else on his mind he wanted to discuss.

I took another confirming glance around the room, a slice of pizza in my hand paused in midair. Once I felt secure in our privacy, I dropped the slice back onto the plate.

"I do enjoy your company, but there's another reason I asked you to meet me here." I took a deep breath. Scott fought back the urge to let out a sigh of relief; this had been on his mind the entire time.

"Keep this very confidential," I prefaced, warning him with my eyes. He nodded in silent consent, urging me to go on. It took effort; it was heavy. "I've thought it over and decided to go through with that thing we talked about," I rushed out.

Scott stopped chewing and lowered his pizza. His eyes widened and darted about, dancing with possibility. He took a big gulp, and swallowed the little ball of tomato sauce and dough that had formed in the back of his throat. "Are you sure?" he choked out.

"I'm very sure. I'm not happy about it, but I'm very sure." I said firmly, looking into his eyes.

"Do you mind telling me what made you decide?" Scott didn't need to finish that question. He knew what I was going through. Or rather, what I had *been* going through.

I picked up my final piece and reached for a couple of napkins. "I've got to leave for class in a few minutes. We'll talk more next time. In the meantime, tell Joe and Linda. Sarah already knows. I think the wives should know. But, you make sure everyone acknowledges how important it is to tell absolutely no one about this."

Scott nodded his head rapidly. "So, when do we meet? I'm excited." He'd completely forgotten about his pizza. It sat there getting cold.

"I'll know tomorrow night. Look, my plan will be thorough. No one will get hurt or arrested. It'll be the *perfect* crime," a smirk, "only way I go. But, everyone has to do exactly as I say." I looked at Scott for any signs of alarm or confusion. Thankfully, there were none. This guy really trusted me.

"We can use the house from now on, if you want," Scott assured. "Linda and Sarah can make sure the kids are gone. What do you think?"

"Yeah. Sounds good, I guess," I said, mulling it over. My tongue darted around in my mouth, checking my teeth for any remnants of the wings.

"I'll let you know tomorrow night. Everyone has to buy in before we go any farther." I sort of half-ass wrapped what was left of my share of the pizza and moved to get up. "I've got to split."

Scott put up a hand, not ready to let me go yet. "Listen. Sit down for ten seconds."

I hesitantly slid back in the booth and placed the pizza-filled napkin on the table. "You're not just doing this for Linda and me, are you?" I shook my head, and he broke out into a grin.

"I can't tell you what a life saver this could be. For all of us. We appreciate what you're doing, little brother." He placed his hand on my arm. There was a light in his eyes for the first time in months. "I won't let you down."

"We're helping each other. It's just that I'll be in charge." I chuckled and got up to leave as he reached up to shake my hand.

We'd made a deal, and there was no going back.

51

It truly wasn't as complicated as one might imagine. I wasn't the typical criminal. I had a grasp on things from two entirely different perspectives; authority figure and rebel. I did my homework, and I planned to orchestrate and direct the show. *Kind of like my first shot at street theater*, I thought to myself. Dissociation to the rescue.

No—this was a different kind of theater entirely. This was theater of the mind. Method acting. The ultimate form of expression. This was my masterpiece. Here was how it played out.

I continued to keep in loose telephone contact with Stu. He'd talked lately about leaving the PD and going back into the food truck business. He kept me up to date on the PD, the guys and Gorsh. I never let him spare me a detail.

I began to go to work with a masterful attitude, strutting around that huge store with the knowledge that soon I'd be robbing it blind. I knew what the future held for these damn people—every last one of them. I could swagger if I wanted.

I decided on Sunday, August 31, for the date. Monday was Labor Day, which meant there would be no armored car pick up over the weekend. That left the Sunday evening shift with all that Labor Day weekend cash.

Someone really should have warned these guys about their predictability. Oh, wait. I already had. But, I confidently counted on the fact that no one ever communicated anything they're supposed to—at least not in Kmart retail.

The work schedule was prepared monthly, so I knew in advance exactly who was going to be there at store closing—a.k.a., when the robbery would take place. I went through those names carefully to see which people needed to be prepared for, and perhaps avoided. Didn't want some "company man" to think this was his moment to be a hero and make everything more difficult than it needed to be. I didn't need any hassles at all.

I knew the closing security routine, where and when it took place. Also, who had to sign off on what, and who had this specific protocol under their supervision.

More importantly, how involved in the ritual was each person? Who actually cared, and who just wanted to get home? I felt it necessary to watch their body language at closing, to thoroughly answer those questions. *Nothing unknown. No guessing.*

During the weeks preceding the event, I casually found out the Labor Day plans for the managers, so I'd know if they had family coming to pick them up, or if they were going to be in a hurry to attend some event. While spending time with each member, I carefully watched for attitude, personality strengths, and eagerness to get off work.

Everything had to be *perfectly* in place when the lights flashed and that curtain went up. There would be no unknowns.

I was doing this for my family, I'd tell myself, for my wife, my daughters, my sister and brother-in-law and their kids. Our wellbeing. But, I couldn't help inwardly chuckling as I pictured one of my wimpiest managers shrieking with panic in his shrill voice when faced with a gun. I was sure the flower he always wore on his lapel would immediately wilt.

I spent a lot of time watching the closing habit patterns of other personnel as well, including the parking lot activity. I made sure I was aware of every nook and cranny in the parking lot.

It was incredibly simple for me to gather all of this intel: walking all over the place and observing everything was my job. It was all I'd known for the last four and a half years.

My security office was next to the cash room office, where they deposited the money at the end of each day. In that office was a bare table, two folding chairs and one huge safe.

The money was counted, signature verified, and placed into a safe every night, to be picked up by the armored truck the next day. I played a minimal role in that process when I worked. It gave me access to the room and the open safe with all the money. Controlling the other two men expected to be in the room would be minimal-to-no-risk. Controlling the entire scene, including the robbers, was my job. And, I was good at it.

By now, I'd developed casual relationships with all the managers, and any information needed was easily retrieved. I felt as though I could control the entire store. Retail management attracts neither intelligent nor particularly brave personnel. They were there to sell you slippers, not to take a bullet.

I also used some of the information I retrieved to set up a memo I'd written, and before I knew it, this operation appeared completely fool-proof.

Walter from Corporate was on vacation for two weeks, which happened to land around Labor Day. I also wrote a memo to Walter about the "state of security" at store level. For example, it would be quite easy to walk into the store through the warehouse area, take a television set and leave undetected. "Very vulnerable to robbery or other types of grand theft," I dutifully reported.

In this memo dated ten days prior to Labor Day, I also told Walt that I'd reported many of the vulnerabilities to "local" store management, and even directly in writing to him, but nothing had changed or was even considered, and the weaknesses remained. I filed away copies of the memos, none which had ever left my purview.

I then reluctantly announced in the memo to Walt that I'd be taking the responsibility, as security manager, to direct a walk-thru pseudo-robbery on August 31, to *test the strength of our systems.* Like a fire drill. I let him know that I'd retained two men to pose as "robbers," so we could properly evaluate any issues or holes within the store's response. "Invoices for their work are enclosed."

One invoice had Scott's signature; the other, Joe's.

Mic check, testing. One two, one two.

I paid both participants out of my personal checking account, noting on the check that it was for "drill-participant fees" and listing the invoice numbers. Both checks were cashed by the guys two days prior to the event, paid by monies I'd borrowed.

I'd submit for reimbursement for this expense, of course. I ended the memo by stating I would be present during the drill to witness and control the testing process.

Had any of this been true, the best-case scenario meant that Kmart's security manager was an obsessive megalomaniac. Can you imagine anyone putting this much effort into staging a *fake* robbery? Primping his own authority until it was expansive enough to move as he pleased without any objection? *This is all very aggressive for a security guy*, I thought. This audacity would undoubtedly get me fired. But, for some strange reason, I wasn't that concerned about it.

I dated the memo one week prior to the event and addressed a stamped envelope to Walt at Corporate headquarters. Then I shoved the envelope in my VW glove department, allowing it to wrinkle so it would show a week's wear.

Ten minutes to curtain, Mr. Ellis.

Should the police happen to come in and interrupt our test, we'd of course cooperate immediately and advise them, "It's just a drill. We represent Kmart corporate, and this is a private business matter."

They'd be shown the guns were empty. I would have a naive look on my face.

If they took this too seriously and decided to arrest us, that was okay. That memo in my glove compartment would eventually explain *everything* to any jury. My wife would testify she failed to mail it for me. Oh, that absent-minded wife of mine. *She's a mother of four, Your Honor. Sometimes she leaves the stove on for hours, Your Honor.* How's that for reasonable doubt?

Both Scott and Joe knew about the robbery decision now, but had no idea how or when it would go down. They also agreed to my first requirement to allow us to move forward: A pledge that this was the very first and *last* time any of us would do anything like this.

I advised them about patterns and MOs, and re-affirmed the necessity to be one and done. On with your life.

Talk about a *Blue Light Special....*

They also agreed to not shop at that store for three years, when there would be protection from the statute of limitations. That should have been a no-brainer, but I wasn't making the mistake of overestimating anyone involved.

One week before the day of the robbery, I met with Scott and Joe at a park and told them exactly what I wanted them to do.

I showed them my hand-sketched diagrams of the store layout. Their routes and timings were marked. We went over it thoroughly.

We went to the store twice during the week for edification. I made sure they came in when the "audience" was not working. I showed each one where to hide and where the cash room was. Routes, speeds, how to knock and enter the cash room. What to say.

Both were to enter the store separately near closing time, go to their predetermined hiding areas, and wait. Wait for me to come get them when the attention of the employees was solely on getting home for the night.

I'd then take them to my office and hide them. Thirty minutes later, they'd hear me and two managers going into the cash room. Twelve, not eleven, and not thirteen, but (*pay attention, Joe*) exactly twelve minutes later, they would exit the locked room and knock on the cash room door.

Instinctively, I'd answer the door, where we'd then be rushed in on and held at gunpoint. Then, being the big security cheese that I am, I'd see to it that everyone complied and remained safe.

How many times had I stood facing this curtain, waiting for it to rise? It would turn things around in many ways.

We'd count the money, divvy it out, and part ways. Everything would be back to normal.

At least, that was the script. But as any fellow theater buff knows, no matter what happens, "The show must go on."

5 2

Days leading up to the event came and went in an anxious blur. I stayed away from friends and social situations, wanting to avoid any chance of distraction. My mind had to remain on the prize. The event approached with lightning speed, yet, it couldn't arrive soon enough.

I was going through my regular routine and acting like myself to the best of my ability, but internally I was in a constant, obsessive state of reviewing and rechecking. All the while, desperately trying to squash down the guilt that was building up inside of me.

Sarah, the girls, and I'd moved into an apartment in Brea a few weeks before, draining our remaining financial assets. I had four dollars and eighty-six cents to my name to last until payday. We couldn't wait another day if we wanted to.

As we kissed goodbye on opening night, I told Sarah I'd call as soon as it was over.

I was extra vigilant in my duties at Kmart that day. I figured I owed them that much. I roamed the store as usual, but this time I was making a mental checklist of the employees, ensuring everyone who was supposed to be there was accounted for, right down to whoever had called in sick that day, and who their replacement was.

The store manager was a tall man, balding at a rapid pace. He was whippet thin and looked like he could snap like a twig in a breeze. Previous experience with him assured me he'd be very compliant and responsive to directions. I couldn't have asked for anyone more perfect, especially considering the fact that I planned to rob him blind in a few hours.

At 6:30 p.m. on the dot, Scott entered the store. He began browsing around, playing the role of casual shopper. I watched his movement, making sure to keep my distance as I did. Looking out for any other employee who may have been paying extra attention to him, and so far, it was coming up roses. No one more than glanced in his direction.

As the clock struck 6:40 p.m., Joe entered the store looking much more nervous than Scott. He started by checking out some merchandise on the south end of the store, and I was hoping to God anyone that noticed him would think his obvious stress was because he was buying a present to make up for a fight with his wife or something. I held in a massive groan. His eyes appeared to dart toward the exit.

At 6:45 p.m., Scott positioned himself at his first hide-in location, in the far northwest corner. I watched carefully to see if there was the slightest indication that anyone had any curiosity concerning Scott. But no one had so much as glanced in his direction; he disappeared with ease.

At 6:50 p.m., Joe had worked his way to his first hide-in location toward the southwest corner of the store. I couldn't help but chuckle to myself. Here was this man creeping through the store, an invisible halo of nervousness bouncing in the air around him, and none of the staff had taken the slightest bit of notice, all preoccupied with the clock. Joe easily disappeared.

Step one had gone very well. Too well. *What was the matter with these people?*

At 6:55 p.m. there was an announcement over the store loudspeaker alerting shoppers that the store would be closing in five minutes, a polite, customer-friendly undertone that everyone should get the hell out.

I looked around the two hiding areas to make sure my guys were alone. I walked to where Joe was and signaled for him to follow me. I took him to the security office and let him in. After ensuring no one was the wiser, I went to where Scott was hiding and signaled for him to follow, repeating the process.

Baldy closed and locked the front doors at 7 p.m. sharp, desperate to keep any aspiring customers out. At 7:08, I walked toward the register area as the last few customer transactions were being completed. I also viewed staff members to make sure nothing was out of the ordinary. Everything seemed to be okay; the anticipation for them to hang up their customer service smiles at the end of day was palpable.

I watched as the last customers were let out of the door and bid, "Have a nice Labor Day," by the unarmed door security guard.

As soon as the doors finally closed, the staff threw themselves into a frenzy, shoving their way through the closing night rituals. I'd never seen these people move so fast.

I looked out into the parking lot, half-expecting to see a gang of cop cars. But, of course not. It was very quiet out there.

Opening night and everything went swimmingly. It felt too good to be true. The remaining staff completed their closing duties and were let out the door. By 7:30 p.m., only the two managers and the security guard remained.

I approached the security guard, wished him the best possible Labor Day, and let him out the door, locking it behind him, while the two men finished their reconciliation of receipts and registers.

Moments later, the three of us walked back to the cash room/manager's office in the southwest corner of the building. We could have heard a pin drop. I kept flexing and unflexing my fingers.

We walked up the short stairwell, past my security office, and entered the cash room/manager's office, locking the door behind us. I was thankful for the continued quiet. It assured me that my soon-to-be assailants could hear our movements clearly.

The store manager opened the safe and started to double-check and sign in cash and personal checks. The money was placed into the safe. Confirmed by Baldy, as Wimpy Man the assistant manager, recorded the movement on his reconciliation sheet. They were so earnest. I almost wanted to tell them it was pointless.

I took note of the position of Baldy in relation to the safe door. The door was huge and heavy, and if he suddenly lunged to close it, I was going to have to prevent that. I didn't know the combination. I casually positioned myself for the possibility a good kick was needed.

Baldy was on his knees, and Wimpy Man sat in a chair. Neither was paying the slightest bit of attention to me.

It was easy to covertly check my wrist watch to see how many minutes had passed since our entry. Eleven. I waited for a minute, then began to talk to the two men about Labor Day plans that called for no answer. I made a joke and laughed at it to cover any sounds from next door or the hallway. They both glanced at me, looking slightly annoyed.

I continued my meaningless commentary, getting no polite response from either one of them at this point when a sharp knock came from the door. Right on cue.

"Don't answer that," Baldy said. *Oh, so now you're talking to me?*

I ignored him and moved to open the door.

Two men burst into the room, pushing me back in the process. They were both armed. The black man began waving his revolver in the air as the tall white one bellowed, "This is a fucking hold-up! Everyone be quiet, look at the floor. Do what you're told, and no one gets hurt. Then we'll be out of here."

Both managers stood frozen. I could see on their faces that it didn't occur to them to do anything but cooperate.

Like any good security person, I put my hands up as I backed up to the safe door. To the naked eye, it appeared this good security person was trying to shield the view of the safe from the two bad guys.

"We don't want any problems," I said, making sure to add a nervous edge to my voice. "Take whatever you want. And please be careful with that gun. Nobody wants to get shot."

Soon Scott had moved both Baldy and Wimpy Man over to the desk and tied them very tightly; his old Army training kicking in. I could tell he was in his element.

Forced to my knees by Joe, he directed me to take the cash from the safe and place it into a trash bag he'd brought. As I did this, Joe placed his gun next to my ear threateningly.

The managers stared at me in silent alarm, right up until Scott tied blindfolds around each of their faces.

Joe encouraged me to hurry the process, aggressively threatening me further for the benefit of the two managers, our men of the hour.

With my background, I was able to withstand the fear of dealing with those two obviously deranged men, efficiently placing all the cash and checks into their bag. As security manager, I took charge of making sure no one was hurt, and I made sure those dangerous fellows got every last dime they came for.

Several moments passed and neither manager had so much as twitched. To their credit, neither had soiled their pants. Not enough audience participation for my taste, but overall, they were doing a great job. I was proud of them.

It almost made me want to hold out a few bucks for them. Buy Labor Day dinner for their families, or maybe pay to have their suits cleaned.

Scott now tied me up as planned. Not too tightly, in case something went awry and I had to get out. Also, I was blindfolded with a very thin bandana that I could see out of perfectly.

Joe and Scott moved to the door with their backs to it and Scott said, "I want you guys to slowly count out loud to two hundred before you even try to get loose.

"We don't want to hurt anybody, so do exactly what I tell you. My partner here is going to wait right outside the office for five minutes. Anyone walks out, he shoots that person, right? You understand?"

"Right," Joe interjected with his chin jutting out. "I'm a damn good shot, too. I'd love to shoot one of you motherfuckers. Try me."

And then, almost to himself, "I wouldn't kill you. Just a knee-cap shot to slow you down." He nodded slowly and threateningly, even though they couldn't see him.

"To two hundred before you even try. Five minutes before you leave this room. He'll be right there watching. Thank you for your cooperation," Scott said, giving us a little salute, even though we were still unable to see.

"Yeah," Joe added. "Don't worry. It wasn't your money."

The door closed behind them, and they were gone just as swiftly as they came, only the shuffle of their shoes hurrying down the stairs as any indication that this had even happened.

Through my blindfold, I squinted in time to see Baldy letting out a huge sigh of relief. Wimpy Man breathily counted to two hundred, his voice shaking with each numeral.

53

"**S**o . . . I don't know if we're going to be able to make it to your mom's house tonight." I paused on the phone for Sarah's answer, watching while several Los Angeles Sheriff Deputies interviewed the two other victims. They were hungry for clues.

A couple of robbery detectives were also on the scene. I was encouraged to telephone my wife, so she wouldn't be worried. They'd informed me this might take a while.

"Linda just called. They both got home okay, everything went well, and Joe has the package." Sarah rushed out in one breath. It sounded like she'd been holding it in for hours.

I turned away, hiking the phone further up my shoulder. "No, honey. I told you I'm okay. Just a little shook up. That's all. I'll see you when I get there . . . maybe a couple of hours." I lowered my voice significantly, taking a furtive glance at the detectives and sheriffs, darting my eyes to make sure I was as alone as I could be.

"Tell them it couldn't be better here. They sent the junior varsity." I raised my voice to a normal level.

"I love you," she said, her voice quivering with nerves.

"Okay, babe. I love you, too."

I hung up the phone just in time to see both managers giving descriptions of the two robbers to the deputy taking the report. Thankfully, their descriptions were far removed from what Joe and Scott actually looked like.

No one seemed to remember much besides the clear presence of guns, even though there was only one, and it was unloaded. Not that they knew that.

Two hours later, details were finished, and I was allowed to leave. Which I took no hesitation in doing. I wasn't feeling much harmony.

As soon as I got home, I told Sarah everything. She was so excited, she could barely keep still as she listened raptly. I took her in my arms, and we danced around the apartment living room for a few minutes, laughing and kissing the whole time. We wouldn't have to live on the streets, secure in a home for the first time in quite a while.

As she listened, she began to complain about not being more involved in the whole process, but other than that, she was completely elated. I was too pumped on adrenaline to realize how insane it was that I was married to someone who wished she was *closer* to an armed robbery.

Around 11:30 p.m., we went to our bedroom and tried our best to sleep.

A few hours later, my attempt was interrupted by the bedside phone ringing. "I'm sorry to bother you, but I had to call," Linda's urgent voice rang in my ear. "We need to get together right now."

"What are you talking about?" I muttered, rubbing a hand over my eyes and feeling the ball of acid in my stomach. "It's two in the morning. They could be watching me right now. Remember?"

I sat up in bed and realized Sarah wasn't sleeping, either. She was right by my side, watching me, her wide hazel eyes blazing in the dark.

"I don't know what to tell you. Joe is acting really weird, and so is Donna. She's throwing a fit, telling him to take the money to the police."

"What? You're kidding me." My jaw went rigid.

"No, I'm not. Here, talk to Scott."

I looked at Sarah and shook my head as I heard the phone being handed to Scott.

"Hey, brother," Scott's voice, normally smooth as caramel, was strained. He'd gone from baritone to tenor.

"What's going on?" I quietly asked.

"Everything will be fine if you can just come over here." He was pleading. "I'll get Joe and the material, you know, 'the material,' and we can separate everything in my garage in an hour. That way, Donna will shut up, and he'll be calmer knowing everything is final. That'll work," Scott spat the words out nervously.

I ran my free hand over my face. "Scott, you know, if they have even the slightest fucking inkling I could be involved, they'd be watching me. Right? And from there, it's not exactly a far step away from you.

"If I'm not a suspect, you and Joe aren't shit to them either. No one knows who you are. Trust me. No one can get to you except through me. Can't you calm Joe down until part of the day is over—like we planned?" I held in a holler.

I could hear a whisper of Linda's voice in the background, coaching Scott on what to say. "I think we got to act fast, brother. They wouldn't be watching you yet." Scott said after a beat. "And Joe has all the material. Who knows what could happen if he slips over the brink?"

"Hold on a second." I put my hand over the phone and lowered it, turning to Sarah. "Joe's freaking out. Scott wants me to go over now and finish things. Split it up."

Sarah didn't hesitate, jumping out of bed. "I'm all for that. I'm going with you."

"What about the kids?" I asked. It felt a little strange going out at this hour.

"That's all right. We'll be home before they even wake up," Sarah said as she began to put her Levi's on with trembling hands. Her eyes were dancing. "Hurry up. Let's go."

This was a Sarah I hadn't seen in a while. The enthusiasm rang through her voice, maybe even hope, something I didn't know she still had—as she brushed parental responsibility aside for us and led me into the night.

"Okay, I've got it. We sit in a circle Indian-style. We'll each count what's given to us by pile. Then, the person to the right will verify count."

We were seated on the garage floor, Linda eagerly taking charge. She felt at home when organizing activities and bossing people around. Now that we'd had the chance to thoroughly calm down Joe, she was firing orders like a drill sergeant. Joe doled out the piles to each person.

Donna left before Sarah and I even got there, which made the process a lot easier. She said she didn't want to be around when "it" was being counted, but I'd bet my share she'd be around to spend it. Her anger and righteousness would be short-lived when she saw their share.

"Okay, listen to me before we start." I eyeballed each of my peers before continuing, making sure I had everyone's attention as they sat around me.

"Make sure you place every single check into the middle, here. No matter how juicy and easy it looks, or how big the amount is. That would include every document or paper that is not cash. Even the canvas bag. Everything. Put it all in the middle." I paused for a moment to calm the room. "Person to the right verifies each count, remember cash only, and everyone keep focused. We can celebrate later. We'll all watch as Scott burns every single piece tonight. It has to happen before we leave. Knowledge is power."

The adrenaline-high kicked in as soon as we began to count, building each time a bill was passed from one hand to another. You'd have thought we'd pounded six espresso shots each.

As far as that garage was concerned, there wasn't a care in the world besides the cash between our fingers. The smell of unearned cash. Transitory, but good for the moment.

They say humor is tragedy plus timing, and now that we felt distant enough from the actual crime unfolding, we were suddenly laughing and joking about it like a bunch of Woody Allens. We strolled through every gritty little detail. "I have a *gub*."

Before we knew it, we'd split the net profits and watched the checks, documents, and anything that could possibly get us in trouble, go up in smoke, including my special memo to Walt.

It felt like a fifty-pound weight had lifted off my shoulders. Despite all the smoke from that guilty bonfire, I was breathing much easier. We all were.

The only thing left was untraceable cash, lots of it.

Any voice of guilt coming from inside my head had died. I somehow had a twisted, self-assured knowledge that all would be well again.

Fuck you, Gorsh—was playing on repeat in my mind. *Too bad I can't rob the police station.*

Right as we were wrapping things up and turning our attention to celebrating, I took center stage. "Okay, this to be said with us all here. Nothing needs to change in our lives. This just never happened, that's all. We never mention it again. Be very, very careful with your spending. We all have enough here to set ourselves straight, which is the sole reason we did this. And remember our pledge: We'll never do this again."

We all looked at each other, nodding in agreement. It all seemed so sincere.

A month later, our family took a much-needed vacation, our one big splurge with our recent influx of wealth. Otherwise, we made sure to keep our living conservative as usual. Not being careful is usually how criminals get caught. *You'd think everyone would know that.*

However, we did buy a house with a minimum down payment and moved our large family into a home again. Our very own, brand-new home—no cement to be found. There was a patio, but we didn't live on it.

I lived with an underlying feeling of guilt every day. Juxtaposed with a newfound freedom. I was a provider. I had provided. Nonetheless, the guilt was heavy and unrelenting. My go-to defense was disassociation and charging forward. I'd learned that long ago.

A few months later, I hired on as distribution manager at E.R. Squibb & Sons Pharmaceuticals, while continuing my studies. I'd always been good at interviews, and Squibb apparently didn't feel a need to contact the PD, which was fine with me. It stripped Gorsh of the chance to try and screw me over yet again. He seemed to be permanently in my rearview mirror. Finally.

The job was a fast learning experience. It had to be. I certainly didn't know what I was doing. I supplied the entire western region with pharmaceuticals and managed all that goes with that: personnel, operating systems, transportation, warehousing and real estate assets. Unlike anything I'd ever done before, I wasn't sure what the hell I was thinking in taking the job. I guess the money gave me confidence, or the lust and drive to ensure I never ran out again. I was determined to stay above water, the right way.

Preparing for the job interview, I drove to the Placentia Library and skimmed through many recent books on distribution and logistics, taking notes and committing them to memory. During the interview, I just told them I could do pretty much everything *(especially crowd-control),* and repeated some of what I'd read at the library with a confident look in my eyes. I assumed the people interviewing me didn't know much about this aspect of the business either. How were they going to fact-check me? I took control of the room like I'd become captain of the damn ship.

Sure enough, everybody seemed to like me, and they hired me right on the spot. Just like that, I had a brand-new career. A career that I hoped would be short-lived.

While everyone assumed I was an old pro, I learned as I went. Staying ahead just long enough to make it. And somehow, I made it. I managed a staff of forty-seven people, and I did it well. Having been a cop granted me with an aura of authority that made leadership second-nature.

This also meant I had to smile as each employee told me what it was they did. Then, I would casually stroll back to my office, quickly looking up what they'd just said. Then, put it together with everything and everyone else. It was exhausting. The whole thing would have been pretty hilarious if I wasn't running around like my ass was on fire all the time, but I began to adjust, and the position eventually became habitual to me.

I had been on a solid upswing, and the comfort of stability had me feeling creative. I came up with a brilliant idea of how to have some more fun with Gorsh. I had been wrong; I wasn't ready to let him go yet. *That was two careers taken, and a family left out to dry.*

I remembered. I never forgot. I never forgave.

I still had the can of Mace in dispute, that beautiful reminder of his loss to me in court. That outrageously profound reminder of what I had done to him. *His earned humiliation.*

But, he needed more. I needed more.

Weeks earlier, I was gifted a copy of *Quotations from Chairman Mao Tse-tung,* a.k.a., a book that could give a far-right conservative like Gorsh a heart attack—something I vehemently felt he deserved. One that would make him flop on the floor in front of everyone, so he could watch them laughing at him as he slipped away.

I put both the Mace and the Red Book in a cardboard box, sealing it generously with packing tape.

Each can of Mace issued was serialized and would be easily traced directly back to me, which was exactly what I wanted. It was my golden idea.

I carefully wiped all surfaces free of fingerprints. *Might match up with* The Phantom. If the Commie book didn't drive him over the brink, the serial number certainly would. I addressed the box to: Chief of Police, City of Buena Park, 6650 Beach Blvd., Buena Park, CA, USA. No return address.

But here was the best part: A friend of mine flew to China routinely as a navigation engineer for Flying Tigers, an international air freight line. He was the person who had jokingly given me the Red Book in the first place. At my request, he took the sealed box on his next trip and mailed it from Communist Red China to Chief Gorsh. I really wanted that postmark. It was like a symphony.

I expected his reaction to be volatile, laced with curse words. *But, what's he gonna do? Huh? Appeal the small claims court decision on the grounds of new evidence? Ha!* It would make him a laughing stock throughout the judicial and law enforcement system. He would have to eat it and be quiet about it.

No, the can of Mace would have the opposite effect. It was now in "his" possession. How could he explain that to the judge without wearing a funny hat? *But, what's he going to do?*

A week later, I received an evening telephone call from Bud Fry. "Ellis, you're crazy. What are you doing? Just when I thought Gorsh couldn't get any more pissed at you—he does. He really wants your ass . . . so bad."

I grinned, cradling the phone between my neck and shoulder as I settled into my desk chair. "Don't worry, this is the last time he'll get pissed at me." Couldn't help but let out a short burst of laughter. "I'm going to leave everything alone. Even though I didn't do anything. Maybe, *The Phantom* did. Seriously. I'm through." *Maybe.*

54

onths later, I was living a normal Orange County life, trying to distance myself from that otherworldly incident and working as assistant to the Dean at Western State University of Law. I was also close to completing my studies, and had my sights set on a soon-to-be-open professor position at Fullerton College. Yet, guilt remained under the surface.

Everything with me and my family had been blissful, but I still couldn't help but notice the spending Linda and Scott had been doing out of the corner of my eye. They'd been burning through their money quicker than planned, and it was starting to not make sense.

A new car here, a designer purse there—it was like they were trying to get rid of their money as quickly as possible. Joe and Donna were also pretty out of control. The four of them were leading lavish lifestyles in West Covina, and they were starting to stick out like sore thumbs. Granted, sore thumbs are more common in West Covina.

I tried to assure myself that what was done was done, and it was their business what they did in the aftermath, but I couldn't help feeling nervous. The vibes didn't seem healthy.

"And, I also have seven years of law enforcement," said Patrick, an applicant to Western State University, with hands folded in his lap. "So that should help with the criminal law portion. Then, I can decide to practice law or stay with PD another ten and start practicing then." Patrick was a police officer eager to advance his career.

My job was to pay attention to him. I also worked with admissions.

"Sounds like you've got your path pretty well figured out, Patrick. I have a law enforcement background as well. I must tell you, you're doing the right thing by continuing your education. I'm always happy to see a police officer working to improve his worth where he is. Or, to even start a new career."

Patrick cocked his head, smiling off into the distance. I imagined he was thinking about his bright future.

The next day, I drove home early to meet the new decorator Sarah hired. I made my normal right onto Williams Dr. toward Musial St. But as I made my way down our street, I suddenly became convinced I'd made a wrong turn.

The grass on the front lawn of our home was invisible—completely masked by furniture that looked more expensive than a year's worth of mortgage payments: glass tables, ornate paintings, lush rugs. It looked like a designer home decorator's fire sale. It was a moment before I noticed my mouth had fallen open.

Parked directly in front of what I still hadn't quite confirmed was our house, sat a large truck with the back door open. Presumably, this was how all this shit got here in the first place. *What the hell?* I stopped my car about fifty yards before the house out of sheer confusion. Stalled in the middle of the street, motor running, but not nearly as fast as my mind. *Please, what the hell?*

My next thought was, who might have seen Liberace's fucking living room broken down and spread out on our front lawn? Who would be talking to whom about this? And when they did, what would they say?

She may as well have put out a flashing neon sign that spelled out:

WE GOT A LOT OF MONEY!

Do I turn the car around, drive really fast and never look back?
Taking much longer to rule out this possibility than one would have thought, I finally overcame my shock and parked across the street. Not by choice. I couldn't fit my car into the driveway if I tried.

I got out of my car and walked across the street warily, briefcase in hand. I passed through the large shadow the parked truck was casting, coming face-to-face with Sarah and a petite man.

"I call myself Chuckie, because my mother always called me Charles. It's my only rebellion." He bent over and giggled ostentatiously, resting his small, soft hands on the pant legs of his thin blue suit. I smiled at his absurdity and nudged Sarah's arm, motioning to the side of the yard, to the only damn place with standing room.

"What is the matter with you?" I asked quietly through clenched teeth, my eyes bugging out. "Why would you do this? Anyone driving by, I mean *anyone*, will see this display. And what the hell are they going to think?"

She laughed and threw her arms around me, no regard whatsoever for the burning look in my eyes. "Don't be so paranoid," Her laughter warmed my neck as she buried her face in it. "There's no obligation here. Just enjoy and have fun. I thought it'd be a nice surprise for you." She withdrew but kept a hand on my right arm, using her other to brush some hair off my forehead.

"Let's hurry up. Take a quick look and get Chuckie's ass out of here," I quipped, moving past her and back toward the van. I wondered if I had overreacted, but quickly rescinded this doubt as I looked around. I could practically feel all of our neighbors watching from the cracks in their curtains and blinds. *What the hell could they be thinking?*

I followed her back to Chuckie's shrill voice, standing by Sarah's side as he guided us through the details of each piece of expensive furniture. I was trying to push my paranoia away, but if anyone out there had any reason to try and link me to a robbery in the recent past, this was their golden ticket. Guilt and paranoia can be heavy bedfellows.

For a full week, I came home from work each night to more furniture options and decorators, until one day I pulled up to find two of my favorite blondes standing on the curb and waiting for me.

"Momma took us to Rose Drive Church today, Daddy. We met the pastor," Annie told me, beaming with pride. She felt like such an adult. The kid really knocked me out. She was growing up so fast, and always trying to be just like her daddy. She called me her best friend. At least, so far.

Kate bolted over to us, never wanting to be left out of a conversation. She immediately threw her head back and blew raspberries out of her mouth, doing her infamous impression of a horse. She wasn't in such a big hurry to grow up. Her thing was making people laugh. She wanted to be the funniest person in the room, everywhere she went. I instinctively put my briefcase on the sidewalk and put my arms around both girls, nuzzling their heads against mine.

"Did Annie tell you about the church?" Kate asked excitedly, staring up at me with twinkling eyes. "It's right over there, really close," she pointed, waiting for my gaze to follow her finger. She watched my face turn and my eyes search.

"Can we go to services, Daddy?" Annie asked. They both stared at me pleadingly.

"Of course, we can," I assured them as Sarah opened the front door and stepped out onto the front porch. *What now?* "We'll check it out on Sunday."

Kate started jumping up and down with enthusiasm. "Can this be our home church?" Annie asked. Perhaps still trying to get over living on a patio for a year. Children can sometimes feel like they have to carry the burden their parents do. She was desperate to manifest some good into our lives, and some stability into hers.

Sarah caught my eye and silently waved me over. She had a frantic look on her face.

I planted a kiss on the head of each girl. "I hope so, honey," to Kate, putting a hand on each side of her golden head. "It'd sure be convenient." I looked up at Sarah and gave her a small nod. "I've got to talk with your mom for a minute. I'll be right back." I squeezed Annie's hand and walked to the front door, leaving the two girls to run around the front yard until they collapsed from mutual exhaustion and joy. *Ah, youth.*

Sarah ushered me in and closed the door behind me. Something was on her mind. I kissed her hello, but her face didn't soften. Her lips felt closed off.

"The worst is happening, Bill. The absolute worst." She aimed her paled gaze at the floor, shaking her head.

"What? What happened?" Sarah still loved to beat around the bush. Sometimes I was okay with playing along. This wasn't one of those times.

"Say it."

She hesitated as long as she knew I could stand before blurting out, "Candy Palermo called me a couple of hours ago. I tried to call you, but you were in a meeting."

"Candy? That's strange. Anything wrong with Stu?" I hadn't spoken to Stu since that day at Kmart. A mixture of reactions bubbled in my chest: nostalgia, anger, guilt, paranoia. Soon, I wouldn't have enough room for oxygen.

"No. Actually, they're on their way over here. Right now."

My blood went cold. "Whoa. Wait a minute. Why are they coming here? It's too soon for that," I said, awkwardly backing away a few steps.

"I know. She just called out of the blue. I couldn't stop her. She said they'd love to see the new house." Sarah's voice sounded resigned. She puckered her lower lip in pout.

"No, not yet. It hasn't been long enough, damn it," I spit, my head shaking no.

"I understand," Sarah answered, keeping her voice level. "But that's not what's happening. I guess they're driving out to her sister's *right now*. They only go once a year, she says, so they want to stop by and see us. Before I could think of an excuse, she said they were on their way. They should be here any minute now."

"Oh, shit. This is not good." I wondered in extreme annoyance how she could have let this happen.

I took a furious glance at my watch, and then at the door. I began pacing, imagining myself tucking my girls in for bed and telling them, "Okay girls, good night and don't let the bedbugs bite, Daddy has to go to prison now." No. That could not happen.

I grabbed Sarah by the waist so I had her full attention. "Okay, look. We have to have the same story. Just remember this . . . ." I told her the story I'd prepared for us. The story I'd been rehearsing for months, the one she'd overheard so many times before, tweaking and perfecting to make absolute sense to anyone who had questions. Of course, I wasn't expecting to have to use this story for another several months if at all. I could only hope this all didn't unravel.

55

The doorbell rang twenty minutes later. Sarah and I jolted out of our seats and moved to answer. A small part of me was excited to hear about what had been going on at the PD and with the guys, but mostly I was anxious as hell to see Stu so soon after Kmart. Too soon.

I could feel sweat forming on the small of my back.

I opened the door, and we stood face to face with Stu and Candy, who greeted us warmly. Everyone hugged each other. After seating, we began with the small talk. How are the kids, how's work, how's the weather, yada, yada, yada?

It was nice to see Stu's familiar smile again. Candy was beautiful, with big eyes and a hearty, contagious laugh. Normally, I'd be thrilled to see both of them, but it had been a while. The four of us just kind of sat in silence staring at each other.

"He's moving on," Stu said to break the silence, surely referring to Gorsh. He glanced around our newly renovated and furnished living room with confusion on his face that he wasn't even trying to mask.

"What do you mean?" I asked, trying to distract him from noticing too much. I felt sweat on my upper lip. "Who's he screwing over now?" I was silently urging him to focus his attention on me, Gorsh, the damn gas prices, whatever. Just not the decorator's wet dream we were living in.

"Why don't we please just move on and forget about that stuff for tonight," Candy said, her voice tinged with exasperation. "It's been a long time since we've seen you guys."

"Yeah. No. I don't want to talk about it either," Stu confirmed, clearing his throat as if that brought finality to his statement, and appreciation to his face.

"And where she stops, nobody knows," I sang. I *must* have been off-key. Does "misdirection" have a key?

Stu looked at me for a moment as he registered. Then his brows narrowed as his head jerked slightly back in question.

"Why concern yourself? It looks like you got it good where you are. This place is really nice, man." He got up out of his chair and moved a few steps, taking a panoramic view of the room. "You going to show us around, or what?"

Candy remained seated, running her hands along the light blue velvet arms of the chair. "Sarah, this is gorgeous." She leaned forward to get a better look at the huge thick round glass coffee table in front of her, held in place by a heavy gold-colored stand. Stu walked the length of one of the walls, which was covered in light blue velvet-flecked wallpaper to match the chairs and couch, nodding in approval.

"I'm going to get us some coffee, if everyone's good with that," I said and moved toward the kitchen, glancing at Sarah. Neither of us had acknowledged their comments. She stared at me, looking like she might start crying any minute. I knew she would soldier on, but maybe a small part of me hoped her nerves would cause her to throw up and freak everyone out, bringing an immediate end to this horror show.

"Show you around when I'm more alert," I motioned to Stu. "Can you give me a hand?"

We both walked into the kitchen. Meanwhile Candy asked about the girls, and Sarah's face practically melted and started dripping all over the floor with relief at the subject change.

I reached into the cupboard to grab four mugs, assembling them on the counter with Stu right next to me. His curiosity hung in the air. It was one of those moments where a word isn't said, but you can hear everything. He knew how much we'd been struggling, if you call living on the patio struggling. Surely, none of this made any sense to him.

I focused all energy on steadying my hands, which were getting a little shaky. I was thinking, *What if Gorsh found out I moved into a new home and asked Stu to check it out?* They had no idea what they were stumbling into. If he was suspicious about me having a housekeeper, I could only imagine how he'd react with this nice new home and furnishings.

I handed Stu the first steaming mug, pouring another for myself. We both leaned against the kitchen counter. I took a sip of my coffee, using it as a shield to hide my anxiety. Felt my tongue go numb from the burn.

Willing myself to breathe evenly, I looked over the mug at Stu. He'd barely noticed me while the coffee had brewed, too busy glancing around the kitchen.

"So, Stu. What do you think?" I grandly waved my left arm around for him to take everything in.

"It's really nice in here, too." He smiled. Wryly, I thought.

"It worked out perfectly. Sarah's parents loaned us the down payment (*yeah right, Mom in a mental hospital, and Dad making drunk driving history year after year*), and her uncle's the broker (*well, he was a cashier*). We took another loan to furnish. And, Placentia is nice. It's like living in the orange groves." I inhaled the scent of these fictitious oranges, performing to the best of my abilities.

"This new job is paying me well. Heck of a lot better than the police department ever did. Payments aren't much of a stretch. It was one of those things that just fell into place." I paused briefly and smiled, "Timing, my friend." It felt like a rehearsed monologue still being refined. I was just hoping Stu didn't think so.

He stood there for a moment as I took another, longer sip. He was just standing there, staring at me. Maybe wondering what it was that he was seeing.

ONE WEEK LATER . . .

"It's about time. This is the third time I've called you in the last half hour," Linda complained. I could hear the phone cord being scraped across the mouthpiece.

"We don't answer the phone during dinner. You know that. What's going on?" I said, already irritated enough to hang up on her. The rest of my dinner felt doomed by her virtual presence.

"We need to talk. When can Scott and I come over and talk with you?" Her breathing was shallow and forced.

I sighed. I was so sick of hearing the words, "We need to talk." My wife already beat me to death almost daily with that phrase. I didn't *need* to talk to my sister.

"Slow down. What's wrong?" I leaned against the wall, waiting for her response.

Silence on the other end. Then Scott's voice crackled over the line. "Hey, brother."

"Hey, Scott," I said, very relieved he'd picked up the conversation. "Why's Linda so uptight? Something happening?"

"Well, she *is* right. We do need to talk about this in person. But, nothing is happening. Everyone's fine. But we should still get together," Scott continued measuredly, "Probably not your house. Maybe a coffee shop."

"Sure. We can do that, no problem. Not tonight, though. Let's do Coco's in Fullerton, State College and Chapman. You know where that is?"

"Yeah. Linda does. When?"

"How about Wednesday night at seven."

"We'll be there."

"You sure there's nothing I need to know beforehand?"

"Let me check with Momma," his voice trailed off as he muffled the mouthpiece. Then, "Oh, yeah. I forgot. Joe might be there."

I immediately rejected that. "No, no. No Joe. It's too early for a damn reunion."

Scott chuckled lightly, "I'll tell him. I just think he wanted to say 'hi,' anyway. It'll just be Linda and me."

"And I'll be alone. See you then." I hung up the phone and looked directly at Sarah, who I'd just realized had been hovering nearby, scowling and gnawing her lower lip.

"Did you know about this call?" I asked with a slight jerk of the chin. I wanted to trust Scott, who'd always been straightforward with me, but nothing about this felt right.

"I don't know what you're talking about. I told you Linda's been calling. She sounds more desperate to get ahold of you each time. That's what I know about," Sarah answered with wide eyes and her palms raised toward me.

When someone was seriously lying to me, it often seemed they only had enough breath to utter the final word of their short monologue. Like they'd fall to the floor if they said one more word. Breathless, their entire energy expended. Sarah stood there, drooping from the weight of her words.

She continued to stare at me.

"I'm going to meet with Linda and Scott at Coco's Wednesday night for maybe an hour. Do you know why they suddenly want to meet with me?" I asked as I watched for her response.

Sarah took a seat, seeming all the while to watch my eyes for a sign of anything beyond that question—anything else that could be going on in my head. "Maybe they want to borrow money?"

"Borrow money? Are you kidding?" My stomach dropped. "How would you even know that?"

I slowly lowered to sit, my mind running over all Scott and Linda's ridiculous amount of spending I'd caught glimpses of over the past few months. What seemed like none of my business at the time was suddenly a very pressing matter.

I should have known. An alcoholic and a fat ass weren't exactly a good pair for financial responsibility. How could I have been foolish enough to think they wouldn't go crazy? Greedily buying new clothes, jewelry, furniture, and God knew what else?

This wasn't a plan to make us millionaires. It was just supposed to help us get things straight.

After watching me for a moment, Sarah tested the waters with a bit more truth. "Actually, we've kind of patched things up, and we've been talking lately."

My eyes narrowed. "So, then you *do* know what they want to talk about."

"No, not really," she backpedaled, shaking her head firmly. "I just know they're about to run out of money." Her thoughts seemed to freeze in confusion. She moved to where I was sitting and took my hand in hers.

I looked at our hands for a moment, "You know, this has been a dark comedy to watch unfold. But, now it's getting to be just dark." I paused a few seconds and slowly shook my head, "Us pitching in when they blew through all their share was never part of the deal."

Sarah squeezed my hand, "I want to go with you Wednesday. I'll get a babysitter."

"No. You're not going. It's better if I'm alone. I don't want this to be a family deal."

Sarah shook her head. "I don't want to be left out. You might be talking about something that affects both of us. I should be there."

"I'll fill you in when I get home. I'm going alone."

I spent much of the next two days wondering about the state of Linda and Scott, and how I could help. Maybe point him in the right direction to get some extra work. Anything.

I asked Sarah to avoid any conversations with Linda until after I met with them. "Let every call go to the answering machine."

56

At 6:55 p.m. on Wednesday, I pulled into the parking lot of Coco's Bakery Restaurant and found a spot reasonably distant from the entrance. We had another month or so before the time change happened. The days never seemed to end in Southern California, the sun was still burning bright in the sky. It was still warm out.

Walking toward the entrance, I could see my two relatives through the restaurant window. Their silhouettes sat facing each other; Linda yammering as usual, and Scott's attentive visage soaking it all in. Nothing new there, but this time, it looked much more serious. Scott was actually listening, after all.

I entered the restaurant, their heads swiveling to take notice. They rose out of the booth, and we greeted each other with hugs. We sat and they half-heartedly asked me how I'd been, but I could already feel the tension coming off their skin like heat.

We shot the breeze for a while, talking about the kids and exchanging photos. I couldn't help noticing all of the pictures Linda pulled out were of their family at fancy venues—way fancier than anything we'd ever known as kids. I felt a wave of resentment going through me as I looked through the photos. It was all I could do to not get up and walk right back out of the restaurant. But, I stayed. I was invested in this meeting.

I still wasn't sure what to expect from this talk, but could already tell it wasn't going to go in a direction I was comfortable with.

As soon as our coffees and slices of pie had been placed before us, Linda finally cut the bullshit. "I don't know what to tell you, Bill." She noticed a look on my face and rushed, "We went a little crazy. That's clear. And now we have nothing. We need some help. All cards on the table." She cut into her slice of pumpkin pie and took a generous bite, avoiding eye contact.

I reacted compulsively, honestly. "Hearing you say that really pisses me off," I spat out without missing a beat. "I talked to you about this months ago. We had an agreement, an oath. You had the opportunity to get where you wanted financially."

The more I talked, the more annoyed I became.

Scott glanced at Linda, guilt painted on his face.

"Not even six months after our investment returns, and you're already wiped clean? Seriously?"

Scott answered, staring at his hands folded in front of him. "Not completely out, yet." He almost whispered, "We've got a few grand."

My eyebrows shot up. For a moment, all I could do was stare back at them. I felt a bonfire between my ears. "I can't believe this. The plan was for it to last you at least two years. Give you time to get a good job." I leaned forward on the table, desperate to get my feelings across. Desperate about a lot of things, as if that would undo what they'd done.

Scott opened his mouth to speak, but Linda put a hand over his and took over. "We know. We know. We've beaten ourselves up about it. A lot. But reality is, it happened. That's where we are now. Do you have any ideas for us?" She was writhing her tongue around in her mouth, both to clear her gums of stray pie crumbs and to covertly express her anxiety.

"I'm sorry for you, and I'll help where I can, but you have to know I really fucking resent this. You go back on the agreement and it becomes *our* problem? All I know is, I did my part perfectly. Exactly as we all said we'd do." My voice was getting quieter as I wound down.

Scott nodded his head, "You're right. No, you're absolutely right."

"Now, I'm almost where I need to be in life, by following the plan." I tapped my right index finger on the table with each syllable, my eyes burning into theirs.

Out of words, we all shut down. For three minutes, silence. Three zombies with tight faces, eating pie and drinking coffee.

Me staring into space; them hesitantly watching me stare into space.

I slowly shook my head. "This isn't right."

They didn't bother to respond.

I could hear the banging plates in the kitchen, the waitresses flying about in their beige and peach uniforms. Diners chewing with their mouths open. *Who the hell raised these people?*

I started to slide across the booth, but stopped, turning back to face them. A deep breath dripping with resignation, "Okay. So, I guess it is what it is. How can I help? What are you thinking of, staying with us for a while? Help getting a job? They're both doable, you know."

Linda spoke, "You know, why don't we get together again in a few days? We're okay for now. You can give it some thought, and we'll also give it more thought. And, next time Sarah should be here. Maybe she'll have some ideas." She was seeking strength in numbers, but I wasn't sure what for.

Somehow, I didn't see how me giving "some thought" . . . or *any* thought to this was going to make any difference.

I stood. "I'll talk to her about it. I'll keep my eyes open for any jobs, Scott. When we get together again, we'll talk more, and I can help you with a resume or something."

Linda slid out of the booth and clasped my left hand with one of hers. It took all I had in me not to rip my hand away like it was burnt. "Thanks for listening. We'll do some brainstorming. I love you." She gave me a kiss. "Say hi to Sarah and the girls for us."

Scott got up, shook my hand and gave me a hug. "Love you, little brother."

57

Sarah and I didn't discuss Linda and Scott's situation the next few days. It was an extremely sensitive issue, and I was doing a good job pretending it didn't exist. But, that didn't stop her from calling Linda on her own time. On a few separate occasions, I'd caught her whispering into the phone, pressed up against the kitchen wall like a spy.

I told her after I'd caught her mid-call for the second time that week, "You need to cut out your calls with Linda until we meet. I don't want any seed-planting from either of you."

"I'm not hurting anything. We aren't even talking about that," Sarah defended.

"Listen to me. I'm not shitting around with you. Cut your talks until we meet again. All talks. You can tell her, or I can." I watched her reaction, trying to pick up what I could from her body language.

"Why don't you relax a bit? It's been six months," Sarah sighed, rolling her eyes.

I went about the rest of my work week trying to not give the elephant in the room much more thought. I played with my daughters and read to them. I thought about how special they were to me. I told them, "It will be a huge challenge, but I'm going to make sure all of you are smarter than Daddy."

Before I knew it, it was one week later and we were back at Coco's.

I parked in the same space and approached the entrance to find Linda and Scott sitting in the same booth. The only differences were, this time Sarah was by my side, and Linda and Scott were radio silent. Contemplative.

Small talk consumed the beginning of the meeting. Much to my dismay, Linda began showing those damn photos again, this time to Sarah. Sarah expressed great interest about each photo and insisted on a description of each venue. I felt the hair bristling on my neck.

Halfway through yet another order of pie and coffee, I was the first to finally speak about issues. *Get in and get out.*

"Scott, I've got names and contact numbers of two managers, good men I know, who said they have openings right now and would probably hire you. They pay well. You'd have to screw it up to not get hired." I wiped my mouth with a napkin while sliding a scrap of paper with names and numbers in someone else's handwriting to Scott.

"Sarah and I can loan you a few thousand, but that's really all we have." They both stared at me without speaking. "Look, I'll help you along the way as much as I can until you're back on your feet. But, this is all I've got." Two pairs of eyes continued to stare. "That's all we can do," I repeated, pausing slightly and then leaning forward. "Tell me you understand."

Sarah nudged me nervously. "Maybe we should talk about it. Maybe there's more we can do," she said through her teeth. Her right knee was jerking up and down involuntarily.

I looked at her, shocked she was springing this on me. Sarah and I had spent the past two weeks discussing in detail how we felt about the whole situation, and up until now she had seemed completely onboard. But all of a sudden, with Linda and Scott here, her opinion had taken a sharp turn.

I resigned myself with a sigh. "Okay, we can talk. But, I think I covered everything."

"Look. We're all thinking it, but we're not saying it," Linda said in one quick breath; a breath she'd been holding in since we sat down. "We want to do it again. We need to." She assumed the posture of a braggadocio teenager.

"Do it again? Excuse me? I thought we had an agreement about even *talking* about that," I said, my eyes flashing instant anger.

Scott nodded, so very understanding. As if this was the first he'd heard Linda speak of this. As if my sister wasn't the type of woman to talk about *everything*, to anyone who would listen, all day long.

She suddenly rose from the booth. "I'm going to the restroom."

Yeah, drop your ticking time bomb and then prance off to the bathroom. Thanks for that.

As soon as she was out of earshot, Scott oozed apologetically, "Before you say anything, I understand completely. Why would you even be slightly interested?"

"One time and out. Do you remember why we don't go back, Scott? Because it gets you caught. It establishes a clear MO. We talked about that. A lot."

I stabbed a finger at the piece of paper. "Call those guys. They'll get some work for you."

Sarah interjected with a strangely disappointed voice, "He probably needs something bigger right now, babe." Compassion was bleeding from her eyes. Her right knee was still jerking.

I felt like I couldn't remember who she came here with.

I gazed around the restaurant for a while, watching other diners distractedly. Scott and Sarah's eyes were burning holes into me. I was careful not to acknowledge either of their existences. It felt fleetingly pleasant and peaceful.

A few minutes passed, and Linda strode toward us, not a care in the fucking world, as if she hadn't just suggested we commit two felonies for the second time. She sat down next to Scott and leaned in, clearly unaffected by the chilling silence that had taken over since she left.

"Okay, so here's the thing, Bill. We've looked at this from every angle. Scott has talked to Joe, who by the way, also learned some tough lessons. We've agreed this definitely has to be done once more. We learned from our mistakes. It'll never happen again."

I ignored her, pressing my hands to my temples. "What happened to *once and out*?" I glared at Scott.

"I'm really sorry, man." He glanced at Linda. "Got a big family like you. Look, we really need you with us. I understand you not wanting to. But, we feel we have no other option. We'll do it completely differently. Nothing traces back to you. I promise." He looked at the table as though suddenly distracted by its presence.

I was barely with them anymore. I didn't look at or speak to anyone. I vaguely felt Sarah's hand massaging my shoulder, and it gave me a slight sense of comfort amidst the chaos.

"What about those two job leads?" I hoped to slice through the haze. To bring in some air.

"We truly appreciate what you've done, brother. But, we've already made our decision. I may still take one of those jobs, but we're going to do this. I hope you can see why."

No, not really.

"What are you guys talking about specifically?" I finally asked. "You best not be talking about doing a Kmart."

"No. No. Of course not. I told you, nothing traces back to you," Scott said soothingly. As if that made any of this better.

"We were hoping you'd go one more time with us," Linda added. Trying to turn on whatever charm she had left. I felt cold all over.

"You decide where. You could put it together. You know you could."

"I won't have anything to do with that. I don't even want to talk about it anymore," I said with finality, but not with the scream I was dying to release. After all, we were in public. "I'm happy with my life. That was supposed to be the end goal for all of us."

"Can't you at least give them some ideas?" Sarah purred in my ear. She now had a hand on each shoulder, distracting me from the fact she didn't seem surprised by any of this.

"No. No. Come on. Leave me alone," I leaned back.

"Sure, *you're* okay. That's great. You know how happy I am for you." said Linda. "But, we had a serious problem come up, and now we need to fix it."

I silently stood up. There was really nothing to say. There was no fucking "we" anymore.

She continued, pretending not to notice that I was standing. "I understand you not wanting to help if that's how you feel. But, we're going to do it anyway. We thought we should tell you, is all."

She took a drink of her ice water, cool, calm, and collected. At least on the surface.

Finally, she looked up at me, forcing my eyes to meet hers. "They clearly don't have your skills. The chance of getting caught is so much higher without you."

She put her glass on the table and quietly added, "Look. If they get caught, you know Scott wouldn't say anything about you. But 'cops tie those things together,' you said that, and who knows what they'd come up with to offer Joe. Especially if they think you're involved."

She paused only slightly, "*You* told us that."

Complete immunity for testimony against me.

"I'm just being realistic," she added, almost smug. "You've got to consider everything."

"She's my freaking sister. I can't believe this is happening. " I shouted, my voice getting out of my control.

It was a couple hours later, and we were home from Coco's. We'd turned on the TV for the girls and they were sprawled out on the floor, enraptured. Meanwhile, Sarah and I'd locked ourselves in my study. I was sitting in my black leather executive chair, drumming both sets of fingers against the thighs of my Levi's.

Sarah was leaning against my desk, directly adjacent to where I was seated, contemplating.

"Well, unfortunately she's kind of right, Bill. She's being practical. They're probably going to mess this up without you. You know that. But they're going to try anyway. They're desperate. You should think about helping a little. This could turn out to be a real problem."

"It's already a *real problem*." My fingers drummed a little faster against the denim.

"Let's think about this. Couldn't you oversee them just a bit to make sure they do it right? You almost have to." Sarah reached her hand to her mouth and began to nervously bite one of her fingernails.

"Help them? Stop it. Do you realize we're not struggling for the first time in our married life? Ever! I know you know what that means. All these years, all this strife and struggle and doing whatever it takes to salvage our dreams for the future. And we're right there. We're right there."

Sarah looked at me silently, but without taking any of it in. Maybe it wasn't still *her* dream.

"I don't know what you do, then," she said, shaking her head. "Scott's okay, but how well do you know Joe? Without you directing his every move? Linda's right. He's the wild card here, without you."

"I understand that. I just can't do anything about it." My gaze appropriately fixated on a copy of *Theatre of the Absurd* lying on my desk. "I'm feeling really screwed, here."

"I say you pay attention to what they're doing and help where you can. You have a family to think about." She left the desk and moved to the chair.

What do you think got us here? But the words didn't make it out of my mouth.

We sat in silence. She in her chair, me in mine. Nothing seemed real. And nothing seemed good.

Finally, Sarah broke the quiet, "I'm going to put the kids to bed. Why don't you relax for tonight? Think about it again tomorrow." She got up to leave and walked to the door, turning around at the frame to face me again.

"You've got time, Babe. They're looking to you for help. I'm looking for your help, too." Her tone was suddenly playful. She bit that fingernail again, not so nervously that time.

"How about after I get the kids to bed," she suggested with a sultry wink.

58

The next several days passed almost without my noticing. I had a lot to think about, and no one to talk to. I often found myself at Hillcrest Park after work, sitting on a bench consumed by my thoughts. Like a movie montage inspiring heavy melodrama and conflict. The park greenery was drained and gray, the day dreary . . . foreboding.

Sarah continued to butter up the idea whenever she could. I didn't give her much opportunity, but she took what she could get. Her needs were simple and transparent: For her husband to stay out of prison. Oh, and more money wouldn't hurt.

Linda and Scott didn't call or pursue me further, but I could feel them coaxing Sarah from the sidelines.

Not that she needed much coaxing.

One sunny day, it all came together in a surreal moment of clarity. Or, perhaps a moment of madness. I'd gone to the Cypress College campus, hoping to see the Dean, my now-absent friend. Since that bullying session with police management, he'd completely avoided me. He wasn't in the office (or so they'd said). *They aren't even trying to be convincing anymore,* I thought as I walked out the door.

On the return trip home, feeling dejected and low, I'd stopped at a traffic signal at Lincoln and Valley View. Paul McCartney was just crooning the last notes of "Let It Be" on my VW Bug's radio.

Waiting for the signal to change, I took a nostalgic look around the intersection. It was the first time I'd been in Buena Park as an ex-cop, and I felt very out of place.

Gorsh's deep, haunting voice whipped in the wind. As my mind was settling into a dark place, "Mama Told Me (Not to Come)" pulled me back to reality and into a better mood.

Before I knew it, I was slapping my steering wheel to the beat as I sang along, flashing sheepish smiles at fellow drivers.

Suddenly, everything came into focus. I'd glanced up just in time to see it in all of its glory. The building was *majestic*, with a beautiful blue sky overhead, making it glimmer like a beacon shining in the distance, calling my name.

The Buena Park Kmart.

Fuck you, Gorsh, I thought to myself. It'd been a while since I'd heard that mantra, but it played on a loop as if it had never left my mind. I'd entered into a delicious contemplation.

My disgust for him and everything he represented coursed through my veins. Suddenly I couldn't remember what was so terrible about the plan. *This would be great.* I felt a surge of strength at the prospect. I could barely remember who else was involved anymore.

I soon found myself parking in the lot and looking up at the Kmart building longingly. I got out of the car and looked both ways to sort of scope out the two huge contiguous stores sitting side by side: Kmart and Vons Market. The traffic on Lincoln was swishing by. I stretched taking a better look at the Kmart side.

From the outside, it looked just like my golden goose from Industry, a reassuring sign. But this was Buena Park. A dangerous home game.

Why am I even thinking about this?

I walked inside the store. It was arranged in the cookie-cutter corporate Kmart setup—if I didn't know any better, I'd think I was back in Industry. I could see the security manager in the middle of the store, but kept my distance. I'd meet him another time.

After walking up and down a few aisles like I was a shopper on a mission, I left without being noticed.

Returning to the car, I noticed my head shaking not in dismissal, but in a surprising and growing change of mind. I felt about thirty pounds lighter than I had those past several days. I practically skipped the remainder of the distance.

There was a lift in my step that replaced the foreboding of the past several days. *I can do this.* This could work with enough creative preparation, and as much control as possible.

Who was I kidding? Of course, I could pull this off.

I kept everything to myself—about as far as the first pay phone booth outside of Buena Park.

"Hello," Scott's velvet voice came on the line.

"Hey, it's me. I'm on a pay phone with no more change, so listen up," I spat out.

"Sure. You got it." I could already feel him smiling over the phone.

"Okay, this is not definite, mind you. Not definite at all. But, I may go ahead with what we talked about. Got to give it some more thought and talk to Sarah. But, I'm calling to make sure you guys don't do anything further until I get back to you."

I was pacing in the phone booth, whipping back and forth in the two-step span I had.

"Oh, absolutely," Scott said enthusiastically. I heard Linda in the background asking who he was talking to. Without lowering the phone, "I'll talk to you after I hang up, sweetheart, okay?" Back to me, "We haven't got that far, yet. Our first get-together is tonight."

"Be sure to cancel that until we talk. I'll call you in three days. Got to sort a few things out." I made sure my voice sounded serious and removed, but a smile crept across my face. What the hell; he couldn't see. "Don't say anything to Joe yet."

"Okay," he agreed. "I promise I won't." He'd do anything I said, as long as it meant there was a possibility ahead.

"And tell Linda to absolutely *not* call Sarah. I want this to come from me, in person," I still lived with the suspicion that my phone was bugged, even though I'd been away from the PD for over a year now. Old habits.

"I can't tell you how much you even *considering* this means to me. Hell, to all of us." Scott said, his usually calm voice beginning to tremble.

"Good. But remember, I'm only considering."

"Understood, brother. Understood and appreciated." His tone assured me that both sentiments were true.

As I hung up the phone, it dawned on me how unusual this call was. No Linda clamoring for the phone, making sure every thought that came in her head was verbalized. I guess she saw the hopeful look on his face and realized it was, for once, time to shut up.

Throughout the day, I considered. I rationalized, thinking about every conceivable outcome. I tried to be pragmatic, business-like, but couldn't help smiling at the ironic *absurdity* of it going down in Buena Park.

It definitely upped the ante for me. This was kick-ass-and-take-names kind of stuff. Gorsh had won a few battles, but I was about to win the war.

That night when the girls were asleep, I led Sarah into my study and shut the door. She took a seat in my desk chair. These late-night meetings were becoming a ritual. I pulled out a folding chair next to her and sat down on it backwards, facing her.

"Okay. It's been kind of crazy. Half the time I don't know how I get from place to place," I began, not wanting to dive into anything quite yet. The eagerness on her face was practically turning me off.

She smiled, "I know. I know. You've got a lot on your mind," her hand rubbing up and down my leg. She looked up through thick eyelashes, waiting for me to continue.

"I called Scott on the way home today and told him, it's absolutely *not* definite yet, but I may go ahead and get involved. Some things I want to look into before committing."

I took both of her hands. "I'll keep you in the loop."

Sarah barely held back her smile. "I think you'll decide it's the right thing," she uttered ever-so-casually.

"I know you do. But, I don't want to talk about it anymore until I decide." I squeezed her hands.

Sarah cocked her head to the side and ran her tongue over her teeth, "Hmm, you know, so we don't have to talk about it…." Her eyes smoldered as her hands coaxed me out of my pants, and within seconds, I was on top of her. Her back arched against the carpet, chest heaving as we moaned together. The rug burns were deep, but neither of us cared.

59

"Please tell him Bill Ellis is here to see him. He's expecting me." The young lady at the Buena Park Kmart returns counter blinked a few times. The dullness of her shoulder-length brown hair matched her expression as she paged for Chuck the security manager to, "Please, come to Returns."

A few minutes of awkward silence later, an amiable-looking man greeted me. And why not? Think of what he was doing for a living. It's not like he had an exciting future before him. This has to be near the end of some line, somewhere, and he'd accepted it.

He was somewhere in his late fifties, graying, pot-bellied and bored. He gave me a hearty handshake and after our mutual introductions, invited me into his office, clumsily offering me a seat and a paper cup of water.

"We heard about that. Must have been scary," Chuck declared from across the desk.

I'd just finished telling him about the terrifying, shit-your-pants experience of being robbed at gunpoint at my last job in security at Kmart, City of Industry.

"One guy held the gun right here at my head during most of it, while the other one unloaded the safe," I said, aiming my index finger to my right temple for added effect. I kept a wideness in my eyes.

"Hey, don't even hesitate if they're armed. Just give them the damn money. It's not worth it," Chuck reassured me with his hands up like a victim in a stagecoach robbery. "It's store policy, anyway."

I nodded fervently, "You said it. The only guy I could really see looked like he was on speed or something. He was sweating a ton. I was afraid he might just accidently jerk the trigger, and there goes half my head!"

Chuck stared at me incredulously like, *I can't believe you went through that and made it out okay, man.*

"I hope you have better closing procedures than at Industry. Staff usually didn't do a thorough check of the store perimeter at closing. We don't have any idea where the robbers got in. No signs of forced entry." I slowly shook my head in dismay.

Proper closing procedures have always been very dear to me, Chucky babe.

"Wow." Chuck was blown away.

"Yeah. I made suggestions for improvements, too, but nothing happened. I wish I could have stayed to help with that, but it got to be too much of a drive from Placentia." I had the answer before Chuck asked the question.

"That's interesting," Chuck pondered. "You know, we have an opening coming up, here. You ought to think it over. It's close enough for you to commute, and we'd love to have you and your experience."

Bingo. Hello, Gorsh. I almost swooned.

"Appreciate that. I do have something coming up in a year. Maybe in the interim, I can help you out. Let me talk to my wife and give it some thought." I smiled at him with an appreciative look, but not a sincere one.

"How do you guys do closing here? Slight differences, I'd imagine."

This was Chuck's shining moment. I could tell he'd been dying for someone to ask him over the years as he delved into excruciating detail. I was sure to respond animatedly to his closing procedure monologue, ready to soak up as much information as possible.

I told him I needed to talk to my wife about the job offer and get back to him. I asked for a schedule of his days off so I'd be sure to not miss him. He wrote out his complete work schedule without so much as blinking.

Two days later I met with Joe and Scott. It was about 6 p.m., and we were alone at Scott's house. Joe had just finished outlining his personal financial woes, which seemed to be identical to Scott's.

We were silent. I was thinking about these people who had somehow turned into a huge burden for me to handle. *What a clusterfuck.*

"I've been thinking about this," I said, breaking the silence. "A lot. In my gut, I know this is an *extremely* bad idea. The thought of you guys trying to do this alone is beyond scary. Frankly, I don't see how it will work. And from what I've been told, neither do either of you."

Both men were giving me their full attention, leaning in. They both agreed with my assessment by nodding their heads with a trace of self-doubt and guilt.

"So, I'm willing to do this once more. And, we do everything afterwards *as agreed* this time."

And just like that, Joe and Scott had won the Lotto. Scott pumped his fist into the air and let out a yelp. Joe slapped him on the back, eyes starting to water with excitement. "I can't believe it," he exclaimed. "This is no longer a suicide mission, man. The cavalry has arrived." He let out an incredulous laugh, pumping a fist in the air.

We all shook hands, something in common once again.

"There's a few things you both have to agree on before we proceed. Number one is the fact that I will not be in the building this time. It can't work that way. I'll strategize the process and I'll be close by, but *not* in the building. Okay?" Two quick nods.

"Which brings me to number two. You must *follow instructions completely, without fail.* Do not use your own instincts. Use my knowledge.

"Number three—and listen carefully—is that we *do not contact each other for at least one year* following. No exceptions to this. We need space from each other for a while. For good reason."

"Whoa," Joe stuttered. "I thought this was family."

I looked at him for a moment, waiting for his words to weigh in the air. My eyes pierced into Joe's face. He couldn't hold my gaze any longer and glanced at the floor. I leaned back.

"Anyway, Scott and Linda are taking their family to Oregon. As for you and I, Joe, we're not neighbors anymore. I'm sure Donna would feel better with the separation anyway. A full year. That's non-negotiable." A year didn't even sound long enough, in my opinion.

Scott sat upright in his kitchen table chair, "Yeah, that makes sense. I'm fine with all of it. I pledge." He turned to Joe, "Neighbor?"

Joe clutched his chest, "Neighbor? What? I think after what we've been through and are about to go through, 'friend' is the tag." He didn't miss a beat. He placed his hand on Scott's shoulder and squeezed it.

"Yeah. I'm okay with all of that, too. Let's do this." He rubbed his hands together.

Scott asked, "Have you decided on where, yet?"

"I have. For me, that might be the best part. We're going to do another Kmart." I paused as they both stared at me with wide eyes. "The one in Buena Park."

Scott blanched, "The town where you were a cop?"

Joe looked at Scott and then at me, feeling he was missing something. "Why would you do that? You got somebody on the inside?"

"Course not. They don't know we're coming." My face stretched into a Cheshire smile. They frowned back at me.

"Is Buena Park actually a good choice? Or just a 'fuck you' choice?" Scott asked. I guess I'd shared a little more with him when we lived together than I'd remembered.

Chuckling slightly, "It's both. Look, if it didn't meet the first qualification of being a great choice, I wouldn't have given it a thought. But the two of them together? Now, that is a bit of poetry not often found in real life."

Joe scratched his head. "Poetry?"

Scott was still wary. "Tell me about it. How does this work?"

"I've been inside the store twice recently, and I'm going again. The security guy's given me all the intel we need without realizing it. This'll work seamlessly. I even know how the police will respond when they get the call.

"This is why we need to be away from each other afterwards. They could be looking at me eventually. I wouldn't want them to stumble on any connection."

Scott had resumed his interest. "When are you thinking it should happen?"

And now, Joe leaned forward, "Yeah. When?"

Their bodies were like mirrors, reflecting their inner turmoil and financial distress. They really needed this.

"It's going to have to be quick. Give me two days to decide when this will go down. I'll give you both a call. We have to be very precise."

Joe nodded his head vigorously. He let out a burst of delirious laughter. "That sounds fucking great."

60

"I want to be involved this time," Sarah breathed into my ear, sounding like one of our daughters when they complained about being left out of a game. She'd been beating around this bush for days now, desperate to be a player. She gripped my back with her hands and wrapped her legs around my thighs, pulling my body closer to hers in bed.

"Sarah, no. You just do what you did the first time, and I'll call you when it's over. You'll be our anchor," I muttered, shaking my head, determined not to let my dick do the talking. A weakness I should have had better control over by now. I moved away from her and rolled over on my back.

Sarah propped her head up with her hand and moved onto her side, facing me. She dragged her fingers across my chest and whispered, "No, really, honey. Being at home, waiting for the call, killed me. I need to be there. It's the only way I can cope with this."

She looked at me pleadingly. "You said you weren't going to be in there. Why can't I just sit in the car with you? An extra pair of eyes. Please?"

She slowly put her head on my chest. I twirled a few strands of her hair with my fingers and ran my hand across her back slowly, contemplating compromise.

"Okay, I'll tell you what we'll do. I'm not going to commit to you being with me . . . ."

Sarah interrupted. "Why not?" The softness in her voice was gone.

"Let me finish. Then, I take questions from the floor." I smiled slightly to cushion the seriousness of my annoyance.

"What I was *going* to say is, I will let you go with me to Kmart tomorrow. Help with the casing process. We'll see where it goes from there. Fair?"

"That's fine with me. Teamwork. What'll I be doing?" Sarah shot back, eyes dancing around the room as she rubbed her hands together.

"I'll tell you in the morning. Let me work it out."

We aggressively threw ourselves back into a passionate embrace, both aware we were done talking. This whole *Bonnie and Clyde* thing had made its way into our bedroom, and we were using it for all it was worth.

The drive to Kmart was silent the next day. Within the silence lived a tension so thick, I could barely breathe. As we neared the exit, I spoke for the first time. "Okay, we can talk about it now. You ready?"

She noticeably perked up, turning her gaze to me with bright eyes. "I've been ready."

I used the turnoff to Orangethorpe Ave. and parked near a pizza parlor right after lunchtime, as planned. The lot was mostly full. I turned off the engine and reached into the glove compartment, taking out a notepad with a pen attached.

It was irrational, but my body buzzed as though I was being watched. Like the PD would give a crap that I'm sitting in a crappy pizza place's parking lot. *Get a grip, here.*

Sarah sensed my paranoia. "Well, come on, let's go. Tell me everything." She was like a kid ready to rip apart her presents on

Christmas morning. The concept of consequence did not seem to be in her wheelhouse—or mine.

It brought me back. I looked at Sarah and her bubbling enthusiasm and couldn't help but chuckle. She did make a pretty cute gangster. I felt a wave of affection for my wife, who wanted to be right by my side through this.

I doubted this was what she had in mind when she vowed to love me for better or worse.

I opened the notepad and showed Sarah a diagram of the Kmart interior, going over what everything represented. All of the aisles and cash registers were noted pretty much by scale, as were the entries and exits. Pointing to the northwest corner of the store, I ran my finger across the west wall. "I want you to find two places where Scott and Joe can hide. This is right next to the cleaning supply section." I glanced over at her.

"You're kidding." she said, raising an eyebrow. "That's it?"

"What were you expecting, a cape or something, Super Woman? This is actually an extremely important part of the drill. You have to be creative and very intentional. Watch the pattern of customers and staff. Watch what they do in various situations, and pick two places least likely to be seen by anyone around closing time."

She stared at me, memorizing every word.

"Then I want you to mark those spots on this diagram. And choose carefully. The whole success of this plan relies on these spots."

"That's not much. What then?" she asked, visibly frustrated. "What are you going to be doing?"

"Don't worry about me. I have my own assignment. If you see me in the store, remember to *not* acknowledge me. Let's synchronize watches. Mine says 2:17."

She sighed and reluctantly lifted her wristwatch, "Mine, too. On the dot."

"Okay, you'll go in first. Look at some merchandise for five minutes like you're shopping, then go to the west wall and do your thing. We'll come back at closing time for a couple of days and watch the activity around those two spots."

"This is really exciting," she deadpanned.

"I'm not finished. Leave the store exactly thirty minutes after you enter. Exactly. As you leave the store, casually walk east to Vons Market. Go in and buy two diet Cokes.

"When you come out of Vons, I'll be there. If not, just kind of hang around the entrance. Be casual." I watched her diligently taking it all in. "And I want that damn diet Coke."

Her icy disposition finally broke and she let out a laugh. "Then, let's go get it."

We leaned in for a quick kiss. Then I started the VW Bug, and we rode. We had the radio cranked up and blaring "She Came in Through the Bathroom Window." With windows down. we belted along at the top of our lungs. I was fleetingly reminded of her coming through *my* window all those years ago.

As we drove past Crescent Ave., I noticed a black and white waiting at the light, an ex-fellow officer at the wheel. I turned right at the very next turn and entered a residential neighborhood. I quickly turned off the radio, as if that made us more invisible.

Seven or eight houses away from the turn, I slammed the car into park with the engine running, with my foot off the brake so taillights would not be lit.

I rested my hands on my pant legs and looked over at Sarah. She was white as a ghost.

"Oh, my God," she gasped. "What are you going to do?"

"Stay calm. I don't think he saw us, but if he did we'll know very soon." I was watching carefully through the rearview mirror. Sarah turned in her seat to see. My subtle gangster.

Even the chance of him seeing us would make further planning useless. Our presence would be recorded in the officer's mind forever and possibly broadcasted right back to Gorsh.

Seconds later, the ominous black and white drove by very slowly—so slowly it looked as though it might turn down the street where we were parked. Sarah gripped my wrist. Other than that small movement, we were completely still and holding our breaths.

The black and white continued south on Valley View, still too slowly for my liking. My VW was not exactly inconspicuous, and known by most on the BPPD. The thought crossed my mind that he could have radioed the PD about spotting me and been instructed to stand by and watch. My upper lip was beginning to perspire. The police unit slowly disappeared from view.

"Oh, crap. It was like he was standing still. Is that right?" Sarah asked, biting her lip.

"Usually you want to patrol very slowly, so you can see what's going on. If you drive too fast everything's a blur," I answered evenly. "But, that seemed way too slow."

"I hope we were a blur to him. Or better yet, invisible."

"Like I said, we'll know soon if he saw us. Let's just sit here for five more minutes and see what happens."

Five minutes passed and nothing had happened; we felt confident again. I put the Bug into first gear, and we continued to Kmart, scanning carefully.

Pulling into the parking lot, I chose a spot considerably distant from the store. Looking back, that close encounter with exposure was a premonition. But, my eyes did not see and my ears did not hear.

61

The following week, I was awakened from a peaceful sleep by four girls bouncing up and down on the mattress, yanking at my free limbs and shouting and laughing.

Little shits, I thought, still groggy. "Come on, Daddy, wake up," they chanted. I wondered if they'd spent all morning rehearsing this assault. I grabbed Mary in a headlock for good measure and growled at the others, curling my lip in an exaggerated snarl.

"Pancakes are ready! Momma wants you to get up," Kate laughed. She hooked her index fingers on each side of her mouth, making a hilarious face at me. *I taught her that one.*

Annie and Claire held my legs hostage, giggling. Meanwhile, Kate tried her hand at stealth by attempting to free Mary from my headlock. Instead, I used my free arm to put her in one. Lots of legs and arms flailing about in fun. We loved each other and always had fun.

"Okay, okay. I give. I'm getting up," I surrendered as I released both heads. I lightly knocked them together like blonde coconuts, causing both to laugh more and to look at me with pseudo-indignation.

Annie lifted her arms and started to dance around, eager to see me get out of bed.

Just another day in the Ellis house. *Only, today Momma and Daddy are going to rehearse robbing a Kmart. Again.*

It could have been a fun family outing really, but we opted for a sitter instead.

As the girls ran out of the room toward the warm and inviting aroma of breakfast, I swung my legs around the side of the bed and sat up. Sarah walked in with a cup of coffee. "Thought you might want this now. How are you doing?" she coaxed.

"I'm fine," I muttered as I took the cup. She left, picking up on my desire for silence. I sat and sipped my coffee, staring at the wall and thinking about the impending rehearsal with Joe and Scott. *Rehearsal. Because this is just another show, another character,* I affirmed to myself.

Joe and Scott entered the store separately. I was in the parking lot, checking for the best place to park and be able to view the action. Both went to their place, designated by Sarah, to get a feel for things, feigning the look of the ponderous shopper.

Joe acted as fidgety as ever. Possibly he wondered if this was a setup—if maybe I was secretly working with the PD against them. With no employees were anywhere near him, he started to look better, seemed calmer.

On the other hand, Scott projected complete confidence in the plan. It was almost nostalgic. I *could really make a lifestyle out of this, if it wasn't for all the damn guilt that came with it,* he thought. He'd been having nightmares ever since our first dalliance with the law, but it felt like a small price for such a guaranteed mass of income. He smiled, unaware that he'd been vigorously balling his hands into fists the entire time.

I was seated down low in the backseat of Joe's car while they followed the process and made mental notes of any questions and comments. Written notes weren't something I was going to risk getting lost and found by the wrong person.

Sarah had done a thorough job with the diagram marking, and I felt comfortable. As long as they followed instructions precisely, everything would go down as planned. We were aware of any possible hang-ups to the plan, and Sarah would be in the car with me when it went down. I was conflicted about this, but familiar enough with the woman to know that if she wanted something, she'd find a way to get it.

"It's not like your whereabouts are a secret to me. I'll just drive over there," she had threatened over and over until I relented, not really seeing the point in arguing if she was just going to do what she wanted to anyway.

Things going wrong never even entered our minds as a possibility, yet again.

A few days later at Denny's, the diagram laid discreetly open for us to view in unison.

I finished eating with Sarah, Joe and Scott.

"It's pretty clear. You just need to pay attention to detail. I'll be close by."

Scott heaved a big sigh, "No questions here. I'm ready to go."

I put my hand over the diagram to get Joe's attention. "Hey. Just remember, get the clean-up guy, Joe. Don't overlook him."

I scrunched up the diagram paper and put it in my pocket. "Any other questions?"

He let out a nervous laugh. "Nope. Guess I'll see you all tomorrow."

woke up with thoughts of things undone, even though my bases were pretty well-covered. Anxieties with no home address. My breathing was shallow.

I floated through my thoughts alone, next to a sleeping Sarah. Considering what was coming, I barely noticed her lying there next to me. The anticipation was much more intense than it had been last time. Somehow, this felt more *real*.

I had to admit, last time was so easy, it was almost fun. But, I wouldn't be able to direct the scene this time around. *What if they went off script?*

In any event, I had to have faith in them. I didn't have much of a choice.

About the same time, as the shaving cream made a steady stream into his palm from the can, Scott eyed his reflection in the bathroom mirror. One of the two bathroom light bulbs was out, and he was having trouble making out his eyes.

At five in the morning, there was barely a ray of sunlight to help him out. He stared at his reflection, peppered in shadows. He was so still, he started to remind himself of one of Linda's paintings. A flat smattering of paint on a surface.

Slightly disturbed, he broke the gaze.

Why the hell am I even shaving? He mused to himself. *Is it really that important that I look clean-cut for this?*

He waded through the plan in his mind for about the millionth time, doing a mental review of every step. Visualizing every move.

He jerked out of his thoughts by a sudden throbbing pain in his neck. He touched his fingertips to the pulsating area and was mildly surprised when he pulled away and saw blood.

"I'd better pay attention before I kill myself," he muttered.

A few minutes later after cleaning up, his zombie-like body found its way to the living room couch. Tortured by his own thoughts, he comforted himself by repeating my words, "The plan is ideal; simple execution is needed. That's all."

He and Joe could do that.

Denny's wasn't too busy yet, but the wait staff operated at a scurry, paying special attention to their senior regulars. The wait-resses may have been wearing Denny's uniforms, but they worked with the care of personal nurses when it came to the Early Bird Special frequenters. They winked and laughed at the old men's jokes, putting up with pinches on the cheek and being called "sweetheart" or "honey." They brought breakfast specials out without taking any orders down, already well-aware what each table was going to request.

The salmon-colored Naugahyde booths were and cracked from years of dining, laughter, and living. Each couple sat at *their booth*, the same one they'd been warming seven days a week for the past decade. Only dire illness would prevent their perfect attendance.

Sarah and I arrived ten minutes early—*the boring middle-class couple*—me staring mostly at the floor as the waitress showed us to a table. We were four blocks outside of Buena Park, and I didn't want any chance of being noticed.

We took seats facing each other. As the waitress left, we stretched our hands over the table and held on tight. We locked our gaze for several seconds, then smiled at each other in determination and squeezed.

I let her fingers slip through mine, and we picked up our menus, dedicated to our role of quiet middle-class couple. I caught a wink from her before she disappeared behind her menu.

As we browsed, my attention was drawn to two black and whites having a ten eighty-seven in the parking lot. Their taillights pointed in opposite directions as they made conversation. They were California Highway Patrol, and not here for me or us. No. They were just talking. Perhaps just having a few laughs around the water cooler. Routine.

But, I couldn't take my eyes off them.

Ten minutes later, a man wearing all black entered the restaurant looking confident as hell. His smooth black hair was combed back to perfection, and a few women glanced up at his handsome face as he passed by—so handsome, they probably didn't even notice the small bandage covering up the razor cut on his neck.

He surveyed the room purposefully, looking over the sea of chattering bald heads and bluish hair. His head stopped moving as he spotted Sarah, and soon he was making his way to our table.

As he approached, I moved to sit beside Sarah, and he slid into my former spot. He wasn't even looking at us. His gaze was out the window to the parking lot.

"That scared the shit out of me. You know I almost ran into a cop car out there?" He carefully watched the lot. "They're gone now," he muttered. "I wonder what they were doing."

I lightly chuckled, hoping to release the tension. "It's okay. Don't worry about it. They were just having a meet-up. Happens all the time."

I paused and leaned in, "The badge doesn't make them clair-voyant, so I think we're safe."

Scott sighed with relief, kicking himself for having such a ridic-ulous, paranoid thought. Then again, it wouldn't have been the first ridiculous thought in his mind that morning. Hell, even that hour.

We leaned in, talking about our bowling team and its upcoming match that evening while waiting for our friend Bernie to join us. Because there was no Bill, Sarah, Scott, and Joe. We were Jim, Mary, Gene, and Bernie—the unstoppable bowling foursome.

The good-time three glanced up in time to see Joe/Bernie enter the restaurant. He looked as though he'd run here, like he was ready to thrust his fist into the air. But with that sense of victory was an underlying sense of fear, like he'd just had the best orgasm of his life only to find out the condom broke. He also looked ready to take flight at the first sign of anything.

He did a quick survey of the restaurant. Too quick to recognize a single face. *Whoa, everyone change their mind?* But, then he noticed Scott's large hand waving him over, and he spotted his bowling team.

As he strode to the table, Scott asked for the house, "Did you bring your ball? I hate having to rent them."

"Yeah. It's out in the car." Joe answered, as he sat and started to eagerly review the menu.

"Did you have lunch this afternoon?" I quietly asked him.

"Yep. Like you said," he responded, peering over the top of his menu.

"Don't order much, then. You need your stomach to be light. Have decaf tea." Joe stared at me for a few seconds, incredulous that I was dictating everything, even his *diet*, but too nervous to protest.

After fifteen minutes of quiet conversation and enough time to assess the room, Sarah looked at me with an obvious question on her face. I nodded.

She took the diagram out of her pocket and carefully placed it on the table.

Scott covered the paper with his hand. "Wait. I got to tell you guys. Neither Linda nor I have slept much lately. I've been reciting the plan forwards and backwards until she falls asleep. Routine was I'd recite our plan until she fell asleep. So, I know this." He smiled triumphantly.

"What are you looking for? Extra credit? Who out of any of us has been sleeping lately?" I spat, done with the light banter. It was time to get serious.

Scott removed his hand in chastisement. I had each of them point to the diagram and verbally go over the exact details of their part in the play. I had to hand it to them, they had it down perfectly, even the blocking.

"Okay, so the only wild card is the clean-up man," I reaffirmed. "You hearing me, Joe? It could all go to hell without him accounted for. *The clean-up man.*"

6 3

S arah and I drove to Kmart, followed twenty minutes later by Joe and Scott. Once they arrived, we drove to a parking lot at Euclid and Crescent. They followed again and sat, waiting for final word from their director.

I pulled into a parking lot across the street from Kmart to get a macro-view; a lay of the battlefield, so to speak. Eventually satisfied with the safety of the location, I drove into the proposed crime scene parking lot and cruised by the store for Sarah to see in the windows and ensure everything was happening normally. I didn't expect a *fire-drill in progress*, but you couldn't be too sure. Like the trial attorney's credo, "Never ask a question you don't know the answer to," we needed no loose ends.

We parked for a few minutes while I took a closer look: scrutinizing cars in the lot, watching to gauge the end-of-night spirit of the staff and customers alike. I searched for a sense of the rhythm, or even a disorder, to the evening.

"Okay. Let's go," I finally said, ready to drive by the store for the last time before the show began.

"How do you feel?" asked my crime partner.

"It's good so far."

I smiled inside. As I pulled into the lot, I saw Scott leaving the small store with a bagged can of Coke. He approached the car where Joe was seated, and I parked right next to them.

"Looks perfect. Piece of cake if done right. Deviate . . . and I can't help you," I said without turning my head to him. "Don't forget afterwards. See you then."

I put the car in gear and drove out of the lot.

Sarah and I moved south on Knott Ave. to Ball Road. We traveled in silence, Sarah stared out the window deep in thought. Meanwhile, I was flashing back to when I used to drive these streets with a badge. A water hose of memories, and the car was loaded with emotional turmoil. There was nothing pleasant about the drive. I also glanced around, continuing to watch for black and whites.

As we reached Ball Road, I turned the car around and headed back to Kmart. The guys should arrive in ten minutes. I wanted to be there for their entrance, to boost their confidence, make sure everything was going well . . . or to know quickly enough to abort if it wasn't.

In a matter of a few minutes, we parked across the street from Kmart. I watched Scott's car pull up and park. He stepped out and glanced around the parking lot a bit. I watched him spot my car. Joe lowered himself slightly into the passenger's seat.

I cruised over to the Kmart side of the street to take a closer look. Feeling that it was clear to do so, I parked about two hundred feet from the entrance, slightly to the side. It was like I had a box seat to the show.

My job of watching was set on autopilot now, as Scott entered looking calm and confident. Determination bled through him. He was definitely in mission-mode.

I waited several minutes, then exited the car, and casually moved toward the front windows of the store. That placed me in a better position to observe as Scott covertly crept toward his hiding spot. I silently wished him well. Every particle in my body buzzed regarding the action.

I turned toward the car, scanning the lot for anything out of sorts. Not too many cars, not too much activity. Sunday evening. *That was right. That fit.*

Satisfied, I walked back. I could make out Joe still slouching in the car, waiting. I nodded slowly as I passed, ever so slightly. His face looked like that of an amateur actor right before opening night. *I'm glad Scott took the car keys with him. Joe might bolt right now.*

I reached my car and leaned in the window, making pointless conversation. Was I calm, was I anxious? My mind wasn't aware of what my mouth was doing. But, my eyes remained focused on Joe. My entire body was frozen, watching him with intensity.

Through peripheral vision, I saw him close his eyes for a moment. It seemed like forever. He finally climbed out of the car and walked into the store, looking heavily yoked. *Shit, I've seen this before. Fight or flight?*

I hoped to God he wouldn't choke. *Or faint.*

I casually walked to the same store window, *just a shopper, checking out the merchandise.* Perhaps my wife sent me to the store, and I just couldn't seem to remember what for . . . husbands are all the same.

I peered in to see Joe milling around at the shoe section, his eyes darting about. He'd made his way to his assigned hiding spot. A bit too quickly, he left my view. I continued to stare nonetheless, slightly unsettled.

I walked back to the car again. The little clock read 7:10. I got in, drove out of the lot, and parked several blocks away; a whole town away. I couldn't even hear Sarah breathe.

Crossing the city limit granted Sarah the comfort to say, "Whew. Whew. So glad to be out of sight. I can't believe this is really happening." She pounded on the dashboard of the Bug and shouted, "YEAH!"

"No, not yet. We say 'YEAH' at the *end*." I eyed her as though she had broken a rule. My face twisted into a reluctant smile.

We drove around Anaheim for twenty minutes before returning to Kmart as planned. The store was now closed for customers; the parking lot, almost empty. I could see the scattered employees working in closing-mode through the front windows. Everything looked peachy.

I finally parked across the street from the store. We waited there for a planned fifteen minutes. Then, I slowly drove the car back to the Kmart lot where we sat still.

Very still.

I focused on the front windows, trying to look like we were there to give someone a ride home; not trying to make any friends along the way.

A group of staff members started to walk back toward the manager's office. Another remained at the front with the manager.

A few more than expected. But, I'd planned for everything.

Sarah strained to see, without making it obvious to customers leaving the Vons next door. "Can you see anything?"

"No, it's too early for that. Watch for people going back to the manager's office."

Joe should be close to getting his man by this time. I peered down the aisle, knowing there was no way I could see. I tried anyway.

My heart slammed against my chest as I clenched my hands into fists on my legs to keep them off the wheel. I moved my head around to see if any police cars were coming into the area. I glanced at Scott's car to double-check there were no obstacles to a quick exit. My ass felt like it was slammed shut.

We waited another ten minutes. It was torture.

Suddenly, the manager appeared to yell something to the rear of the store. He and the other man began walking back toward the office area.

"Shouldn't be long now. Looking good," I enunciated as they disappeared toward the back.

"Can you see Joe or Scott?" Sarah asked.

For the first time in months—no—for the first time since we'd smoked that pot and hatched the idea all that time ago, I heard doubt in Sarah's voice.

"They should be in the back area now. In a minute, we'll see them move across that main aisle."

Sarah rolled her window down to breathe, taking huge gulps of the cool air. Her whole body buzzed with . . . *fear*?

We voraciously watched the manager as he approached the group surrounding his office. It appeared small talk was made, and they disappeared toward the office.

The night seemed so quiet. I could close my eyes and imagine I was the only one on the planet. I kind of wished I was.

Our four eyes remained locked on the manager's office.

After several minutes, Sarah broke the silence, "What could be going on in there right now?"

Slowly, I turned my head toward her, and raised my eyebrows. "Hopefully, a successful robbery. Isn't that why we're here?"

"No. I mean what kind of problems are they having, if any? I mean, what's going on?" she mumbled to herself, beginning to rock back and forth slightly.

"Don't worry. They've got a crowd, that's all. It'll take longer. When we see movement, take your spot. They're going to be nervous."

"Facing for yes, back to them for no?" She smiled and cocked her head slightly. "Just checking," said with comic disdain in an obvious attempt to suppress her body shakes.

I turned to her and took both of her hands. "You sure you're okay?" I searched her face for any problems, any last-minute change of mind. Exactly the reasons I knew she shouldn't have been here in the first place.

"I'm fine. I'll be fine. This is exciting, is all." She slowly shook her head, "I feel like a current of electricity is going through me."

I let go of her hands and kissed her on the cheek. Suddenly, I noticed movement in the middle of the store. "What the hell?"

Someone was making his way down to the middle aisle to the entrance, in full stride. I sat up a little in the seat and leaned forward to focus as it dawned on me; *someone was escaping.*

I felt like someone just threw a hardball at my stomach. *Oh, shit! No.* "It's the clean-up guy. I can't believe this."

Fernando picked up the pace, all of his focus on the front of the store. But, it seemed like he was in the store alone. No other movement. No one looked for him.

Sarah finally noticed him. "Oh, my God! Bill, he's going to get away. We have to stop him."

"We can't stop him. It's too late. Look at him."

The door seemed to fly open, and Fernando blazed through it, headed straight to Vons. He almost fell twice in his abject fear, but adrenaline helped to right him each time.

I can't do anything about it. I can't even start my car and run the bastard down. It is too late.

Sarah opened her car door. "I've got to warn them."

I grabbed her by the arm to keep her from leaving, but she struggled to get free. "We've got to help them." Tears appeared in her eyes.

I kept a firm grip on her arm. "We can't even *get* there before the cops are here. Do you understand? What kind of help is that?"

She continued to struggle to free herself, failing to listen to reason. I twisted her toward me, and grabbed her other arm with my free hand. Trying to get her attention, "Stop it, damn it. You stay in this fucking car!" I hollered.

She finally gave up the battle, slinking back into her seat. I reached across her trembling body and slammed the door shut. She sat there, staring straight ahead. Defiantly.

"That man just ran into Vons to call the cops. They could be here in seconds. We don't know where they are coming from. That's the deal. You understand? We don't know where they are." I gave her a moment, hoping she could process this.

"I still say I go in there and warn them." She edged toward the door handle. I grabbed her wrist.

"Knock this *off!* I'm not screwing with you."

Somewhere in the back of my mind, I registered my heart rate quickening.

Within seconds, the first black and white crept into the lot. Red lights on, no siren.

Then another.

Another . . .

Two more...

I slouched down and pulled her with me, our heads dragging across the leather.

Sarah slowly turned to look at me, with that face that had been melting me since I was seventeen years old.

But my eyes remained dead cold.

64

Gorsh's voice boomed over the police radio, "My ETA is one minute. Have everyone stand down until I get there." His left foot pressed down on the floorboard for no apparent reason.

He turned to Pense seated next to him and elbowed him on the shoulder, "Shit, call the press. You heard 'em. They got hostages." He let out a resounding, "Yee-haw!" as they approached Crescent.

With no cars in the intersection, they had the right-of-way with a green light, but he just had to activate the siren as they drove through. "Here comes the cavalry!"

The corners of Pense's mouth lifted slightly. *Fucking nut.*

He held up a bullhorn, dangling it in front of Gorsh like a carrot, "Here you are, darling. You've waited all your life for this."

"Don't be a smart-ass. It could be you in my sights next." Gorsh glanced at Pense and jutted his jaw toward him . . . then laughed heartily.

He still needs my loyalty after all, thought Pense.

A small crowd of people gathered in the parking lot. In addition, people driving by on Lincoln Ave. were curious about the red flashing lights on the police cars. Cops stood all over the place. Whatever was happening might suddenly get very dramatic. The night was quite dark.

Occasionally, a passerby couldn't take it and had to drive onto the lot to see what was happening. This was an attraction they didn't expect, and it was all free. *I wonder if they have refreshments.*

The crowd continued to grow and interact as the siege continued, every member offered a different version of what might be happening. One person saw nothing; another saw tanks. Gorsh's dramatic arrival was barely noticed with everything else going on.

With the wind knocked out of his sails, it kind of made him want to go back out and arrive again. Maybe use the siren more. Maybe jump out of the car before it completely stopped.

"I'm going to take a run by and see what's going on," I said at about that same time. We're parked on the north side of Lincoln, just east of Euclid. It was the first word said by either of us for what felt like an eternity.

Watching from a distance as the clean-up guy escaped, the quick and silent arrival of the police all caused our minds to go blank with shock.

Sarah absentmindedly shook her head, not wanting to go back, but she felt the Bug's engine start and begin to move westbound toward Kmart. By the grimace on her face, I could tell she felt in the pit of her stomach every piece of asphalt we drove over.

As we approached Valley View, the show was still on; the small crowd gathering was clearly very interested. People stretched and swiveled their heads to see everything going on. They chatted about perceived updates constantly. I looked at Sarah. Her eyes were locked on the scene.

I turned left on Lincoln and drove past the store slowly to get a better look; it felt surreal. The store was surrounded, but the police maintained their positions slightly away.

It appeared to be a standoff, or a stare down. I knew they had at least six hostages in there, and the possibility of positive outcomes didn't look good. Fortunately, Joe and Scott were not carrying loaded weapons. The planned intent was one of suddenness and diversion—not danger.

The police, of course, didn't know that. And, if the guys performed as rehearsed, the hostages weren't aware of that either. But, if even one of the hostages was familiar enough with firearms and took a good look at the weapons that carried no bullets, this could get much worse for Scott and Joe.

At the last moment, I turned into the Kmart parking lot, west end.

"What are you doing?" Sarah's first startled words in minutes. Her feet dug into the floorboard, bracing for the unknown and the fear that came with it.

"I don't think they'll notice me. I'll stay on the edge." It came out as an aside.

I was focused on what was ahead. I shifted the car into park.

Once I had a good visual of what was going on, I told Sarah to stay put. I left the car to carefully make my way to the edge, or better, the middle of the crowd. Everyone had common sense enough to have moved away from the obvious danger at the front of the store, yet still had a pretty good view of the action.

I tucked in between a few people and found myself within arm's distance of a couple of cops. My heart raced. *Feels like a damn reunion.* Except none of my old friends noticed me. I had worked with every single cop present, and not one of them noticed me.

Gorsh stood next to his police unit about thirty yards away, holding up the bullhorn. He wasn't speaking into it, just holding it up frozen in midair—frozen in time and posing as General MacArthur. Silently hoping the press and public were taking their photos.

Several minutes later, the shrill of the telephone ringing broke the silence in the manager's office. Everyone held their breath. Scott stared at Joe, who moved his gaze from the hostages to meet Scott's.

Another ring. Another. Silence.

Bob took the opportunity to squeak out, "Don't worry, that's my direct line. It's not a store call."

Before he continued, Scott commanded, "Don't answer that phone."

"What?" Joe said with bewilderment. "That could be the cops. We could make a deal," through clenched teeth.

As the phone continued to shriek, Scott pressed, "Yeah? What kind of deal would that be?" He squared his stance in front of Joe, forcing himself to be the center of attention now. "We're surrounded. I don't see where we have much room to negotiate here. You'd better accept that tonight, we're going to jail."

Joe shook his head in denial. "No. No. There's a way out of this. You'll figure it out. I'll figure it out. Whatever. We got hostages," he spat out.

"We have to use that. We can get out of this. Keep thinking." He looked at Delores for a moment, calculating. "If any one of you has an idea how to fix this, speak up." He leaned in, "It's for everybody's good." He looked a tad too maniacal to successfully solicit help.

No one answered. Most kept their gaze on the floor; some had their eyes closed as if the fear had put them in trance. Silence.

The phone rang again. Startling all, as if they'd never heard it before.

"That's my line again," Bob muttered to the floor apologetically. "Store line doesn't come through after hours. A service handles it."

"You getting anything, yet?" Joe asked Scott with desperation. He was beginning to get palpitations from the thick, blinding anxiety.

"Yeah. I'm getting that we surrender. We're in a shit storm. This can only get worse, and every option ends with us losing." His shoulders slumped and both arms dangled at his sides; the gun threatened to slip out of his hand.

"That's bullshit," barked Joe. "We got to see this thing through." His body was taut and the outline of his jaw moved forward.

Manager Bob took another pathetic stab at leadership. "Let me talk to them," he pleaded with a trembling voice. "We can get you guys out of here."

"Shut up, Bob, before I knock you the fuck out," Joe snapped, taking a huge step to lean in on Bob's space with a clenched fist.

Bob stared back, unaware his mouth had almost come off its hinges.

Suddenly, a bull horn invaded the silence of the store. "This is Chief of Police, Dilbert Gorsh of Buena Park," the voice growled.

Scott motioned for Joe to watch the hostages while he moved from the office to the store to better hear the rest of the announcement.

He had already heard a couple of announcements saying the police were there and the store was surrounded, but this was a new, much more menacing voice.

"We're aware you have people in there. Stay calm and expect phone contact."

Gorsh's voice continued, "We want everyone to stay safe. You must surrender. There's no way out. We'll wait as long as you want; just don't hurt anyone. I'm going to call you now. Please, answer the phone and let's talk." He paused briefly and then repeated, "Please, answer the phone and we'll talk. That's all for now." He briefly thought of saying, *Over and out*, but decided against it.

Scott glazed over, his shoulders slouching further as he turned back to the manager's office. For a brief moment, he felt totally detached from the situation.

There is hope, Joe thought to himself from his post in the office. *We can talk. Yeah, that's it.*

On Scott's return, Joe sprung into action. "Let me handle the call." He was already preparing the single negotiating skill that had seen him through thirty-eight years of life—throwing himself on the floor and having a fit.

"No one's going to handle the damn call," Scott answered, back to life. "Not the next time. We need to talk about this more. I'm not ready yet, and you look like a fucking madman."

He felt in control of the room again. He straightened his posture, willing himself to stay in control.

Gorsh remained standing next to his police unit, still those thirty yards away.

He just finished giving his third announcement to the hostage takers, and the crowd was electrified with confusion and adrenaline. Nothing like this was showing back home on TV, that's for damn sure, even on those new color sets.

Everyone had an opinion, and they all wanted to give it at the same time. A local radio station's truck entered the lot, ready for any action that may or may not go down.

"I can't believe this is happening..."

"My husband said they have hostages in there..."

"Man, I wish I'd brought my camera..."

I could be completely nude, and no one would look twice.

I observed everything from where I stood: The police and their activities, their individual personalities reacting just as I'd expected; the robbers and their individual personalities screwing up as I *should* have expected; the hostages, about the only ones I didn't know much about; the crowd, of which I was a part; and then myself, on the edge, in the darkness.

It was a well-lit action movie set.

And I was the only one who knew the extent of this plot. My thoughts bounced against the parameters of my mind, and I silently hoped my head wouldn't explode.

This had gone way beyond any conceivable plan.

I glanced over to see Pense sitting in the driver's seat. Next to him stood Gorsh, partially shielded by the open car door. Pense looked up, "Okay, Chief. We got the line again. They didn't answer first go around."

"You ready?"

"If you still say so," Joe answered, resistance on his stoic face.

"I'll talk to them. You see another option?" Scott challenged.

Scott and Joe stared each other down, waiting for the phone to ring again.

It eventually did, and it seemed to get louder with each ring. Scott pressed a button for the office line. "Hello?" he spoke tentatively into the mouthpiece.

Joe watched him, his body signaling growing resignation. His shoulders were squared, but without any real force.

Gorsh's voice boomed through the line attached to his car radio. "This is Chief Gorsh. That was me on the bullhorn." Always making sure he received proper credit for everything he did.

"I want you to stay calm and know we're not coming in there, right now. So, relax for a minute. We don't want anyone to get hurt."

"We don't either," Scott exhaled.

Gorsh continued, attempting to persuade the gunmen to let the hostages go and surrender. He stood there all wound up to lead the parade, but there wasn't one.

He had no idea that was exactly what Scott wanted to do, and he didn't stop to entertain this possibility. Scott couldn't get a word in edgewise.

Gorsh was bathing in the drama. Not much of a chance for glamour in a town whose main attraction was Knott's Berry Farm. He always took what he could get.

I knew just where to look. Moments later, I saw the slow-but-steady movement of a person inside the store. It appeared to be a hostage that had been released. She stumbled toward the front door on giraffe-like legs, slightly disheveled and in a daze.

Okay, time to leave.

I avoided any eye contact, making sure to not so much as brush up against anyone as I made my way back to the car. Not that it mattered anyway; everyone else remained focused on the store entrance.

Two minutes later, I slowly drove off the lot for what felt like the umpteenth time that night. As we left the driveway, Sarah rose in her seat and peeked around to watch the still-unfolding scene. She was in total disbelief.

I drove in silence, turned left on Valley View to go home and relieve the baby-sitter.

I had great fear inside myself, of course, but the autopilot had kicked in and outwardly, I was eerily calm. Police training and experience had overwhelmed my honest and logical intuition, and changed my conscious mindset forever. Every breath became strategic. Every emotion was put on hold.

We entered the freeway to the sounds of the first frantic radio report of a "robbery in progress."

"I'm being told, Jim, the remaining hostages are apparently now leaving the store one at a time," the reporter slowly announced, as though the speed and impact of his voice might play a role in endangering a hostage.

I stared at the road, heaved a deep sigh, and slightly shook my head. "They're done. They're toast. I can't believe this. I did my job. Joe didn't get the clean-up man, like I instructed *a million times*. They screwed up the plan. They didn't follow it." I shook my head again.

"Hell, they owe me thirty percent of the money they didn't get," I said in a bizarre attempt at levity.

I still stared ahead, barely aware Sarah had begun to quietly cry next to me. "We're driving to Linda's house," I announced, more to myself than anything.

"I don't want to use our home phone, and we've got to get there quickly." *What a time to be low on change.*

I glanced over at her face. "Hey. Hey. Calm down," my voice softened. "You'll be okay, darling. That's all over with now." I reached over and raised her chin, "We've got work to do. Just breathe deeply. Okay? We'll be there in twenty minutes."

She still couldn't speak, but forced a smile and rested her head on the back of the seat. I noticed her right foot tapping nervously from the corner of my eye. We drove in absolute silence for fifteen minutes, until I turned my head to her, waiting for her to look at me so I could say, "This is just the beginning...."

EPILOGUE

My father, Bill Engle, passed away on December 23, 2021. He was 80 years old, fiery as ever, and surrounded by his family—his true and lasting legacy; his forever loves.

Although he is no longer on this Earth, he is far from removed. He survives in myself and my five sisters: as a part of our DNA, the fabric of our lives. We see him in each other's faces and hear him in our laughter, and his incredible story is one that will live on forever.

Watching my father leave this world was the hardest thing I've ever had to do. He was surrounded by his wife (my mother) Lori Marie Engle, and three of his daughters: my sisters Cindy and Lisa, and myself. As my sisters sang hymns of comfort, my mother and I held his hands and whispered into his ears, ushering him into the arms of his Savior as he took his last breaths—something he'd dreamed of for his entire life. As difficult as it was, I can't deny the tinge of magic that enveloped us that day.

Moving this story forward without him has been daunting to say the least; something that was never part of our plan. But I am honored to share his beautiful life with the world—to tell the story he spent so many years building. And man, did that guy pump out some compelling content.

Thank you for your successes, Daddy, but even more so, thank you for your failures. Thank you for reminding me time and again exactly how to pick myself back up when I've fallen, and thank you for leaving me the tools I need to share your strength with the world. Until we meet again.

www.ingramcontent.com/pod-product-compliance
Lightning Source LLC
Chambersburg PA
CBHW020603270326
41927CB00005B/157

* 9 7 8 1 9 6 0 0 5 9 0 4 8 *